EXECUTIVE SPEECHES

Tips on How to Write and Deliver Speeches from 51 CEOs

Brent Filson

John Wiley & Sons, Inc.

New York • Chichester • Brisbane • Toronto • Singapore

This text is printed on acid-free paper.

Copyright © 1991, 1994 by Brent Filson
Published by John Wiley & Sons, Inc.
Previously published 1991 by Williamston Publishing Company.

IBM® is a registered trademark of International Business Machines Corp.

WordPerfect® is a registered trademark of WordPerfect Corporation.

Microsoft® Word for Windows® is a trademark of Microsoft Corporation.

The purchaser may make backup copies of the enclosed disk for his/her own use only and not for distribution or resale. The publisher assumes no responsibility for errors, omissions, or damages, including without limitation damages caused by the use of these forms or from the use of the information contained therein.

Grateful acknowledgment is made for the right to reprint excerpts from *Talking Straight* by Lee Iacocca with Sonny Kleinfield. Copyright © 1988. Reprinted with permission of Bantam Books, a Division of Bantam Doubleday Dell Publishing Group, Inc.

Library of Congress Cataloging-in-Publication Data:

Filson, Brent.
   Executive speeches : Tips on how to write and deliver speeches from 51 CEOs / Brent Filson.
     p.   cm.
   Includes index.
    ISBN 0-471-59931-X. —ISBN 0-471-59932-8 (pbk.)
    1. Business communication. 2. Public speaking. 3. Oral communication. 4. Public relations. 5. Chief executive officers--United States. I. Title.
   HF5718.F55 1994
   658.4'52—dc20   93-26409
                                           CIP

Printed in the United States of America

10 9 8 7 6 5 4 3 2 1

CONTENTS

1. WHY THE SPEECH *1*

Executives must communicate *2* CEO communication *3* Express ideas to get ahead *3* Every executive's job *3* The speech as history *4* The speech as Proteus *4* More speeches needed *4* Better speeches needed *5* Inspiring business speeches *6* Heaven, divorce, headlines and war *6* The speech as message and massage *7* Speeches trigger success *7* **20 reasons why speeches are vital to an executive's success** 1. Communicate change *7* 2. Provide continuity of change *8* 3. Help transform a company's culture *9* 4. Communicate a vision *10* 5. Influence industry *12* 6. Influence investors *12* 7. Increase learning *13* 8. Promote social values *14* 9. Broaden business contacts *15* 10. Enhance sales *15* 11. Advance marketing *16* 12. Increase your value to your business *17* 13. Increase your promotion opportunities *18* 14. Position yourself for career changes *19* 15. Enhance business growth *19* 16. Promote technological and statistical understanding *20* 17. Be newsworthy *20* 18. Communicate a turning point *21* 19. Make meetings productive *22* 20. Build teamwork *23* Summary *24*

2. THE AUDIENCE *25*

Be yourself by knowing yourself *26* Knowing yourself helps liven up your speeches *26* The hardest thing in life *27* Tape yourself *27* Cultivate critics *28* Encouraging feedback *28* Be outrageous . . . in practice *28* Pare down *28* Just speak *29* Live the examined life *29* **19 techniques**

7. HUMOR *125*

8. WRITING THE SPEECH *143*

9. DELIVERY *161*

PREFACE

THIS BOOK IS FOR the executive who wants to be not just a better public speaker, but a better communicator. That's because the executive's speech is the moveable feast of business. When you begin to master the art of the speech, you become a better leader by broadening and enriching a variety of communication skills.

For years, I've been helping a select clientele of successful, high-level executives become more effective communicators by working with them on speeches and communication strategies.

During this time, we worked best together not when I talked and they listened, but when we shared our experiences and knowledge.

So, pooling and sharing resources are essential features of this book. As an executive, you don't have the time or margin-for-error to try untested communication techniques. You need techniques that have worked again and again, not in theory, not in a classroom, but on the front lines of communication engagements.

It makes sense to learn these techniques from executives who themselves are successful speakers and communicators. But unless you take a business sabbatical, you won't be able to contact many of them. So, I've done it for you. The tips found in this book are the distillation of my own experience as a speechwriting and communication consultant, the experiences of executives I have worked with and the experiences of 51 other CEOs. In addition, I have interviewed security analysts, production company specialists, public relations executives, executive search consultants, speechwriters, and other communication experts for their suggestions.

CEOs are the focus of my research because they are the change masters of business. To lead effectively, they must deal with change. They must be able to look around corners and see what others don't see. They must have a vision of where their businesses are headed in changing marketplaces and of how the people in the businesses are going to get there. Finally, they must motivate people to achieve the vision.

Three criteria were used to select the CEOs to be interviewed. They are helping lead changing businesses in changing marketplaces. Their businesses are achieving good results. And they believe strongly that speeches are important to the success of their business.

Although this book is about the experiences of CEOs, it's for *your* success, your success as an executive, as a speaker, as a communicator. Like a CEO, you have to understand your job and the jobs of the people you lead within the context of a changing business and changing marketplace. You have to develop goals for your team and inspire people to attain those goals—objectives directly related to your speaking abilities.

So here's to your moveable feast. May it be bountiful, now and for a long time to come.

Bon appetit!

ACKNOWLEDGMENTS

THE FIRST CEO I interviewed for this book, David Coffin of The Dexter Corporation, gave me advice that I used throughout my research. When I told him that I wasn't sure that busy people would find time to talk to me, he said, "Don't worry. People will talk to you. Even when busy, most people still want to help. Just ask." I took his advice. I asked. And people helped. In helping, they gave two valuable things: their knowledge and their time. So I'm more grateful than I can ever say to everyone who helped me on this journey. Thanks to all the executives and communication experts who consented to be interviewed.

Thanks to the secretaries of the CEOs who helped smooth the way in so many ways.

Thanks to my "target audience" Jo McCoy for her patient analysis of the manuscript.

Thanks to Rob Kaplan for sharing his knowledge and experience.

Thanks to Ray Shepard for his friendship, advice and encouragement and for being one of the true heroes of my life.

Thanks to Uwe Wascher for teaching that marketing is philosophy in action, that the status quo is *always* wrong, and that you are not engaged in marketing if you're not having fun.

Thanks, of course, as always, to Magalis and our children.

And thanks to all the executives I've worked with throughout the years. No one can teach well without learning; and in my teaching and consulting, I have learned that when the game is on the line, the clock moving, and no time-outs remain, what you do is who you are; and who you are is often what you've become by giving, not getting.

AUTHOR'S NOTE

ALL OF THE CEOs—except two—were interviewed while in office; and those two, Joseph Rice and Robert Mercer, were interviewed only a few months after they retired. But, since time and chance happen to CEOs as well as the rest of us, some of the 51 may no longer be in the same position when you read this book. Some may have retired or changed businesses or even changed careers. But in this book, they will always be "the 51 CEOs". Because no matter where they have gone or will go, the advice they gave, as CEOs, during my nine month season of interviewing in 1989–90, is advice for all seasons of your career.

INTRODUCTION

D ON'T JUST READ this book, use it. That is, don't read it front to back: use it as a reference book—a recipe book. Keep it on the shelf beside your desk. Before you give a speech, check the book out. Try several techniques for one occasion and others for another occasion. Work on improving step by step and year by year.

I'm not offering a quick and easy system for preparing and delivering speeches. One fact stood out in my interviews: No single system of writing and delivering speeches is effective for every person. There is no quick and easy way. There is only what works—and what does not work. Finding out what works and what does not involves working hard, taking risks, and being persistent. Whether you face an audience of two or two thousand, it is not what system you have studied that is important, but instead what you know and how, in the best way possible, you can be yourself.

Heavyweight boxing champion smokin' Joe Frazier said: "You can map out a fight plan or a life plan, but when the action starts, it may not go the way you planned, and you're down to your reflexes—which means your training. That's where your roadwork shows. If you cheated on that in the dark of the morning, well, you're getting found out now under the bright lights."

To be an effective speaker and communicator, you have to get the lonely road work in. There are no shortcuts. You have to make your own way and create your own system. This book helps you do it through the experiences of successful communicators.

For instance, if you want to find out how best to understand your audience, turn to Chapter 2, "Audience Analyzers" and use William C. Ferguson's (CEO, NYNEX Corporation) technique of understanding the audiences within an audience; Mylle H. Bell's (BellSouth's Director of Planning and Development) method of actually polling the audience just before you speak; or Linda S. Mathieu's (CEO, TEFRA, Inc.) way of letting the audience actually determine the talk. There are no guarantees—just simple, proven methods of achieving good communications, methods you have to learn and practice during your personal equivalent of dark-of-the-morning road work.

Since this book is not about formulas, but about experiences, don't get confused if you read conflicting advice. For instance, Dr. T. J. Rodgers (CEO, Cypress Semiconductor Corporation) will not deliver a written speech. (If he wants to distribute copies of his talk, he writes the speech fully—*after* he has delivered it.) But John O'Brien (CEO, Grumman Corporation) insists that he and his top officers write every speech they are asked to give. Rodgers and O'Brien are *both* right. That's because preparing and delivering good speeches is not a science but an art. Like any art, it takes years of hard work, often trying out what may appear to be conflicting techniques, before you can be an overnight success.

Finally, don't be easy on this book. Use it for years. Write in it. Travel with it. Shape its advice to your individual talents and skills. Put it into action. Learn from it. Grow by it. Succeed with it.

Then you, the executive, will be able to do it right under the bright lights.

HOW TO USE
THE DISK

DISK CONTENTS

OVERVIEW

The enclosed disk contains speech guidelines, tips, and questionnaires on how to write and deliver speeches from the book *Executive Speeches: Tips on How to Write and Deliver Speeches from 51 CEOs* by Brent Filson. The speech guidelines are provided to you in three formats, ASCII, WordPerfect, and Microsoft Word for Windows:

- [ ] ASCII is a standard text format for IBM DOS files. These files have the extension ASC.
- [ ] WordPerfect has the extension WP5.
- [ ] Microsoft Word for Windows has the extension DOC.

System Requirements

The enclosed disk requires an IBM® PC family computer or compatible computer with 256K minimum memory and the following:

- [ ] IBM PC DOS or MS DOS 3.1 or later
- [ ] A 5¼" disk drive
- [ ] WordPerfect® Version 5.0
- [ ] Microsoft® Word for Windows® or any other word processor that can read ASCII files.

Optional equipment includes a DOS compatible printer and a popular word processing package like WordPerfect or Microsoft Word for Windows to read and print the questionnaire or guideline files.

HOW TO MAKE A BACKUP DISK

Before you start to use the enclosed disk, we strongly recommend that you make a backup copy of the original. Making a backup copy of your disk allows you to have a clean set of files saved in case you accidentally change a file or delete a file. Remember, however, that a backup disk is for your own personal use only. Any other use of the backup disk violates copyright law. Please take the time now to make the backup copy, using the instructions below:

If your computer has two floppy disk drives:

1. Insert your DOS disk into drive A of your computer.
2. Insert a blank disk into drive B of your computer.
3. At the A:>, type DISKCOPY A: B: and press ↵.

You will be prompted by DOS to place the Source disk into drive A.

4. Place the first disk into Drive A.

Follow the directions on screen to complete the copy. When you are through, remove the disk from drive B and label it immediately. Remove the original from drive A and store it in a safe place.

INSTALLING THE DISK

The enclosed disk contains 14 individual files in a compressed format. In order to use the files, you must run the installation program for the disk.

You can install the disk onto your computer by following these steps:

1. Insert the *Executive Speeches* disk into Drive A of your computer. Type A: \ INSTALL.
2. The installation program will be loaded. After the title screen appears, you will be given the options shown in **Figure 1**.
3. The following Menu selections will be listed: Edit Destination Paths, Select Destination Drive, Toggle Overwrite Mode, Select Groups to Install, and Start Installation.
4. The **Destination Path** is the name of the default directory to store the data files. The default directory name is **SPEECHES**. To change this name, press ↵, hit the letter **P**, and type in the name of the directory you wish to use and press ↵.
5. **Select Destination Drive** gives you the option of installing the disk onto a hard disk drive C:\ or the drive you wish to install the files onto. This option can be seen in **Figure 2**.
6. The **Select Groups to Install** option, allows you to install each group on the disk one by one. The groups on the disk are broken into three different formats; ASCII, WordPerfect, and Microsoft Word for Windows. For example, if you only need to install the ASCII files, then you would select ASCII format as shown in **Figure 3**. If you wish to install the entire directory at once, tab down to Start Installation and press ↵, as shown in **Figure 3**.

The files are now successfully installed onto your hard drive.

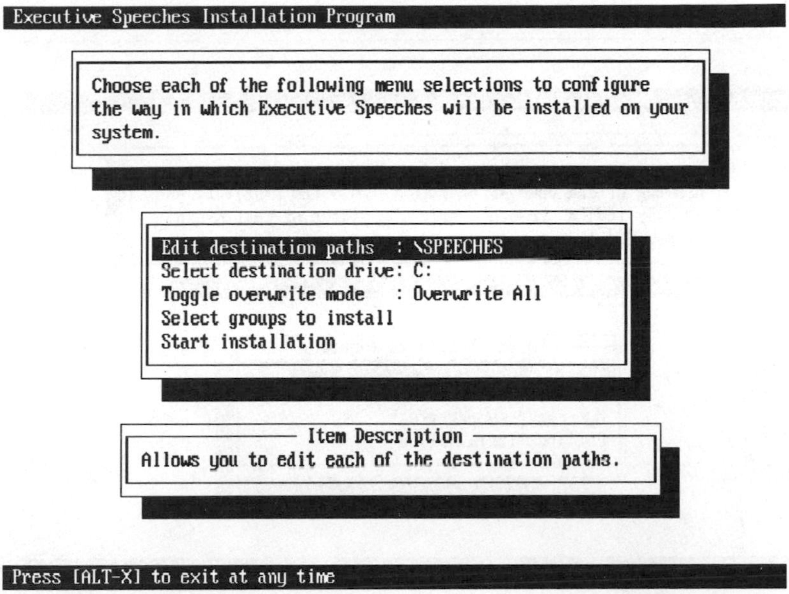

Executive Speeches Installation Program
Choose each of the following menu selections to configure the way in which Executive Speeches will be installed on your system.
Edit destination paths : \SPEECHES
Select destination drive: C:
Toggle overwrite mode : Overwrite All
Select groups to install
Start installation
Item Description
Allows you to edit each of the destination paths.
Press [ALT-X] to exit at any time

Figure 1.

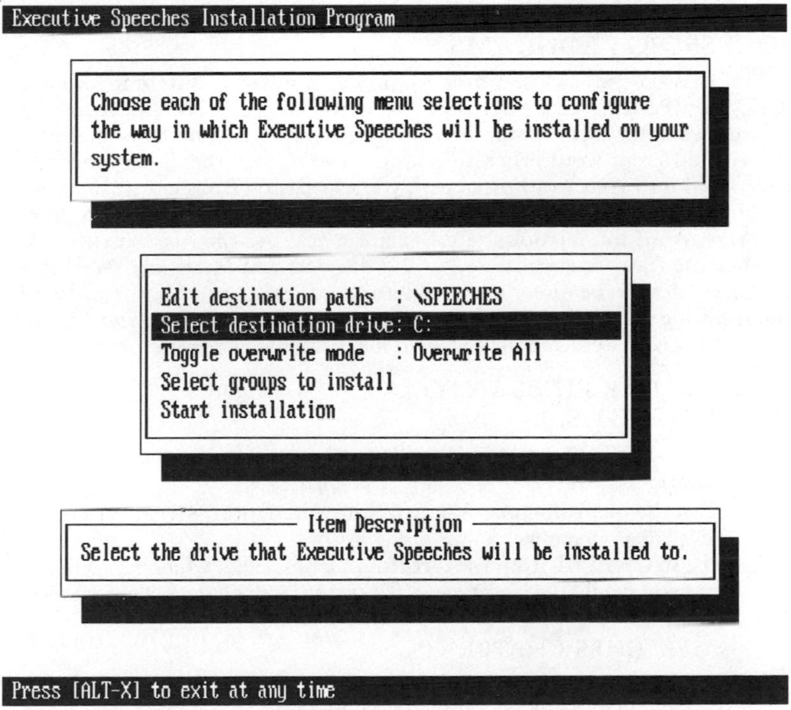

Executive Speeches Installation Program
Choose each of the following menu selections to configure the way in which Executive Speeches will be installed on your system.
Edit destination paths : \SPEECHES
Select destination drive: C:
Toggle overwrite mode : Overwrite All
Select groups to install
Start installation
Item Description
Select the drive that Executive Speeches will be installed to.
Press [ALT-X] to exit at any time

Figure 2.

Figure 3.

READING FILES INTO WORD PROCESSING PROGRAMS

The files on the enclosed disk are provided in three different formats; ASCII, WordPerfect, and Microsoft Word for Windows. ASCII format is standard format for DOS computers. Using this format, a number of different users with different word processing programs can read the disks. Once the file is loaded into your word processor, you can customize them to suit your individual needs. This means regardless of your word processing program (WordStar, Word for Windows, etc.), you can still use the files on the disk.

Since the files are also offered in WordPerfect and Microsoft Word formats, these files can be directly loaded into WordPerfect and Microsoft Word without having to convert the format. The ASCII, WordPerfect, and Microsoft Word formats were supplied to help meet the user's requirements.

READING THE FILES INTO WORDPERFECT 5.0

To read the CHAP01 file in WordPerfect, merely follow these steps:

1. Load the WordPerfect program as normal.
2. When the blank document screen is displayed, press SHIFT-F10 to retrieve the document.
3. Type in CHAP01 from the directory SPEECHES, which is the document you would like to retrieve. To open the document, type the following:

   C:\SPEECHES\CHAP01.WP5

4. Press ↵ when you have finished typing in the filename.
5. To print the document, press SHIFT-F7.

You can make any changes or revisions to the document. When you are through editing it, you can save it under a new file name before you quit.

READING THE FILES INTO WORDPERFECT
FOR WINDOWS

To read the files into WordPerfect for Windows, merely follow these steps:

1. Load the WordPerfect for Windows program as normal.
2. Select OPEN from the FILE menu.
3. The OPEN FILE dialog will appear, as shown in **Figure 4**. At this box, make the appropriate selections for the drive and subdirectory of the document you want to review. For instance, to open the file CHAP01 located in the SPEECHES subdirectory, you must select the SPEECHES subdirectory.
4. Under the FILES option on the left side of the dialog box, enter CHAP01.WP5 as the file name.
5. The file will immediately load into WordPerfect for Windows.
6. To print the file, select PRINT from the FILE menu.

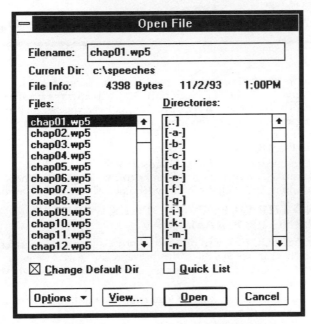

Figure 4.

READING THE FILES INTO MICROSOFT
WORD FOR WINDOWS

To read the file into Microsoft Word for Windows, merely follow these steps:

1. Load the Word for Windows program as normal.
2. When the Untitled document is displayed, select OPEN from the FILE menu.
3. The OPEN dialog box will appear, as shown in **Figure 5**. Make the appropriate selections for the drive and subdirectory of the document you

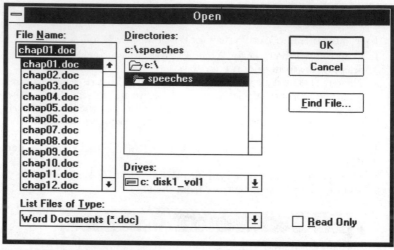

Figure 5.

want to review. For instance, the file will be located in drive C under the directory SPEECHES. To open SPEECHES, type C:\SPEECHES under the file name and click OK. Alternatively, you can click on the directories box to select the appropriate drive and subdirectory.

4. Under the FILES option on the left side of the dialog box, enter CHAP01.DOC as the file name.

The file will immediately load into Microsoft Word for Windows.

You can make any changes or revisions to the document. When you are through editing it, you should save it under a new file name before you quit.

READING THE FILES INTO OTHER WORD PROCESSING PROGRAMS

To use the ASCII files with other word processing programs, refer to the documentation that accompanies the package for instructions on *Using ASCII Files.* Often, the procedure is very similar to those listed above, with two primary steps:

1. Identify the file you want to load from the subdirectory and indicate the filename to your word processor.
2. Identify the file as a DOS text file.

After these general steps, most word processing programs will immediately load the file.

USER ASSISTANCE AND INFORMATION

John Wiley & Sons, Inc. is pleased to provide assistance to users of this package. Should you have any questions regarding the use of this package, please call our technical support number (212) 850-6194 weekdays between 9AM and 4PM Eastern Standard Time.

To place additional orders or to request information about other Wiley products, please call (800) 879-4539.

1

Why the Speech

An executive does nothing more important than speak.
JERRE L. STEAD,
CEO, Square D, Inc.

Many students who work summers at our plants then go back
to school in the fall ask me what courses they should take to
be best prepared for business. I always say, "Take all the speech
courses and communication courses you can. Because the
world turns on communication."
JOHN H. MCCONNELL,
CEO, Worthington Industries, Inc.

The leaders of organizations are people who understand com-
munication. If they didn't, they wouldn't be leaders.
LESLIE H. BUCKLAND,
CEO, Caribiner, Inc.

As I get older as a manager, I realize how little memorandums
accomplish, and how much personal appearances accomplish.
JOHN J. BYRNE,
CEO, Fireman's Fund Insurance Company

L ET'S NOT BEGIN the way so many typical public speaking books do—with a hand-holding, hand-wringing session of me commiserating that you have been given an invitation to speak and isn't it too bad that you feel nervous but not to worry because we'll solve your problem together.

Baloney! Being an executive, your chance to deliver a speech is like being confronted with a high voltage cable lying exposed at your feet. If you pick it up the wrong way, you'll get a serious shock. But if you know how to handle it, if you plug it in, it can boost both your business and career.

EXECUTIVES MUST COMMUNICATE

Most executives get nervous before giving a speech. Thomas A. Murphy, former chairman of General Motors, admitted to nervousness so intense before every speech that he was almost physically sick. Yet, Murphy knew that public speaking was so important that, as CEO, he accepted invitations to speak more than once a week. Because giving speeches enables you to extend and strengthen your influence as an executive, you shouldn't be defensive about them. Go on the attack and seize the moment. Make the most of the opportunity, and give a speech that exceeds your audience's expectations. The results may well exceed your expectations.

To be a successful executive, it's not enough to know your business. You must communicate your business. It's not enough to be a leader. You must communicate leadership. Communication isn't simply moving information. It's moving people by using information; it's transmitting a conviction from one person to another.

CEO COMMUNICATION

Gerard R. Roche, chairman of the executive search firm of Heidrick & Struggles, Inc., believes executives must continually sharpen their communication skills. As an executive search consultant, he's got to know what makes executives effective and how good executives communicate:

"I address a number of business graduate schools a year, and I tell them that their courses are so overloaded with analytical studies and accounting and financial analysis and statistics and all these quantitative, measurable subjects that the students and the schools neglect one of the most important management skills of all: the ability to communicate. When a CEO walks into his boardroom and there are twenty-two members there and he has to speak to them and communicate to them about the condition of the company and what he wants to do and where he wants to take it, his success or failure in being persuasive has a lot to do with his communication skills. There are virtually no successful CEOs who are not skilled communicators."

EXPRESS IDEAS TO GET AHEAD

Clearly, communicating with precision, clarity, and power isn't just a CEO's job, it's the job of every executive. Clark A. Johnson, CEO of Pier 1 Imports, says: "As I moved up in business, starting at the bottom as a lumber salesman, I watched how successful executives dressed and behaved. I saw that there was a strong correlation between their ability to express ideas and to get ahead."

EVERY EXECUTIVE'S JOB

I submit that this ability is closely associated with the speech, not speech as a faculty of thought, but the speech as an oral communication to an audience to obtain a result.

In learning how to prepare and deliver a good speech, you develop good communication skills—poise, articulation, the ability to assess and speak to audience needs, flexibility, conviction, and insight—communication skills that are also leadership skills.

THE SPEECH AS HISTORY

Few human activities have been more effective in shaping history than the speech.

Whether we think of Homer chanting the *Illiad*; Lao Tzu expounding on the Tao; Buddha, Christ, Confucius, or Muhammad teaching their followers; Caesar exhorting his legions; Hōjō Tokimune rallying his armies against Mongolian invaders; Faraday lecturing on electricity; Churchill in Fulton, Missouri; Kennedy in Berlin—all testify that if you want to communicate an idea, wrap it in a human being.

Even though we live in an age of sophisticated communication technologies, the speech is still a key, if not the key, to persuading people, compelling them, inspiring, and converting them.

THE SPEECH AS PROTEUS

Let's not think of a speech as merely a formal exercise in oratory before large numbers of people.

Speeches can be informal ways of communicating. They don't have to be prepared, they can be impromptu. They don't have to be one-way communication but can be give-and-take dialogues.

When counseling a subordinate, you're giving a kind of speech. When making a presentation to customers, you're giving a kind of speech. When trying to persuade your business team to take a certain course of action, you are giving a speech.

MORE SPEECHES NEEDED

A common thread in many interviews for this book is that increasing business competitiveness requires that more and better speeches be given.

Joellen Brown, Director of Executive Communications at Bell Atlantic Corporation, says: "It's extraordinary how much time and attention senior executives devote to speechwriting these days. Raymond Smith, our CEO, gives on average one formal speech a week and meets in informal discussions and groups more frequently."

Xerox Corporation's Communication Director, Joseph M. Cahalan, observes that the number of speeches given by top executives at his business "has increased dramatically in the last four or five years. We wrote more than 150 speeches for our top four or five executives last year."

The experiences of Xerox and Bell Atlantic are the rule—not the exception—in U.S. business today. Yet, running counter to the *need* to give more speeches is a common perception that executives' speeches are about as interesting as dry rot.

BETTER SPEECHES NEEDED

A speech can be a springboard or a snare. Raymond Price, Jr., former speech writer for Richard Nixon, bemoaned in the *Wall Street Journal*: "Why do corporate executives make such deadly speeches?"

Clearly, many corporate speeches seem to come off an assembly line like cans of potted meat. Too many executives can relate their experience as: "I came, I saw—I flopped."

But many executives—including those in this book—are making speeches that are dramatic and effective.

You can do it too. You *must* do it. "If you want to be a business leader, you have to learn to speak in front of people," says Uwe S. Wascher, head of world marketing for General Electric Company's $5-billion-a-year plastics business. "Speaking is one of the ways you carry out your management responsibilities. If you want to be the person who determines strategies, then you have no other choice but to be a good speaker. If you aren't, you lack something as a manager."

There's no secret to learning how to speak well. You don't have to be born to the calling. It takes knowledge, practice, and determination—and the use of proven techniques.

INSPIRING BUSINESS SPEECHES

Take Union Pacific Railroad's Michael Walsh. Since becoming the railroad's president in 1986, he's shaken the operation to its rail beds by eliminating management layers; spreading responsibility; investing in new plants, equipment, and technologies; and taking on the challenge of transforming the focus of the railroad's culture from one that serves the needs of its managers to one that serves the needs of its customers.

To communicate his message of change and challenge to Union Pacific's some 30,000 employees in 19 states, Walsh has instituted "town hall" meetings in which he travels to a work facility and delivers a prepared speech to employees. Then after a break, he'll answer questions—not for a few minutes but for several hours. Afterwards, he'll have a separate meeting with executives. Then he travels to the next facility and does it again.

HEAVEN, DIVORCE, HEADLINES, AND WAR

There is Martin C. Miler, CEO of Hibernia Corporation. Miler often begins his speeches this way:

> *There are a lot of things I want to discuss today. One is heaven; another is divorce court; another is marriage; another headlines. I want to read you some poetry, and we should discuss a global war. We are going to discuss our standard of living, curriculum, your raw material and your finished goods, and why you are in the front lines of the roaring war to be fought in the* 1990s.

Since becoming CEO in 1972, Miler has helped transform a backwater bank operating in a single New Orleans parish into the largest bank in Louisiana. In the process, Hibernia has racked up 16 straight years of record earnings—in a state with a depressed economy. Miler's success stems from his empowering Hibernia's employees with broad responsibilities and his communicating effectively. He's not a dull man. He doesn't run a dull bank. ("If you run a dull business, few people will be interested in what you say," he says.) And he doesn't give dull speeches.

THE SPEECH AS MESSAGE AND MASSAGE

John W. Rowe, CEO of New England Electric System, is another example. He says: "I enjoy giving speeches. I work at it. I think about them a lot before I give them. I think about them a lot when I'm doing them. I pay attention to those people out there in the audience."

Rowe's speeches are entertaining. ("I see myself as a kind of Herb Shriner at the podium," he says.) But they also have a message: that New England Electric is a responsive and responsible business. And his speeches are helping him get that message across to a variety of civic and government organizations as well as to security analysts. "When John Rowe is at the podium, he shows that he runs that business," says Edward F. Gaylor, portfolio manager for Dean Witter InterCapital.

SPEECHES TRIGGER SUCCESS

Mike Walsh, streamlining an old railroad; Martin Miler, empowering employees to achieve record earnings; John Rowe, going on the stump to build community and government support for his utility—these and other executives in this book demonstrate that an executive's speech doesn't have to be like a dose of NyQuil. It can be interesting, humorous, dramatic, insightful, and vital to a firm's success.

20 Reasons Why Speeches Are Vital to An Executive's Success

1. COMMUNICATE CHANGE

Rapid, deep, powerful change is transforming the business of every executive I interviewed. Their markets are changing, their customers changing, their manufacturing methods changing, the structure and size of their businesses changing, and their technologies changing.

When a business changes, good communication is needed, communication by leaders to people inside and outside the business, communication to define the change and enable people to adapt to and even to shape that change.

Andrew H. Hines, Jr., CEO of Florida Progress Corporation, says: "In times of change, it's extremely important for business executives to give good speeches. Otherwise, a lot of people will have their imaginations drawing the wrong pictures for them."

Change, Communications, and Dexter

Talk about wrenching change! David L. Coffin, CEO of The Dexter Corporation, has his hands full. In the 1930s, Dexter's chief product was tea bag paper. Today, the firm, founded in 1767, the oldest on the New York Stock Exchange, is producing high-tech, specialty materials for such markets as aerospace, medicine, food packaging, electronics, automotive products, and industrial fabrication and assembly. And it's expanding around the world. He's got a lot to communicate.

"If we didn't change, we'd be out of business," Coffin says. "So change itself is not an issue with us. The issues are what and how to change. A lot of people in Dexter didn't understand what a global business is and what it means to be in that business. We just keep beating away at communicating what being global means to Dexter. People have to feel the need to be on the right boat, going in the right direction. And speeches are an important way to communicate these things."

2. PROVIDE CONTINUITY OF CHANGE

Few large U.S. businesses have changed as profoundly during the 1980s as General Electric. In 1981, when John F. Welch, Jr., became CEO, the corporation was composed of 350 businesses and major product lines, with products ranging from ballpoint pen tips to nuclear power plants.

Today GE has consolidated to 13 businesses: all global, all leaders in their industries; and GE's earnings are more than two and one half times what they were in 1980.

Although GE has changed radically, the themes Welch has communicated throughout the decade have remained the same. General Electric speechwriter, William K. Lane, Jr., says that it was Welch's constant reiteration of those themes that helped change the corporation and its culture:

Establish Groundwork for Action

"Communicating has been a very important element in Jack Welch's success. I couldn't say that formal, standup speeches did it. But his constant talking of the themes he stressed right from the beginning—being number one or number two in every business, taking ownership of your business, being candid, seeing things as they really are and not as they should be—themes that many businesses are struggling with now—he started communicating back in 1981. I remember when he first started articulating these ideas, many people thought that next week there would be different slogans. But he kept it up and kept it up. He began to back it up with actions. We sold our housewares business, our TV business, our toasters business. Can you imagine GE without toasters? That was a cultural shock of the highest order! But if the businesses weren't number one or number two in their industries, we got rid of them. So Jack not only communicated ideas, he backed them up by actions."

3. HELP TRANSFORM A COMPANY'S CULTURE

"Speeches are very important to our business," says John O'Brien, CEO of Grumman Corporation:

"First of all, I can't give an external speech without first thinking of how it is going to be received internally by the 30,000 people who work here. My position in regard to people outside the company will effect people inside our company one way or the other. If I am going to take on the Secretary of Defense, they have to decide if I'm going to win the battle or the war.

Think Differently

"My speeches are designed primarily for communicating where I want the company to go. What I want at this stage is for the company to change its culture. . . . I want people to think differently. I want them to question why they are doing what they are doing when there is a better way to do it. I want them to change how they do things. I want them to know why we have to change."

Floor-By-Floor

When Edward J. Noha became CEO of the CNA Insurance Companies in 1975, the business had to change or go under. Having lost $200 million that year, CNA was practically insolvent. Noha faced a turnaround challenge of epic dimensions. He knew that before he could change the business, he had to first inspire and change its employees.

When he arrived at CNA, he was asked to talk to CNA's some 12,000 employees over a loudspeaker. He recalls that he rejected that idea:

"I told them, 'No, I'll go floor-by-floor. I want them to see me. I want to shake their hands. I want them to talk to me.' So I went through this building floor by floor—44 stories. I talked to groups of 15 to 20 employees. I worked six months straight, seven days a week, making sure I met with every person there, doing operating reviews at every level, reorganizing the company, and moving it forward."

Today, CNA is one of the leading insurance organizations in the United States, and it all began with Noha's person-to-person style of communication.

4. COMMUNICATE A VISION

To be an effective speaker, an executive must not only understand what does change—but what doesn't change.

And what doesn't change in the world of most successful executives are values and vision.

Vision is the power of seeing new realities.

Communication is convincing people to attain those realities.

And values unite the executive's team in going after the vision.

Nevius M. Curtis, CEO of Delmarva Power in Wilmington, Delaware, has relied on speeches to clarify what doesn't change in a changing world.

Galactic Gulf

When he became CEO in 1980, the blue collar/white collar gulf was of galactic dimensions.

"I found out that workers had a strong feeling of disenfranchisement from those decisions that affected their jobs and their futures. So it was clear back then that it was time to change the way we did business in every area, to break down barriers between workers and executives, and workers and customers. And first and foremost, there had to be a vision! A vision is the crucial underpinning for change. The vision we developed was that we at Delmarva are creating a work environment in which all employees have a feeling of self-worth; that they are using their God-given talents; and that their daily work is of value. Speeches have been extremely important in helping us attain that vision. In order for a vision to become reality, it has to be articulated, almost ad nauseum. The mistake is to think that if we say it once, it will be absorbed. But to get it absorbed, you have to repeat and repeat it and constantly refine it."

Constant Dial Tone

NYNEX Corporation's CEO, William C. Ferguson, observes that speeches are essential for communicating vision and direction to the business' some 90,000 employees. "To communicate vision, you have to have what we call constant 'dial tone.' You can't expect to give one speech and have it absolutely understood and embraced. You have to continually talk about it and elaborate on it and find better ways of saying it."

5. INFLUENCE INDUSTRY

No business operates in a vacuum. Out beyond the front doors are not only customers, but also competitors, investors, media, government officials, and the public at large. View your audience as merely an internal one, and you eliminate a large number of opportunities to advance your business.

Florida Progress' CEO, Andrew Hines, says, "A company can't remain silent in the industry or the area in which it operates, so its executives must speak to that industry and to the community."

BellSouth Corporation's Director of Corporate Planning and Development, Mylle H. Bell, says: "BellSouth is a leader in the telecommunications industry. Therefore, it's critical at this time to be a leader in shaping the ideas of what the industry needs. Having our executives give speeches to groups outside the corporation is an important way to accomplish this."

Sexier, Faster Company

The CEO of Cypress Semiconductors Corporation, Dr. T. J. Rodgers, says that when he worked at Advanced Micro Devices from 1979 to 1981, he was impressed that Jerry Sanders (AMD's founder) "didn't just talk about microprocessors and RAMS and profits and losses. He typically latched onto some significant issue, often a national issue, and raised that in public and the industry. We at AMD felt that we worked for a sexier, faster-moving company, with more vision for the future than its competitors. So when I founded my own business, I set out to be a publicly visible company both for the sake of our employees and our investors."

6. INFLUENCE INVESTORS

Dr. Robert A. Fildes, CEO of Cetus Corporation, a California biotechnology company, says that the speech is a primary tool for communicating to the investor community:

"We spend a lot of time convincing investors that bio-technology can be turned into a profitable business. That entails our giving speeches to groups of potential investors. It's important that you know where you are taking the company and can articulate that in a clear way to those people. It's my impression that they want to know what makes the CEO of that company tick. They want to know how convincing he is as an individual, how excited he is about the future of his company, and how he plans to go forward and build this business that he has this dream for. Often when people are talking to me, instead of talking about products and numbers, they spend most of the time talking about how *I* think and how I would deal with problems, how I feel about the management team. If you can't get up at the drop of a hat to explain what you are doing, and why you are excited about what you are going, you're not going to survive."

Investing In People

T. J. Rodgers observes that giving speeches to investors, for instance:

"Forces me to think about where we are going, what we are doing, what can I tell investors about why we're so good. What can I tell them that I don't want the competitors to hear. Investors all tend to look forward. So you have to make projections: technical, political, strategic projections—which people find interesting. Venture capitalists are much more interested in me and our people than in our business plan. Of course, if you have a terrible business plan, it can kill you. At our original meetings with our first major investor, he said, 'We are big fans of T. J. Rodgers but we are not big fans of your business plan. But we can work that out.' "

7. INCREASE LEARNING

Articulating your ideas is not only an act of communication, it's an act of learning too.

The psychologist B. F. Skinner said that "The paper I complete has almost no resemblance to the paper I set out to write. I learned what I had to say."

Learn By Speaking

New England Electric System's CEO, John Rowe, says that when he makes a speech he usually learns:

"Four times as much as anyone listening learns. Trying to communicate with others, to give speeches, requires that you first learn the subject yourself. You are learning while you do the outline, learning while you mull over what you are going to say, and you are even learning while you are actually speaking. When you get up in front of a group of people you respect and want to depend on, you don't want to seem like a fool. You want to say something that makes sense. The act of speaking forces me to take three or four threads of some issue I was working on and weave them together, and then stand by it all. During the work day, you often hide from those ultimate resolutions. When you get up in front of employees, they don't want to hear that you are hiding. They want to know what you stand for."

GE's William Lane says: "Preparing for a speech is an opportunity for Jack Welch to sit down with a tape recorder, take time out from day to day business, and think and talk about what makes the company go."

8. PROMOTE SOCIAL VALUES

It's often said that labor is useless without capital, capital impotent without executive leadership, and executive leadership powerless without the community's sanction. Corporate profits should be viewed not as a function of greed, but as a vote of society's confidence.

As businesses come under increasing public and media scrutiny, executives are having to speak out on how their activities benefit not just business but society. You can't beat the speech as a means of communicating sincerity and integrity.

The Washington Consulting Group's CEO, Armando C. Chapelli, Jr., says, "Speeches given to community groups and nonprofit organizations are very, very good for our company. Those speeches can create a good perception of the corporation and also enable us to attract talented people. So speeches are great for recruiting, great for opening up new business opportunities, and great for developing community opportunities."

9. BROADEN BUSINESS CONTACTS

We miss success if we miss the opportunity. By giving a speech, an executive can broaden professional contacts. It doesn't matter if your business is bricks in Baton Rouge and you're addressing woodworkers in Washington—practically every speaking opportunity enables you to increase the number of people who view you as an effective executive.

"Giving speeches is a key way I let increasing numbers of people know about my business and me," says Linda S. Mathieu, CEO of TEFRA, Inc., a third-party retirement plan administration firm.

Barbara Walden, CEO of Barbara Walden Cosmetics, observes that in speaking to a variety of audiences, she has made a great many business contacts. "Giving speeches, I've had the opportunity to meet many business leaders," she says. "We would get together and chat, and I would learn a lot from them: about running a company, about promoting from within, about being a good boss."

10. ENHANCE SALES

Every sales presentation is essentially a speech. If communication is transferring a conviction from one person to another, then sales is transferring a conviction from seller to buyer. A good salesperson doesn't simply list benefits and features of a product. If communicating such lists were the only thing that mattered in making sales, customers would be sent brochures or video tapes, and salespeople would look for other work. But salespeople make that vital contact: personal contact. "If you want somebody to take notice, you have to deliver the message personally," says J. Bruce Llewellyn, CEO of the Philadelphia Coca-Cola Bottling Company. Because each customer is different, each sales pitch must be different. Salespeople that are practiced in giving speeches are better able to think quickly on their feet and tailor their ideas to each situation.

11. ADVANCE MARKETING

Speeches can also enhance marketing thrusts.

Many executives I interviewed assert that business people must understand that sales and marketing are totally different activities.

Sales is goal-oriented. Marketing is growth-oriented. Sales focuses on selling and serving current customers. Marketing focuses on getting new customers. When you sell, you ask for customers' business. When you market, you position your business in such a way that customers often ask for your business.

You don't sell products when giving a marketing speech. You define your audience's needs and offer solutions to their problems, often without even mentioning your business or products (See Chapter 4).

Marketing Competitiveness

Dr. Armand V. Feigenbaum, CEO of General Systems, Inc., delivers speeches around the world on competitiveness and quality. In most speeches, he's not selling his products: he's selling answers to the challenges of competitiveness. He's marketing:

"I gave one of the keynote speeches in Detroit in the New World Automotive Congress. I didn't talk about my business products. I talked about systems that drive quality in the auto industry. The speech was well received and got good notices in the press. And it had a favorable consequence on our marketing. Clearly, our business in the auto sector, which was already good, found in the next three months an additional surge forward."

Marketing Health and Fitness

Sheila T. Cluff knows the value of using speeches as a marketing tool. She is CEO of Fitness, Inc., a spa and health product business in California.

"I'm in business to help improve people's health and the quality of their lives," she says. "I give many speeches around the United States. I personally love to share information about health and wellness. It's a great joy to capture an audience, to have a give-and-take with that audience. I'm not talking about my business. I'm talking about *their* health and well-being. But the message is there anyway, the message that my business can meet their needs. And it's a more powerful message for my *not* having said it."

12. INCREASE YOUR VALUE TO YOUR BUSINESS

The executive who can prepare and deliver the timely speech, the well-crafted speech, the speech that changes or reinforces perceptions, is an executive who is tremendously valuable to a business.

John Rowe's value to New England Electric System extends beyond his ability to keep the utility running smoothly. Rowe is in constant demand to give talks throughout the community. Not just because he is a good speaker, but because when he does speak, he is the embodiment of the utility. Since the performance of a speaker is not just who he is but who he is *perceived* to be, Rowe's podium successes increase public goodwill for the business. He says:

A Speech Is a Sell

"A speech is a way you sell yourself. In a job like mine, if you sell yourself well, it gives you some modest credibility. At the same time, you sell a few very basic ideas about your company. Selling those ideas and gaining that credibility can make the difference that if you screw up, somebody will call you up and tell you you've screwed up, and not call the governor first. My kind of business is here for the long run. Speeches are more like lubricant to create a broad base of goodwill in the community. It's not as if I'm out there to sell one specific piece of real estate and if I sell it, retire to Florida. I sell trust."

13. INCREASE YOUR PROMOTION OPPORTUNITIES

Often the best way to stand out as an executive is to stand up and speak—and speak well. A single, awkward speech before the wrong audience can undo years of quiet accomplishment. It can leave the audience thinking that you cannot communicate (and lead) effectively.

On the other hand, a strong speech before the right audience can give your career a quick, powerful boost.

"Speeches have been very important to my career," says John J. Byrne, CEO of Fireman's Fund Insurance Company. "I have been chosen for jobs often because of the reputation I had as a speaker."

In the Spotlight

"I've seen many executives who aren't shining stars in the company make a name for themselves by doing a meeting well or giving a presentation well," says Vincent Sottosanti, CEO of Aniforms, Inc. "It's the one time when you are on stage, the spotlight is on you, and many people are going to form an opinion of you. You want the audience to say that you are intelligent, well organized, and articulate."

Career Booster

Gary E. Nei became CEO of Lyphomed, Inc. at the age of 45. He says that an important factor in his success has been his ability to give good speeches:

"Thinking back across my career, I can see that important speeches delivered at the appropriate time helped, to a large extent, to put me where I am. On a number of occasions, I had taken over a new division or there had been a turn-around situation in the business where people's expectations were particularly acute. Giving a speech, I had a chance to create an initial good impression. That first occasion you speak to your people is an opportunity to tell them where you want the business to go. If they can identify with you and with what you say, you're halfway home. When you finish, you'll know they're following you and not second-guessing you."

Speeches and Career Paths

Delmarva Power's CEO, Nevius Curtis, asserts that he looks for the ability to speak well in public in assessing executive performance. "We are very fussy in our company about who gives presentations and how they are given," he says. "They have to be succinct, to the point, well done. If you can't handle that, you are not going to be a top executive at Delmarva."

Keep Improving

Keep improving as a speaker. Keep doing speeches well. You'll find that you may be asked to start substituting for people who are not speaking well.

14. POSITION YOURSELF FOR CAREER CHANGES

Significant advances in business take place when a person, for one reason or another, is forced to change fields. Career advancement isn't just about going up; it's also about going sideways or even getting out of one field and going into another. In giving speeches, you are compelled to learn new things, involve many different people in your ideas, and so expand career and change-of-career opportunities.

15. ENHANCE BUSINESS GROWTH

"In several instances," said one CEO, "speeches helped us buy a company because people selling their company were looking for somebody they could be comfortable with. At the podium, I was able to come across as a person they wanted to do business with."

"Public speaking is an essential part of our businesses growth," says George L. Pla, CEO of the Cordoba Corporation. "Basically our business is in land use, urban planning, and those are broad and hot topics. I get to speak in a lot of private and public forums. In addition, we require that each of our offices be a player in the market they are in. They have to be very involved in the community, which means their executives have to do a lot of public speaking. So the Cordoba Corporation has a very high profile in Los Angeles. That's helped our ability to recruit."

16. PROMOTE TECHNOLOGICAL AND STATISTICAL UNDERSTANDING

Because a speech is one of the most personal forms of executive communication, you can't separate what you say from who you are. You might be talking about facts, but you are also communicating, whether you know it or not, *beliefs*— your beliefs about the way to dress, the way to articulate, the way to engage an audience, the way to use or not use visual support, the way to carry yourself, the way to gesture, the way to develop and meet objectives.

If you just want to communicate facts alone, send a brochure.

Speeches offer unique opportunities to communicate technological and statistical concepts. There is a great demand for specialists, such as technologists and accountants, who can communicate their knowledge in simple, clear terms. Specialists who wish to advance their careers must view that communication as essential for their success.

17. BE NEWSWORTHY

It's a sales maxim that satisfied customers can often sell your products better than your best salespeople. That's true for publicity as well.

"The obvious thing missing in almost all corporate speeches is newsworthiness," says John F. Budd, Jr., vice chairman of the public relations firm Carl Byoir & Associates, Inc. "Most companies don't make news in the area they want to make news, and most reporters don't interview the companies' executives on the subjects they want to talk about."

Often, the best publicity is *free* publicity, the publicity you gain when influential people not connected with your business are so inspired by your message that they become self-appointed promoters of you and your products.

In giving a good speech, you develop the issues you want developed, the way you want, when you want, and so create opportunities to make converts to your cause who will spread your gospel far beyond the room in which you talk.

18. COMMUNICATE A TURNING POINT

History is replete with people who changed the course of events by giving speeches.

As an executive, you probably won't be engaged in turning the tides of history, but by giving a speech, you might be able to make a major difference in the course your business is taking.

Joseph A. Rice, CEO of Irving Bank Corporation, gave a speech in Saratoga, New York, in 1975 that came to be called the "Saratoga Speech" in the way that sports fans call the 1950s Giants/Colts overtime contest "The Game" or the Ali/Frazier bout in the Philippines, "The Thrilla In Manila"—a sobriquet suggesting that, at least in New York banking circles, history was made.

Breaking the News

New banking laws went into effect that year that permitted statewide bank branching. Rice says:

"Before that, banks were only permitted to have holding companies made up of individual banks. We at Irving Bank had acquired 14 banks with individual names, banks that were key participants in individual markets. But with the change in the law, it was clear that this type of confederacy was not the most efficient way to run a large banking organization. So changes had to be made. And one way to make those changes was to remove their independence and place them under the same name and same strategic banner. Since I had just been named president of the holding company, I was given the task of breaking the news. I did it with a speech, the famous 'Saratoga Speech.' "

"Good Buddies" No More

The audience was composed of the banks' CEOs. They wanted to hear that we were good buddies as always. But I was there to tell them that the 'good buddy' era was over. The new approach had to be presented crisply, unequivocally, and in a determined way in order to create the change we saw to be necessary. The speech was simple and direct. I made it clear that whatever we would do from now on together was going to be in the best interests of the business as a whole. And if the best interests were served by merging the independents, then we were going to do it!

"Well, the coughing began. I saw faces getting red. We had the possibility of rebellion in that room! Before, the language had been 'partnership.' But now with the change in banking laws, 'partnership' was suddenly a clear cop-out. I made sure they understood that words like 'partnership' and 'independent' were no longer operative. Instead, words like 'integration' and 'coalescence' were. Talk about communication! This wasn't a message any of these people wanted to hear. But they heard it!"

19. MAKE MEETINGS PRODUCTIVE

"Catching a fly ball is a pleasure," said former New York Yankee outfielder Tommy Heindrich, "but knowing what to do with it is a business."

Large-scale meetings and conventions can be a pleasure to attend—but knowing how to use them productively is a business, sometimes a very big business.

Taking people away from their jobs, flying them thousands of miles and putting them up in the best hotels for a business meeting is an expensive investment. It's an investment that should pay off in better training, better communications, more productive employees, better morale, and a better understanding of the business' strategies and goals.

"When you want to give people a new direction in business or reinforce an old direction, hold a meeting and have the leader speak to them," says Leslie H. Buckland, CEO of Caribiner. "Meetings change people's minds. Memos seldom do. Videos seldom do. Throughout history, the great leaders of armies, religions, and political organizations understood that when they wanted to inspire people, they gathered them together in a special place and spoke to them."

An Executive Must Speak

"Companies can spend a great deal of money, sometimes over four million dollars, on speech support and communication for a single meeting," says Aniforms' Vincent Sottosanti, "but no matter how much they are spending, somewhere along the line, an executive has to get up and give a speech. All the rest is paraphernalia and show business. You may have live entertainment, all the bells and whistles of communications, and a fullblown show, but if the executive is ill prepared, he's hurting his career and his business."

This may be the only chance you have to talk to these people this year. Don't waste money by giving a mediocre speech. Make it worth their while and the business' to communicate a message that will stay with them long after the meeting is over.

20. BUILD TEAMWORK

General Electric's Uwe Wascher says that speeches are inherently team-building mechanisms:

"An audience is a kind of team. Because they are more or less interested in what you say, they usually have a common goal. Let's say you put another audience and another speaker in the very next room. He can talk on a different subject or even the same subject as you are talking on. If you remove the wall, you could have two teams, each with its own beliefs, ready to go in its own direction."

SUMMARY

Speeches come in many varieties—from formal platform type to informal, give-and-take, one-on-one sessions. They are not just tools to communicate, they are themselves the very essence of executive communication. So when you are asked to speak, don't think you have a problem, *know* you have an opportunity. Be an exceptional executive by being an exceptional speaker. Now let's examine proven techniques that will help make you exceptional.

2

The Audience

The most important advice I could give an executive: Seek every opportunity to give a speech.

ROBERT E. MERCER,
Retired CEO, The Goodyear Tire & Rubber Co., Inc.

Never give the impression that you haven't prepared. Why should I sit there and listen to somebody who didn't think enough of the audience to prepare?

WILLIAM C. FERGUSON,
CEO of NYNEX Corporation

Don't waste people's time. If you can't get up there and make it worth people's while to listen to you, don't do the speech.

ARTHUR BROWN,
CEO of Hecla Mining Company

Many times in giving a speech, I say things that I not only didn't plan to say but didn't know I knew.

CLARK A. JOHNSON,
CEO of Pier 1 Imports, Inc.

If all my possessions were taken away from me with one exception, I would choose the power of speech. For by it, I would regain all the rest of my possessions.

DANIEL WEBSTER

I T'S BEEN SAID OFTEN that communication only happens when the other person gets the point. The fact is, communication can't happen unless you yourself get the point—the point that *you* want to make.

To give an effective speech, you must know who you are, what you want, why you are there, what you want to say, and how you are going to say it.

Only then can you begin analyzing an audience.

BE YOURSELF BY KNOWING YOURSELF

"Any individual who is giving speeches has to be clear about his or her beliefs," says Hibernia Corporation's CEO Martin C. Miler. "If you have that sense of clarity—then you can move on to technique."

Daniel E. Evans, CEO of Bob Evans Farms, an Ohio-based restaurant chain that is expanding throughout the South, says: "One of the things I made up my mind to do many years ago when I first started giving speeches was to be myself, whatever that is. If that isn't good enough, they'll have to get somebody else to give the speech. You can't be what you're really not."

KNOWING YOURSELF HELPS LIVEN UP YOUR SPEECHES

Fitness, Inc.'s CEO, Sheila T. Cluff, says: "You have to know yourself as a speaker. That comes from having a passion for what you do. And having the knowledge and expertise in your field. When you have a good sense of who you are, you can package that knowledge and the passion and have the audience sitting on the edge of the chairs waiting to hear what you will say next."

Knowing who you are entails knowing where you came from. Lupita Armendariz is the Equal Opportunity manager at NASA Johnson Space Center in Houston, Texas. Part of her job is to recruit minority students into college engineering programs. That entails giving many talks before many different groups. She says:

"I grew up poor in south Texas in an Hispanic community and had to overcome many obstacles in my life. It's very important that I am honest about who I am so that I can make genuine contact with the audience. If I am talking to women, I want to relate to them through my professional and personal experiences. If I am talking to students, I want them to identify with me, identify with the fact that maybe we share a similar background but that its possible to go on, get an education, overcome adversity in life."

THE HARDEST THING IN LIFE

On a freeway, I pulled up behind a car and read the bumper sticker: WATCH OUT FOR THE PERSON BEHIND ME.

Wondering who that person was, I suddenly realized it was me. I had better watch out for *me*.

I don't want to make too much of bumper-sticker philosophy: but that particular sticker makes a good point. It's a point made by the Ancient Greek philosopher Thales who said that *the hardest thing in life is to know yourself, and the easiest thing is to give advice.* And it's a point made by Pogo, who said, "We have met the enemy and he is us."

TAPE YOURSELF

Of course, Thales and Pogo didn't have access to a video camera and VCR. Those tools can help us know ourselves better by enabling us to see ourselves as others see us. In any case, if *you* have access to them, use them. If you hire a coach, require that he or she use them.

CULTIVATE CRITICS

Every speaker should have a way of getting feedback on how well you are communicating.

Goodyear's Robert Mercer says:

"It's vital to have a critic that you can trust and believe in. Otherwise, you can't improve. Our public relations vice president was one such critic for me. My wife was another. My speech writer, a third critic. I tried to make sure that one or more of those people were at every speech I delivered and that I was given an honest appraisal of my performance."

ENCOURAGING FEEDBACK

Square D Company's CEO, Jerre L. Stead, is transforming the organization from being product-based to being customer-based by increasing the sales force and worldwide distribution network and by moving into specialty niches. "I work hard at getting honest feedback from our employees about my performance," Stead says. "I encourage employees to write letters to me. During the last three years, I have personally answered 4,500 letters."

BE OUTRAGEOUS . . . IN PRACTICE

People with a chance to observe the great actor Lawrence Olivier in rehearsal were often shocked. Instead of seeing a consummate technician learning his part with poise and confidence, they saw a buffoon—the renowned Olivier shouting absurdly, gesturing outrageously, leaping foolishly about, gibbering, and guffawing.

This was the madness in Olivier's method. "Never be afraid to be outrageous," he said. In that way, he got to know the full dimensions of the character he was playing.

PARE DOWN

As rehearsals went on, Olivier would pare down his acting to synchronize with the character. But he claimed that those

early stages of rehearsal were the key to a successful performance.

So take a tip from Lawrence Olivier: get to know yourself
better by being outrageous when you're alone practicing: Leave
the script behind, make dramatic gestures, get away from the
podium, and march, shouting your lines up and down the
aisles.

Often we can't be effective speakers without first going
through a period of speaking ineffectively. We have no idea
how good we'll ever be as long as we assume we can't be
different—and better.

JUST SPEAK

Football can be a complicated game, but the late Big Daddy
Lipscomb viewed it in simple terms. The former all-pro tackle
with the Baltimore Colts said, "I just wade in and pick up ball
players until I come to the one with the ball. Him I keep."

Take that approach with speaking. Just "wade in." That
is, stand up time and time again before live audiences — and
just speak!

If you have never been scared or embarrassed or hurt before
audiences—you probably haven't given many speeches.

And if you haven't given many speeches, you have yet to
discover who you are when you stand alone to speak to people.

LIVE THE EXAMINED LIFE

Those are a few ways to analyze yourself. It's hard to do.
It takes years to do. It takes nerve. It takes a willingness to
risk failure. It takes living the examined life. But it has to be
done if you are to speak well.

Yet, knowing yourself is only half the battle. As Menander,
the ancient Greek comic writer, said· "In many ways, the saying
'Know yourself' is not well said. It's more practical to say,
'Know other people.' "

Let's examine how we go about knowing other people, the
other people who are the audience. If they aren't receiving,

you might as well not be sending. Understanding the needs of the people you are talking to is an essential prerequisite of communication. A top real estate salesman, who is blind, said that he doesn't have to see through his eyes because he sees through his customers' eyes. The best speakers have the knack of seeing through their audiences' eyes.

Here are 19 tips for doing that.

1. KNOW WHEN NOT TO SPEAK

Often, the problem for the executive isn't the lack of opportunities to speak. The problem is knowing when *not* to speak.

"Sometimes the best kind of audience analysis you can do is the one that leads you not to give the speech," says United Technologies' speechwriter Laurence Cohen.

So, before you accept an invitation, understand what the audience wants from you, what you want to say to the audience, and if the two "wants" mesh.

Audience Needs

It's relatively simple to assess the audience's needs. At a minimum, you should contact the person organizing the event, as well as somebody else connected with it, and ask what's expected of you. Of course, the audience's expectations may involve several agendas (See Chapter 4).

Let's say, though, that your audience's expectations have been clearly described. The rule of thumb in this case is simple. TEFRA's CEO, Linda S. Mathieu, gives this tip when she says: "Know more than the people in your audience."

If you don't know more, learn more. If you can't learn more before the time to speak, don't give the talk.

General Systems Company's CEO, Armand V. Feigenbaum, agrees: "Never—and that's a big word but I mean it— never accept a speaking commitment for which you are not expected to do extremely well."

2. KNOW WHAT YOU WANT REPEATED

"Know what you want the audience to repeat back to you at the end of the speech," says Lawrence J. Schoenberg, CEO of AGS Computers, Inc.

U.S. troops had a saying in Vietnam: *payback is a bitch*. This saying can be applied today in giving speeches. Payback is what the audience thinks or does at the end of your speech. Did you convince them? Will they take the action you want? Will the press report things accurately?

To make sure that the payback is right, think about what you want it to be and how you are going to get it—not when you are standing at the podium and are about to conclude your talk, but well before that: when you have been given the invitation to speak and are deciding whether or not to give the talk in the first place.

Responsibility

"There is a great responsibility in giving a speech," says Syntex Corporation's CEO, Paul E. Freiman. "That responsibility is not to blow smoke at your audience. Give them something substantial they can take away. You really have to prepare your thoughts well before giving a speech. That's the single most important thing I've found in giving speeches."

3. KNOW WHAT THE AUDIENCE WANTS CHANGED

Who you are as a speaker is what you think your audience is. If you think that your audience has no more flexibility and understanding than a block of wood, the chances are you'll give a wooden speech.

Instead, if you view your audience as needing your message, as being open to humor, persuasion, and change, if you view yourself as the best person to bring this message, then your speech has a good chance of interesting them, changing them, and moving them to action.

"The more important the speech," says Square D's CEO, Jerre Stead, "the more time you spend not on the speech alone but finding out what is going on with the audience."

4. KNOW THE AUDIENCES WITHIN THE AUDIENCE

NYNEX Corporation's CEO, William C. Ferguson, advises that in analyzing an audience, speakers should pay attention to the audiences within the audience. View the audience not as a single entity, but as a collection of groups.

"Giving a speech is the next best thing to having one on one discussions with people," he says.

When you understand the needs of various individuals and groups within the audience, you better understand the audience's general needs.

Audience Investigation

Martha S. Hicks, CEO of Harwell-Hicks Real Estate Research, also emphasizes understanding the needs of the different groups in the audiences she speaks before:

"I give many speeches. It's a way of getting more and more people to know about my company. When I'm invited to speak, I ask the person who extended the invitation what the mix of the audience is, what the topic is for the day. I put my research skills to work. I call board members of the group. I call people I know and ask if they know anything about the group I'll be talking to. To a large extent, the mixture of men and women in an audience determines the kind of talk I'll give. In an audience with a lot of men, I am very aware of coming across with confidence and power. Because often, men will probably be wondering, "What can she show me that I already don't know?" We women have to be perceived as positive and persuasive and be respected for that."

Leadership Is Mobilizing People

Mylle H. Bell of BellSouth does much of her audience research just before she gives a talk:

"It doesn't do any good to be dead right about your subject if nobody in the audience is with you. This is especially so in regard to executive leadership. Being a leader means mobilizing people and having them be so turned on by what you say that they act. So, in speaking to an audience from a leadership position, it's important to know what interests them. In speaking, the issue is not to force the audience into your brain, but to take what you know and translate it into their context.

Polling the Audience

"Before the speech, I mill around and talk to people in the audience. I'm not the kind of person that sits and meditates before giving a speech. People are usually there for a reason. Let's say they are interested in international education. So you take a kind of poll: ask what their concerns are, assess their level of sophistication in the subject so you won't insult them by talking above or below them. By talking to the audience beforehand, you can also find out who are your friends and often your enemies too, the people who are going to be skeptical of your message."

5. LET THE AUDIENCE DECIDE THE TALK

Mylle Bell polls the audience before giving the speech and then makes adjustments in what she will say.

But TEFRA's CEO, Linda S. Mathieu, doesn't prepare her speech until after her speech has begun.

"The topic I deal with, retirement planning, can be very intricate. So I start out asking them, why have they come to hear me talk? I get feedback from them right away, right away assessing their knowledge level. I ask them, 'Are you here because you have your own business and retirement plans?' I ask how many are self-employed. How many are incorporated. I get a show of hands. So I come to understand what area I should target. In this way, the talk I give is decided by the audience."

Barbara Walden Cosmetics' CEO, Barbara Walden, says that conversing with members of the audience before she speaks has changed her ideas of what message she should deliver. "Many times I have showed up at the social hour before I was to speak and, in getting to know some of the people I would speak to, changed my entire speech. I left it at my table, got up, and just spoke from the heart."

6. KNOW THE PHYSICAL ENVIRONMENT

No audience is an island. It's not only influenced by the various groups within it but also by events and ideas of the past and present as well as expectations of the future.

So analyze the place the audience is in. Understand the importance of the room where you're speaking, the building that houses the room, the city the building is in, and even the region surrounding the city.

A short time ago, I helped create the communications' strategy for a General Electric marketing meeting. The marketing division had rung up two successive years of record achievements. The trouble was, they were operating in an intensely competitive market where the ladder of success was, in fact, a greased pole. So, the marketing people had to be convinced to redouble their efforts in the coming year. Since the meeting was being held in the Dominican Republic, home to pirates during the Spanish Main sea wars of the 17th century, the marketing director thought of the theme: "The Year Of the Pirate."

No Turning Back
Excerpts from his keynote speech:

> *We're going to make this the year of the pirate. It's not just a fancy slogan. It's a spirit . . . a focal point of action. It has everything to do with why we're here . . . what we want . . . where we are going.*
>
> *The pirates I'm talking about flourished during the Caribbean sea wars of the 17th century . . . on this island.*

*They were outnumbered . . . yet they halted Spanish sea
trade practically in its tracks. They were simple outcasts . . .
yet they conquered sophisticated military defenses. They were
underdogs . . . yet they constantly turned the tables on their
opponents.*

*Desperation shaped them. Often, they punched holes into
their ships' hulls, starting the ships sinking, before grappling
with an enemy . . . so when they fought there was no turning
back.*

*They conquered because they were more determined,
more resourceful, swifter, and smarter than their opponents.*

*That's what this meeting is about. It's about our bring-
ing the spirit of the 17th century Carribean pirates through
a time tunnel and into this business.*

*It's about our becoming pirates . . . pirates in business
suits!*

Metaphor and Message

Clearly, we weren't recommending that the marketing division throw out grappeling hooks and, bristling with cutlasses
and blunderbusses, board and seize the offices of its competitors. But the message was clear: be lean, be swift, be smart,
be bold. A message that would be repeated many ways during
the meeting and during the year to come.

Avoid Cliches Associated With Place

Make sure that you understand the genuine environment.
I avoided pirate cliches and researched facts about 17th century
Caribbean pirates. I found out that they started as outcasts on
the island, making a savage living hunting wild pigs and cattle,
the name buccaneer coming from the racks they used to dry
strips of beef that they smoked in cigars and pipes, the Carib
Indians calling these racks "boucans," and the hunters taking
the name "boucaniers." I found out how they really lived on
the island and surrounding seas (their desperate life drove
them to put to sea in simple canoes looking for extra income),
and I put those facts into the talk.

If the nuggets in your speech are made of fool's gold, the
speech itself will ring false.

7. KNOW THE PSYCHOLOGICAL ENVIRONMENT

Audiences come loaded with psychological concerns: prejudices, fears, ambitions, hopes, vices, dreams, anger, love. As an executive speaker, you have to get a sense of those concerns.

Of course, one way to do that is to read the faces and reactions of people while you are talking to them. (See Chapter 11.) But getting immediate feedback can be most effectively accomplished when you have analyzed your audience before you speak.

Audiences Are Issues

Every audience is an issue. And every issue is a slice of drama.

A New York theatrical producer/director gave me an invaluable tip about writing for an audience when he said: "For every character in a play, you must understand two things: what does the character want and what's at stake for that character?"

The same can be said for every audience. When assessing psychological concerns, think of the audience in terms of a character in a play. Answer the questions: What does the audience want? What is at stake? When the stakes for the audience are high, your opportunities to succeed as a speaker are great.

8. KNOW THE ELECTRONIC CAPABILITIES

- ☐ If you are going to use visual support, is it compatible with the wiring and outlets in the room where you are going to speak?
- ☐ Do you want the lights to be dimmed? Can they be dimmed? Where is the switch that dims them?
- ☐ Can you change slides by pushing a button on the lectern? Or does somebody have to run the projector while you speak?

- ☐ Does the lectern have a light to illuminate your notes? If you wear glasses and might be bothered by glare, can the lectern light be adjusted?
- ☐ Is there a microphone on the lectern? Are you going to be anchored to the lectern and its mike because there is no other way to be heard over the sound system?
- ☐ If you want to move around when speaking, can you obtain a lavalier or lapel mike?
- ☐ Can the speaker volume be turned up or down at the lectern? If not, where is the volume control located?

9. KNOW THE STAGE

- ☐ If you move about when speaking, can you do that on this stage? Will the stage be open, or cluttered with tables or chairs? Does the floor of the stage have raised areas or recesses that you might trip on?
- ☐ Is there a lectern? If not, think of what you are going to do with your script or notes while you talk.
- ☐ If there is a lectern and you intend to use it, will it accommodate your notes? Can its height be adjusted? If you are short and might be hidden by the lectern, make sure there is a riser to stand on. Make sure it's in place before the audience comes into the room. You don't want to be looking for a riser or adjusting it while the audience is waiting to hear your first words.

10. KNOW THE SEATING

What seating arrangements are there: auditorium style, banquet tables, or boardroom table?

In general, a wide, shallow seating arrangement is preferred over a long, deep one. One executive I worked with gave a speech to 1,000 people in a hall so long and narrow he was practically out of sight to the people in the middle of the room, let alone the back. We found out about this problem in advance and were able to set up monitors from the middle on back so that the people in the Siberia section could at least watch the speech on television screens.

Are the chairs moveable and can you adjust their arrangement before the audience sits down? The best arrangement of chairs is often a concave semicircle.

If it's an intimate arrangement such as a boardroom table, avoid reading a prepared script.

If it's an auditorium or banquet table arrangement, will people in the back of the room be able to hear you without a mike?

If note taking is important, will people be able to take notes from where they are seated?

Can everyone in the audience get a clear view of you at the podium or will they have to adjust their chairs before you speak?

11. KNOW THE TIME OF DAY AT WHICH YOU WILL SPEAK

If you are giving a pre-dinner speech, be aware that they may be anxious for you to make your talk short. If you speak after the dinner, they'll tend to be drowsy, so you'll need to add spice to your talk either through visual aids (see Chapter 10) or through audience participation (see Chapter 5).

12. ANALYZE CONTEXT

Find out the total program context in which you will be speaking.

Will the program last for a day or more?

Is there a central theme to the program and a separate theme for your segment?

If it's an annual event, who gave the speech last year? Square D's CEO, Jerre Stead, says, "It's very important for me to understand what the audience has been told by past speakers." Find out what those speakers have talked about. Try to get a copy of that talk. How was it received by the audience, by the media? What did the speaker do well? What did the speaker do poorly?

How different do the organizers want this year's speech to be? How similar?

Speechwriters as Information Sources

What does the speechwriter say? Speechwriters can be important sources of information about audiences. Often, their knowledge and insights span the breath of the organization. If the organization has a speechwriter, or if you can find a speechwriter who has written for executives who have spoken before to the organization, seek him or her out.

If your audience will hear other speakers during the meeting, find out what the other speakers will be talking about.

Find out how the organizers view your speech within the context of other speeches.

Find out if your speech will be part of a panel discussion.

Find out if a Q&A session will be appropriate.

13. THE AUDIENCE AND ALCOHOL

A poet said, "I drink to make people interesting." When an audience drinks, the speaker often becomes less interesting—through no fault of her own.

Alcohol is a dark alley down which many speeches are led to be mugged. Xerox Corporation's Director of Corporate Communications, Joseph M. Cahalan, says:

"One of our senior executives has made it a policy not to speak after alcohol is served. If he is speaking at a function at which there's alcohol, the order will be speech, cocktail reception, dinner—not the other way around, which is traditional. In the best cases, people who drink before a speech will be drowsy. In the worst cases, you may get heckling or clinking of glasses, or people not paying attention or leaving early to go to the toilet or because they have simply lost interest."

Find Out "When"

So, when you're invited, find out if alcohol will be served. If so, can you determine when it will be served? If you can, make sure that it will be served after you speak. If you cannot determine when, then shorten your speech considerably.

But don't rule out taking advantage of the pleasures of moderate drinking. A speechwriter for a CEO of a $10-billion-plus company says he doesn't mind that his bosses' audience has been drinking. "If they're drinking, you can take more risks with humor."

14. KNOW THE SIZE OF THE AUDIENCE

Know in advance how large the audience is going to be. This is especially important if you are deciding whether or not to read a script. A skilled speaker can read a speech well—but only to a large audience (generally speaking, more than 50). Reading a speech to a smaller audience in more intimate surroundings is a tough sell. The smaller the audience, the more your speech should resemble conversation. And who can *read* a conversation?

One very successful executive I wrote for was invited to speak to hundreds of students at an Ivy League business school. We researched and prepared a helluva speech. Anticipating a large audience, he decided to read from script, at which he is a master.

Stranger in a Strange Land

He arrived at the administration offices and introduced himself to the receptionist. She seemed surprised to see him. She made a hasty phone call. After awhile, an embarrassed man appeared and conducted the executive down a long hall. Ahead, the door to what he thought was the auditorium swung open. He stepped into . . . a small classroom! Only a half a dozen students were there. A couple of them were glancing at their watches as if wondering when he was going to be finished—and he hadn't even started!

It turned out that there had been a scheduling snafu. The auditorium speech had been canceled, and we weren't told about the cancellation. At this time, students were in classes. He had been brought to this room just so he could speak to somebody.

How can you read a speech to half a dozen students? My client didn't. He's a gentleman, so he put on his game face and shoved the prepared text in his pocket. He gave brief, extemporaneous remarks, answered questions, and then left.

The lesson to be learned from this experience is the old Russian proverb that Reagan repeated to Gorbachev during their summit conferences: "Trust but verify."

15. KNOW YOUR TIME SLOT AND STICK TO IT

There are immutable laws in life: for example, never buy a VCR on the sidewalk from a guy who is out of breath.

And never step up to the podium to deliver a speech without knowing how long you are expected to talk.

Whether you think you have ten minutes and the agenda calls for you to speak for an hour, or you think you have an hour and the agenda calls for a ten minutes talk, the fact is, you're ambushed.

Scope out potential ambushes well in advance. Xerox's Joseph Cahalan says: "You can make friends with a short speech, enemies with a long speech."

Every long speech has a short meaning, so there is no excuse for exceeding your time limit. In fact, a good technique is to always shave five minutes off your alloted time.

Disappearance Makes the Heart Grow Fonder

Don't even give the appearance that you are going to speak longer.

AGS Computer's CEO, Lawrence J. Schoenberg, tells of the occasion when he was speaking at a high school graduation ceremony:

"The mood of the crowd was somewhere between excitement and riot. Not an easy audience. I started speaking. I had notes on two three-by-five cards. Just two cards! After five minutes, I got through the first card, and visibly turned it over. A groan went through the audience! They were watching my cards! They saw I had another one, and the speech was going to go on. Well, I told a quick joke and closed."

So be aware of what you bring to the podium. A telephone book-size manuscript or a single sheet of paper communicate different messages. If the audience thinks you'll read the telephone book, forget about trying to win their whole-hearted support.

16. KNOW WHO WILL INTRODUCE YOU

Introductions can be like movie cartoons, injecting humor, change-of-pace, and new perspectives before the main feature.

For instance, New York Senator Chauncey Depew, a noted wit and orator in the early part of the century, was introducing President William Howard Taft.

Taft, who weighed more than 300 pounds, much of it in his belly, got up to speak.

Chauncey cried out, "He's pregnant!"

Taft took a step forward.

Chauncey cried out again, ". . . with conviction!"

Taft took another step forward.

Again Chauncey cried out, "He's pregnant with courage!"

Taft reached the podium and said, "If I *am* pregnant, and it's a girl, we'll call her Conviction. If it's a boy, we'll call him Courage. But if it is only gas . . . we'll call it Chauncey Depew!"

Don't Waste the Opportunity

Don't waste the opportunity the introduction presents. The person introducing you can communicate insights into your life and work that you cannot.

Introduction comes from the Latin, meaning "to lead inside." So the introduction is the way into your speech. Make that way interesting and easy to negotiate.

Point-Counterpoint

"One of the great opportunities that business leaders have," says Syntex's Paul Freiman, "is that often the people who introduce you tend to overblow things somewhat. It's a point-counterpoint opportunity for you."

But don't respond with cliche humor: "Thanks, John, you read that just the way I wrote it." or "After that introduction, I can't wait to hear what I have to say." If your repartee isn't fresh, you're starting the speech in a hole.

Introductions Are Mini-Speeches

An introduction is a small speech in itself. It should have a beginning, middle, and end. It should be focused on one idea, and it should have humor and insight. Find out who will introduce you. Tell the person that the introduction is very important to you. Offer to provide suggestions for it or to even write it.

Shiny-Ass Bookkeeper

Bob Evans Farms' CEO Daniel E. Evans and his chief financial officer make many speeches together, first one talking, then the other—both to employees and outside groups.

Evans often engages in a brief routine with his chief financial officer when introducing him. Evans says: "I'll introduce him as the executive vice president and chief financial officer and treasurer of the company. Then *he* gets up and says: 'I appreciate that introduction,' (turns to the audience) 'Around the office, he calls me a shiny-ass bookkeeper!' That introduction always gets a laugh. And it leads effectively into his talk."

17. KNOW HOW YOU SHOULD DRESS

Remember to ask how the audience will be dressed. Are business suits or casual wear required? As a speaker, you should try to dress on the level of formality dictated by the audience's dress—never below it.

18. KNOW THE ATTENDEES

Arthur Brown, CEO of Hecla Mining Company, finds it useful to obtain a list of attendees. And if it's an annual event, the attendees from last year as well. He says: "Very often you know one or two people in there. You can learn a great deal from them."

19. KNOW THE AUDIENCE'S VALUES

"In assessing an audience," says The Washington Consulting Group's CEO, Armando C. Chapelli, Jr., "it's important for me to understand what value system they hold. What they believe in. To me, a good speech is rooted in values. It's not simply facts and figures. If the speech is linked to the audience's values, to what they deeply believe, then they will walk away with a sense of meaning rather than a sense of just having been fed information. So I want to know what the audience needs. Not what they have. If I know what they have, I can guess what they need."

SUMMARY

"I don't care what audience we are talking to," says Square D's CEO, Jerre L. Stead. "There are a lot of people who wish they weren't there."

Knowing the audience—whether they want to be there or not—begins with knowing yourself, knowing your capabilities and limitations on the podium, knowing what you can speak about, and knowing what you *want* to speak about. Knowing these things, you can begin to assess the audience itself. Put the "audience analyzers" to work. Know the audience better than they know themselves. Then you are on the way to giving a talk that changes people from wishing they weren't there to being glad they are there.

3

The Single Idea

I don't always tell them what they want to hear. When you tell them what they want to hear, they might whistle and cheer and give you a big hand when you're finished. But you might not have said anything to bring about a long-term solution. So I always tell them what I think they ought to know and how I am prepared to help them accomplish the task.

EDWARD J. NOHA,
CEO, The CNA Insurance Companies

If one is a master of one thing and understands one thing well, one has at the same time insight into and understanding of other things.

VINCENT VAN GOGH

The most important thing to remember in regard to giving speeches is to be prepared. When I'm well prepared, I'm anxious to give the talk. I feel good about giving it.

WILLIAM C. FERGUSON,
CEO, NYNEX Corporation

The worst thing you can do is ramble. That's instant death.

ALLEN G. HASSENFELD,
CEO, Hasbro, Inc.

I'll pay more for a man's ability to speak and express himself than for any other quality he might possess.

CHARLES M. SCHWAB,
Industrialist

A PLAYWRIGHT CAME INTO the office of Broadway producer David Merrick and started talking about his play. Merrick stopped him. He took out a business card. He said, "Write what your play is about on the back. If you can't, you don't have a play."

The same with speeches. The most effective speeches have at their core a single idea that can be written concisely. Keeping your speech focused on a single, concise idea creates a focal point for reflection and action, helps provide structure and continuity, and enables people to remember that speech long after you have delivered it.

You might say, "Wait a minute, I have three or four or five or six things to say to this audience. Not just one."

Okay, say them. But make sure that they grow from, and loop back into, your core idea.

A SPEECH ISN'T AN ESSAY

A speech isn't an essay standing on two feet. An essay relies on formal grammar, structure, and rhetoric to analyze, speculate, or interpret. A speech, on the other hand, relies on your speaking conversationally to the audience. It should be informal. It often breaks rules of grammar. Its end isn't so much to analyze or interpret (often those are means to the end) but, in most cases, to move the audience to take action. A speech is done with broad brush strokes, an essay usually with subtle strokes.

SELLING YOURSELF

There's also another important difference. Aetna Life & Casualty speechwriter Stephen R. Maloney says, "You are not only dealing with concepts, but you are selling those concepts too, and selling yourself."

To best sell concepts and yourself, keep your speech simple, avoid an over-abundance of detail ("If you're not confused," a veteran congressman told a freshman colleague, "you haven't heard all the facts."), and nail your speech to a clear, central idea.

ONE CHANCE

When giving a speech, you've got one chance to obtain your objective. But if it's a good speech, with a strong core idea, one chance is all you need.

Just as an audience leaves a good Broadway play whistling and humming the tunes, so your audience should walk away after your speech is finished with your thoughts and cadences echoing in their minds.

By repeating a single idea many different ways, you enable it to live and grow in the minds and hearts of the audience long after the speech is over.

WEAVING IDEAS

Pepsico's speechwriter Steven Provost says that many executives are afflicted with the "kitchen sink" syndrome. "They want to throw everything into their speeches but the kitchen sink. I tell them that they have to evaluate the whole, not just the individual parts."

Bob Evans Farms' CEO, Daniel E. Evans, says that he almost always ties his speeches to a single theme. "I start with it. I weave it through the middle. I end with it. If anything bothers me when listening to speeches, it's usually a person starting off one way then wandering around."

WRITE THE LEAD

Xerox Corporation's Director of Corporate Communications, Joseph M. Cahalan, says: "I'm a former journalist. When writing a major speech, I try to first write the press release for that speech—at least the headline, such as 'Xerox Executive Challenges . . . ,' then the lead under the headline. What would that lead, that nugget, be? Once I've found that, I have something to build the speech around."

John J. Schiff, CEO of Cincinnati Financial Corporation, says that a speech is essentially a sell. "When you are trying to sell something, you're better off if you sell one thing at a time."

Robert Fildes, Cetus Corporation's CEO, says: "In writing my speeches, I always boil down what I want to say into what I *have* to say. That helps ensure that the audience walks away with a very clear idea of what I've talked about."

WHALE SANDWICH

BellSouth Director of Planning and Development, Mylle H. Bell, adheres to the single-idea technique. For instance, she gives many speeches on the importance of education. One of her most effective speeches was called "The Whale Sandwich." She says: "It was tied to the image of the world media event of two whales being trapped in ice. I was saying that just as those whales were trapped in ice, our children are trapped in ignorance. If the U.S. and USSR can come together to free two whales, why can't we mobilize and educate our young people? One theme. One image. It worked."

CREATING, LOADING, AND TRIGGERING THE CORE IDEA

It's not enough to shape your speech to a single idea. You have to make sure it is the right idea for that audience. If it is the wrong idea—i.e., if it doesn't come from your knowledge and convictions, if it doesn't strike right into the heart of the audience's needs—then, from the start, you are heading off target.

To ensure that I pick the right idea when I write speeches, an idea connected both to the speaker's purposes and the audience's needs, I've developed a three-step process for creating, loading, and triggering core ideas.

1. CREATING THE SINGLE IDEA

First, assess your needs as an executive and a speaker; then, assess the audience's composition and needs using the techniques we've just discussed.

Research contemporary issues and ideas—issues and ideas found not just in business publications but also in nonbusiness sources, magazines such as *Rolling Stone* and *Science News*, late night TV comedy, talk shows (tape programs on your VCR to watch during your free hours). "I don't read the *Wall Street Journal, Fortune, Business Week*," says Cypress Semiconductor Corporation's CEO, T. J. Rodgers. "Not that they are worthless. Frankly, when I get in an airplane and read them just for something to do, I think I really should spend time reading them. But the fact is, I read publications like *Scientific American* and stay current on a shallow level on such subjects as astrophysics."

Detective Stories

Thomas Edison believed in the value of reading in a variety of fields. He said: "I read two morning and three evening papers and most scientific publications. Sometimes I dip into a detective story—even Macauley did that.

"I recommend only books in which things are described plainly, by analogy to things everybody knows . . . . I use my books to prevent waste of time and money by not repeating what others have already done. We live and grow by knowledge."

Ongoing Research

Your research should be ongoing. You should continually have your antennae out for interesting ideas and events happening in the world outside your business and use your discoveries to invigorate your speeches.

Issues Are a Lens to the Future

In addition, don't just take issues, events, and discoveries at face value. Make them a lens through which you look into the future. What are those issues changing into? What aspects of your business—products, R&D, people, marketing, training—are involved in those changes?

You're not expected to predict the future. Winston Churchill said, "A successful politician must foresee what will happen tomorrow, the next month, and next year—and explain why it did *not* happen." You just have to grasp essential changes taking place currently in our world.

For instance, how might breakthroughs in superconductivity, neural network computers, or nuclear magnetic imaging affect the markets in which you are introducing new products? Or how does Woody Allen's latest movie relate to your new R&D thrusts? How do the latest environmental issues being analyzed in subcommittee hearings on Capitol Hill affect the future of your industry?

Develop Ideas

Knowing what you want to say, what your audience wants to hear, and what fresh perspectives new issues may provide, you now can write down ideas that may serve as the speech's core.

Use the typical brainstorming technique of writing many ideas without judging whether they are good or bad. At this stage, it doesn't matter what the idea is, just as long as it can fit on the back of a business card.

Submit those ideas to an imaginary audience. Challenge that audience to think about themselves in new ways, to act, to think about your business in new ways.

Come up with 20 or 30 ideas. Then put the list away. Let it percolate in your subconscious for 24 hours.

2. LOADING THE IDEA

Select the single idea that will drive your speech. It doesn't have to be one of the many you wrote down, but it may be a synthesis of a number of them. It might not even be on the list. Often, the act of trying to come up with ideas will kick-start your subconscious so that the appropriate idea bubbles up when you're having breakfast or driving to work.

The Fundamental

Many executives don't have to go through a process of analyzing and selecting ideas. They already have ideas at hand, ideas by which they have been living for years and that are fundamental to their personal and their business' success.

CNA's Edward J. Noha says, "If you follow all the reprints of the speeches I gave since becoming CEO in 1975, you'll see that they all have very consistent themes: establishing closer agency/company business relations, responsibility, and integrity."

Cypress Semiconductor's CEO, T. J. Rodgers, declares that most of his speeches revolve around one of three ideas: startups and how to do them, Japanese competition, and management systems for a small company.

Lyphomed's CEO, Gary E. Nei, uses such concepts as "Quality is in this room."

Worthington Industries' CEO, John H. McConnell, says the majority of his talks are based on the business' style of "achieving high productivity, profit sharing, and employee involvement."

Hillenbrand Industries' CEO, W. August Hillenbrand, observes that nearly every one of his speeches revolves around three concepts: total customer satisfaction, continuous improvement, and being a people company. "I repeat those concepts in every speech I give," he says. "I can't remember when I didn't use them in every speech. People will forget. You've got to keep hitting it, hitting it, and hitting it. People won't get tired of hearing it if you go out and do it."

Helping Others

Delmarva Power's CEO, Nevius M. Curtis, asserts that the core idea of most of his speeches is "helping people better themselves so the company comes out better."

Pier 1 Imports' CEO, Clark A. Johnson, says, "My speeches are tied to the customer. You get everybody in the organization going in one direction and that is having 100 percent customer focus."

Nevada Power Company's CEO, Charles A. Lenzie, says that during the past few years, "My speeches have been connected to a single idea: growth. The utility has to grow to meet the growing demands of our customers."

Take It Apart

Embedded in the single idea is the structure of your speech. So take the idea apart. Core ideas are like subatomic particles. Each is a rich amalgam of other units. Just as you can smash particles with atomic colliders to separate subatomic units, so you can take your core idea apart. Examine its subunits. Reorder them. Reassemble them.

For instance, if your idea is "quality is in this room," you have two major elements to work with: quality and the people in this room. Books have been written about quality, people power, and people power enhancing quality. "Quality is in this room" is not only an idea that can be written on the back of a business card, but also an idea that can generate volumes of material.

3. TRIGGER THE IDEA

Put it into action in your speech. Each main point should grow out of that idea. Every paragraph, every sentence, every word should be linked to the idea. You should begin with the idea and end with it. When you are finished talking, your audience should have that idea, and the points you have developed through it, strongly established in their minds.

SUMMARY

Each speech you give should be based on a single idea. A core idea is a flashpoint of thought, a linchpin for structure, a trigger for action, and an aid for the audience's recollection.

You can develop and use the idea through a three-step process of creating, loading, and triggering it. Keeping your speech grounded in one idea can make the difference between the audience guessing about what you're saying and knowing exactly what you're saying.

4

The Opening

Half the deed is done if a beginning is made.

HORACE

First command the audience's attention. That means standing up there and not speaking until the audience becomes quiet.

PAUL E. FREIMAN,
CEO, Syntex Corporation

Speed isn't that important in stealing bases. It's the first two steps that count.

WHITEY HERZOG

A bad beginning makes a bad ending.

EURIPEDES

An executive's legitimacy as a leader comes from the people below, not the people above. His or her success depends on subordinates signing up for the vision, in effect, saying, "It's okay for you to tell us what to do."

CLARK A. JOHNSON,
CEO, Pier 1 Imports, Inc.

A UTHORITY IS A POOR EXCUSE for leadership. A good executive directs people to do a job, while the best executive inspires people to want to do the job.

So beginnings are very important for executives. Trying to inspire bored or angry people is a catch-up game no leader relishes.

Every CEO and top executive I interviewed agrees. I'm sure you agree, too. So let's skip the why of making a good beginning, and go right to the *how* of it.

Here are 32 ways to open your talk.

1. TELL THEM WHAT THEY DON'T KNOW

General Systems Company's CEO, Armand V. Feigenbaum, says:

"A very effective opening is to start off with some points of which we as a general systems company are aware and the people in the audience may not be aware. For instance, I gave a speech to industrialists in Brazil. I told them that the assumption that their nation will not be a serious competitive power is absolutely wrong, that, in fact, Brazil could very well beat Japan in terms of economic might in the next ten years."

This opener is like a football bootleg play: a thrust in the opposite direction of where people think you will go. Your unexpected thrust is usually against the grain of a strongly held assumption.

Don't Trick the Audience

Taking issue with such assumptions that people in an audience hold isn't difficult. Often, those assumptions are based on erroneous facts or faulty reasoning. The effectiveness of this opener centers on your understanding what assumptions the audience holds, then making sure that you marshal sufficient arguments against those assumptions.

Be careful: the football bootleg is a trick play. This isn't a trick opener. If the audience feels tricked, they'll resent you. Instead, they'll accept your changing their perceptions only if their self-interest is advanced, e.g., if you can enable them to achieve better productivity or quality.

2. BURY YOUR LEAD

Pepsico's speechwriter Steven Provost says:

"Often in the beginning of the speech, I bury the lead. I put the central point I want to make not right at the beginning but two or three minutes into the speech. I subscribe to the 90 second theory. You have 90 seconds to gain their attention. Ninety percent of speakers spend that time saying, 'It's great to be here, thanks for inviting me,' and totally blow the 90 seconds. When you thank people, nobody believes you're sincere. I go for the dramatic opening, the dramatic statement that will make the audience sit up and think, 'I want to hear this person!' Then I inject the lead a few minutes later on."

By burying your lead, you raise the opportunity to get attention in a variety of ways. Watch out, though, that your opener is not so interesting that everything else—the lead, the middle, the conclusion—pales by comparison.

3. DISGUISE THE LEAD

This is a variation on "burying the lead." Start by listing facts that seem unrelated to your talk. The list forms the structure of the speech, and as you talk, the facts illuminate your main points.

Hibernia Corporation's CEO, Martin C. Miler, opened his speech to the Southern Business Administrative Association by saying that he wanted to talk about "heaven . . . divorce court . . . marriage . . . poetry . . . a global war."

It's as if Miler had gotten himself juggling plates in the air. The audience, wondering how he will pull it off, is eager to hear more.

As Miler went on, he tied those facts directly to his message of United States businesses having to be competitive in a global marketplace. If you don't connect the facts to the audience's concerns, the audience may not think your speech is credible.

4. CREATE SHARED OBJECTIVES

Xerox Corporation's Director of Corporate Communications, Joseph M. Cahalan, says that he often begins a speech with the speaker establishing shared objectives with the audience.

"Certainly, you don't use phoney flattery," Cahalan says. "So you find out what is important to the audience. Let the audience know that the speaker knows who they are—that he acknowledges and appreciates them."

Avoid Banalities

Make the shared relationship both heartfelt and concrete.

It's not good enough, for example, to say that your business and the audience share a concern for the betterment of education. Instead, be specific. Say that you know that many people in the audience are involved in a program that provides counseling for high school students who are dropout risks and that your business also understands the importance of reducing the number of dropouts, since it spends more than $50,000 a year upgrading poor math skills of newly hired employees.

5. GREAT MOMENTS IN HISTORY

Every business is shaped by dramatic moments. Use one of those moments to open your speech.

The Dexter Corporation's CEO, David L. Coffin, used this technique to begin a speech before the Newcomen Society, a

British-American group devoted to the advancement of materials science and technology.

Water Bourne Deposit

My Fellow Members of Newcomen:

On May 1, 1854, Mr. Charles Haskell Dexter of Windsor Locks, Connecticut, had a note maturing at a Hartford bank. It was unthinkable that an obligation of Mr. Dexter's should not be met when due, but the great flood of 1854 had raised the level of the Connecticut River to astonishing heights, and communications between Windsor Locks and Hartford, Connecticut, had been completely cut off.

Mr. Dexter's financial integrity was exceeded only by his resourcefulness. He promptly chartered the little steamboat G. P. Goodsell of Springfield (Captain John Abbey commanding) and cast off for Hartford. Since the bridge at Hartford was under water, Captain Abbey piloted his vessel over the eastern approach to the bridge, back across the river, up State Street in Hartford, Connecticut, and finally moored alongside of Bull's Drug Store on Front Street. Mr. Dexter disembarked and paid his note at the bank as it came due.

One Speech's Importance Lasts Decades

Though Coffin delivered this speech more than three decades ago, he says it remains one of the most important speeches he has given for the business. "Most businesses that Dexter has affiliated itself with or acquired have been family businesses," Coffin says. "People who are thinking of selling their interest to Dexter have read the speech and like the family feeling it conveys."

Would It Make the Movies?

This opener combines drama, character, and business activities. But make it brief, and make sure that the drama and the characters you describe interest your audience. Often, what seems a dramatic moment in your business holds no interest for the audience. Use this test: would it make an interesting scene in a movie? If so, use it. If not, dump it.

6. FRESH RECOLLECTION

The CEO of Florida Progress Corporation, Andrew H. Hines, Jr., says he uses the **Fresh Recollection** opener often:

"Reference some event of the day and tie that back to the speech. Suppose you are addressing a meeting pertaining to the financial health of your company. You could say, 'As I was driving here to give this speech, I saw a four-car pile up. All that suffering and the thousands of dollars in costs. And it could've been avoided.' Then bring that back to the subject of the speech, saying how foresight is important to the financial well-being of the business. An opening like this is more effective if you can cite the unusual."

Be Genuine

Make sure that your example is genuine. If the audience thinks it's contrived, they might not give credence to the rest of your speech.

This opener can be especially effective if you plug it into one already written for the speech.

You could say, "I was going to open by talking about how productivity improves economic prosperity. But I was in a traffic jam on my way over, and I've been thinking that prosperity can often impede productivity. We are all relatively prosperous enough to own cars—but how can we spend a productive day stuck four hours in traffic?"

7. GET THEM MOVING

Demosthenes said that the three major objectives of oratory are: "Action. Action. Action." He was talking about having the audience moved to act after the speaker finishes.

But Fitness' CEO, Sheila Cluff, often gets the audience to move before she begins her talk—by putting them through low-stress exercises.

"While I have them doing some innocent exercise, I'll do a running commentary, tell some jokes. Then when they are warmed up, I get serious and say, 'You've all been good sports.

What I'm really getting at is your working exercise into your business life.' So in opening this way, I've developed rapport. Gotten in some humor. And I'm ready to give my speech."

Audience Resistance

Be careful using this opener. Getting an audience off the chairs and having them move about may alienate them. They came to watch you in action, not to have you watch them.

Take a light-hearted approach to this opener. Use self-deprecating humor. And make clear that it's all being done in a spirit of fun to reveal and advance the speech's message.

8. JEOPARDY

Describe a time when you were in jeopardy: an operation, a car accident, a war experience, etc. Describe your genuine emotions. Make the experience vivid, your emotions extreme. That moment is a slingshot—propelling you and the audience into the body of your speech.

I helped the head of a manufacturing division of a fast-growing business write a speech that he delivered before some 400 of his managers. Having been recently promoted to the position, he was trying to invigorate the division by challenging those managers to give more power and responsibility to people they led. He said:

Cliff Hanger

Three years ago, I found myself falling off a 250-foot cliff.

This wasn't a dream. This was real!

A 250-foot granite cliff with nothing at the bottom but rocks.

If I hit those rocks, I'd be killed.

As the granite face of the cliff went rushing past me, I was about as scared as I had ever been in my life.

And the thing was . . . I hadn't fallen off that cliff by accident.

I had jumped!

I was participating in an Outward Bound Program in Maine.

Learning to rock climb and rappel. But learning . . . most of all . . . about myself . . . and about my companions.

About dealing with stress and fear. About teamwork. About relying on other people.

That sensation I experienced falling off that cliff may be similar to the kinds of feelings many of us are experiencing in regard to the challenges that face us.

We're being challenged to fundamentally change the way we view this business . . . the way we view our jobs . . . and the way we view our relationships to the people we work with.

Teamwork and Challenge

He explained that his fall was broken by ropes tying him to companions standing on the cliff top and that the experience taught him a lesson that applied to the challenges he and his managers were facing: teamwork helps you overcome personal fears so you can succeed in a greater cause.

An Emotional Bond

This opener helps create a bond with the audience. Be careful that you don't seem boastful. You're not extolling your personal strengths but underscoring your *humanness*, the fact that you, like everyone else in that audience, have experienced episodes of extreme emotions, fear, anger, exhilaration, etc.— episodes that changed your life.

Don't draw it out lest the audience start thinking, "Get on with it!"

Finally, make the bridge into your speech vivid, logical, and quick.

9. YOUR BEST SHOT

Don't thank them for inviting you. Don't say how glad you are to be there. Immediately, hit them with your best shot.

General Electric Company's CEO, John F. Welch, Jr., started a recent talk this way:

What I'd like to share with you this evening is one view of managing in the 1990s—the style of leadership, the type of companies, the kind of nations that will be winning or losing as the next century approaches.

This type of opening is a drag racer start: a quick, rubber-peeling get-away before the audience has hardly gotten settled.

The danger: don't let your high octane beginning peter out in the middle so that you drift to a hesitant ending.

10. FROM VIDEO TO REAL LIFE

You're sitting in a sales meeting audience, watching a film of natives chasing a desperate man, dressed in khakis and pith helmet, through a jungle. Suddenly, the screen goes blank and up onto the stage, trailing vines, shirt tattered, helmet skewered with arrows, leaps the man. Gasping for breath, he stumbles to podium, grabs the mike, staggers to the audience, and rasps:

"It's a jungle out there in our sales territory!"

It's not a reincarnation of Stanley Livingston—but the business' general manager. He's come to give a speech about sales challenges for the coming year.

And he's just delivered the video-to-real-life opener.

Genre

You are only limited by the films and videos you can use. Focus on genre: horror, space, western, detective, gangster, love, comedy, sports, and adventure. Video your own action—or get permission to use copyrighted material. Ensure that the bridge between video and real life is logical and that the person who comes on stage is either the person who was on the screen or closely resembles him.

Finally, load the bridge with humor. The audience will laugh when the real person comes on stage. But that is only the beginning of the laughs you can get. Three or four one-liners should help smooth the transition from the opener to the body of the speech.

The advantage of this opener can also be its disadvantage: high interest. If you don't follow with an interesting speech, your audience may wish your beginning was the ending.

11. TRUE FEELINGS

When Oliver Cromwell reorganized his army, he said that he wanted not large numbers of soldiers, but honest leaders. "When leaders are honest," he said, "honest men will follow them."

The audience will forgive many faults: shyness, halting speech, bad jokes—but not a lack of honesty or a lack of integrity.

An effective way to communicate honesty and integrity is to share your true feelings.

"I never gave them hell," Harry Truman said. "I just told the truth, and they thought it was hell."

Partners and Competitors

Speechwriter for United Technologies Corporation, Laurence D. Cohen, says:

"If a speaker feels some trepidation about the audience, whether they are going to like him or whether he has the right message for them, I suggest that he or she take that emotion and use it in the introduction to the speech. Tell the audience you feel trepidation. Often, you can make it the basis for humor. For instance, if you are speaking to an audience that is composed of people both for and against you, you might say, 'I see people out there who are both my partners and my competitors. Sometimes you are both at the same time. It's very difficult for me to imagine what I can say that will make everyone happy in the end.' Speakers have to understand that their honest feelings help them a lot with an audience."

Avoid Mea Culpas

Be careful, though, about admitting that you have a case of speaker's nerves. What you may think is an honest admission might be construed by the audience as irrelevant to their needs.

12. THE HOT KNIFE QUESTION

Ask the question that cuts through issues like a hot knife through butter. It's not enough just to open with asking any question. This opener is about asking *the* question that galvanizes the audience's attention.

AGS Computers' CEO, Lawrence J. Schoenberg, says, "I view a speech as something that stimulates thinking, not changes thinking. I'd rather make sure the right question is asked rather than get the right answers."

In opening with a question, make sure you understand what the audience, and the audiences within that audience, want. If your hot knife question interests some members of the audience, but leaves other members cold, you're beginning the wrong way.

Technological Hot Knife

I helped a technology executive open a talk to the people who reported to him this way:

> *The question isn't what are we going to do at this meeting. The real question is whether we should be here at all! Wouldn't it be better for this business if we were back in our labs?*
>
> *What do you think? (PAUSE) What's the answer to that question? (PAUSE)*
>
> *Here's my answer. I'm here. And here is why I am here.*

Then he went on to give a strong speech about the principles he believed his technology department should operate by.

13. THE CLASH

I've talked about citing a shared relationship with the audience. Often, your opening can be even more effective if you cite a *clashing* relationship.

CBS founder David Sarnoff said that he was actually grateful for his enemies. "In the long-range movement toward progress, a kick in the pants sends you farther along than a friendly handshake."

I'm not advocating that you make enemies of your audience. But you should consider once in awhile giving the audience a kick in the pants—in the interest of progress.

A Nibbling of Ducks

For me, listening to speakers mouthing empty expressions of being flattered that they were invited to speak is like getting nibbled to death by ducks.

United Technologies' Laurence Cohen says:

"I refuse to write 'I'm happy to be here.' You already have a modicum of goodwill when you come to the podium. So you don't have to say, 'I'm happy to be here.' That puts an unnecessary barrier between you and the audience. I even go so far as to write speeches that begin, 'Traditionally, you are supposed to start out by saying, "I am happy to be here." In fact, you should know that often I am *not* happy to be here.' Then go on with the speech."

Sweet Science

Like boxing, clashing with the audience is a sweet science. Don't come at them like a barroom brawler. The clash you initiate should challenge, not insult, them.

Be like turn-of-the-century heavyweight champ, Bob Fitz-simmons, who said, "I believe in being gentle and knocking them out clean with one good punch."

Be intelligent. Be understanding. Don't crack demeaning jokes, be they racist, sexist, ethnic, or jingoistic. Don't make fun of people they know, the group they belong to, or political leaders they may admire.

Clash with *issues*. Take exception with their *assumptions*.

14. REITERATE GOALS

A business and its executives can't score without goals. So begin by reiterating the goals of your team, the goals of your business, even the goals of your industry.

Pier 1 Imports' CEO, Clark A. Johnson, says that when he opens a speech to employees, he always:

". . . gives them a good dose of the party line. And that's simply based on the idea that we are in the business of helping our customers better than anyone else can help them. Communication is like vitamin C: It gets dissipated very rapidly. So when I'm speaking to Pier 1 people, whatever the setting, whatever the opportunity, I'm always starting by talking about our business' goals. Goals have to be consistent. Often you get tired of saying the same things over and over. But it is a winning strategy to keep it up. Making the same old things seem fresh is like using 'Hamburger Helper': creating different ways to say that we are in the business of helping the customer better than anyone else."

Context Is Marketplace

Though your goals remain relatively constant, their context, the marketplace, is constantly changing. Every time you open by describing goals, talk about context, talk about marketplace, talk about what the new stakes are, talk about how people are going after the goals in different ways. There are countless ways to perceive and strive for goals.

Square D Company's CEO, Jerre L. Stead, says:

"A lot of people have said to me, 'Jerre, you keep going over the same things time after time.' I reply, 'You bet!' People need to hear a very consistent message from the top, so it's very important that they hear what you say . . . what you say . . . what you say, over and over. I try to ensure that what I say is fresh by reading a lot of newspapers and magazines (at least ten a week) and looking for new ideas that tie back to the subjects I'm driving home."

15. THE HOT KNIFE FACT

Like the hot knife question, the **Hot Knife Fact** cuts quickly to the essence of things.

General Systems' Armand Feigenbaum says:

"We have a reasonable pattern to begin many of our talks. That is, we start where the audience is, make that recognition of respect, then bridge to that situation where we can responsibly bring something to them. We make it relevant to them. All in the first minute or two. We take quality, which is an area with a lot of dimensions, and make it real to them. For instance, if we are talking to an audience where customer service is an important competitive issue, we might give them the fact that more than one third of all resolved customer complaints in their market still leave a dissatisfied customer."

Toyota and a Falling Log

Cypress Semiconductor Corporation's CEO, T. J. Rodgers, said in a speech to the Armed Forces Communications and Electronic Association:

> *If I asked you who is more productive, the average American or the average Japanese, how would you respond? If I asked from which country the United States imported the most, which would you name? And if I asked you what country owns the most assets in the United States, which would you name? If you answered Japan three times, you were wrong each time. The average American is actually twice as productive as the average Japanese. What is happening is that the average Japanese is getting more productive faster than the average American, closing the gap between us. That growth-rate difference is indeed a bonafide problem, but we should not exaggerate it into a second place claim for America. We import more from Canada than we do from Japan. If you were going to be hit by our largest import, you would be hit by a falling log, not a Toyota. Finally, the Japanese have only recently surpassed the Dutch in ownership of American assets to assume a relatively distant second place behind the British.*

16. TELL A *BAD* JOKE

The most commonly used opener is to tell a joke. Many executives spoil their beginning by inadvertently telling a bad joke. But you can make a successful beginning by *deliberately* telling a bad joke.

Make the bad, good! That is, make it be a unique transition into your lead.

Here's a bad joke opener I used for an executive giving a talk to a manufacturing audience.

Death By a Thousand Cuts

He said:

> *Some people start off with a good joke. But I'm going to start off with a bad joke.*
>
> *The joke is this: A manufacturer complains to his friend that Japanese competition is making him lose thousands of dollars a day.*
>
> *"Why don't you close down?" the friend asked.*
>
> *"How can I close down? I've got to make a living!"*
>
> *That's a bad joke because it describes businesses in the United States during the 1980s. Closed plants. Layoffs. Slashed benefits. Shrunken R&D. Forced retirements. Outsourcing. Down-scaling. Restructuring. They are the signposts of business during the past few years . . . signposts pointing one way: toward an economic death by a thousand cuts.*

Getting Down from an Elephant

Of course, the executive *announced* that he was going to tell a bad joke.

A riskier approach is to tell the joke as if you intend to get a laugh. Start out with as bad a joke as you can think of—"I sometimes wonder: if you get obscene phone calls, do you have sexual hangups?"

or:

"How do you get down from an elephant?"

"You don't. You get down from a duck."

The Reaction Is Your Springboard

You may or may not get complete silence. You may even get a laugh—most likely a derisive laugh, the kind that a bad pun often triggers.

Your audience's silence or derision is your jump-off point. ("I haven't got a reaction like that since we introduced our new product that bombed last year.")

There is great danger and opportunity in the bad joke opener. Make sure your transition phrase clearly connects with their reaction to your joke. Which means you should have several phrases handy and be ready to adapt quickly.

17. COLLAPSE TIME

Today, physicists treat time as if it's a chunk of matter. Time can be stretched or compressed. It can even undergo phase changes, analogous to boiling and freezing, in which its basic structure changes radically.

I'm not going to provide a dissertation on the nature of time. The point is that openers can be made effective through the dramatic use of time.

I talked about the opener that focuses on a point in time: i.e., Coffin's Newcomen speech.

But there is also the opener that is made dramatic and informative through the *collapse* of time.

Peyton Place Shock

A speech given by Xerox Corporation President, Paul A. Allaire, at Worcester Polytechnic Institute started this way:

> *It's good to be back home!*
> *I entered Worcester Polytechnic Institute in 1956, and I couldn't help in preparing for tonight's talk to ponder how different the world was then.*
>
> *We still liked Ike and re-relected him.*
> *Martin Luther King was just emerging as the leader of the growing civil rights movement.*
> *Soviet troops marched into Hungary to quell a revolution.*
> *Transatlantic cable telephone service was inaugurated.*
> *My Fair Lady made its debut on Broadway, and Elvis Presley became a star.*

We were shocked by the novel **Peyton Place** *and the movie* **Baby Doll.**
And Japan was admitted to the United Nations.

How long ago those events seem. In the ensuing years, we have had seven new presidents of the United States. The civil rights movement has made real progress. The Soviet Union has shown signs of openness or "Glasnost." Electronic communications have revolutionized the way we communicate with one another. **Peyton Place** *seems tame indeed! And Japan has become a world economic power.*

Collapse Is Context

Allaire's opener led into a speech about business competitiveness in today's global marketplace.

By collapsing the time in which events take place—events *are* time—Allaire put his speech in a dynamic context.

When you open with a **Time Collapse,** always give it a dramatic interpretation (e.g., "Our company has achieved record growth during the last three years. But if we're not careful, that growth is the seed of failure!") Clearly, your interpretation has to be logical and consistent with the events you describe. But if you don't make it dramatic, you put your speech at risk.

18. STRETCH TIME

This is one of my favorite openers. Instead of collapsing a number of events into a value-laden dynamic, take a moment in time and stretch it across a sequence of events that may span years or even centuries.

I wrote the keynote speech for an executive speaking before a New Orleans economic association.

We stretched time this way:

In the year 1700, *just before New Orleans was founded, two enemy ships . . . one French, one British . . . met on the Mississippi just a few miles from here.*

The area was a howling wilderness, inhabited, according to Spanish legends, with fierce giants sporting gold rings in their noses and guarding rivers of gold that ran to the sea.

But the captains of both ships knew that the area was also a strategic junction of river and sea. They knew that who controlled this juncture might control a continent.

English Turn

The ships approached warily. The French was a sloop of four guns. The English a frigate of 16 guns.

The captains hailed each other. Clearly, the English could easily have overwhelmed the French vessel. But the French captain made a convincing case that he was only the scout ship for a large French naval force upstream.

The fact was, there was no French force within a thousand miles of the sloop.

But the English captain believed him! Immediately, he turned his ship about . . . hence the founding of the term of contempt used a great deal in this region, "English turn" . . . and sailed away into the Gulf.

In a moment of time, a single decision was made . . . a decision turning on the audacity of a French captain and the cautiousness of an English captain . . . a decision that ultimately resulted in New Orleans being founded not by the British but by the French.

Three More Examples

Brief moments of decision or activity can trigger far-reaching results. For instance, here are just a few from the history of science.

The moment in 1589 that two cannon balls of different weight, dropped by Galileo Galilei from the Leaning Tower of Pisa, struck the earth at the same time, a 2,000 year old Aristotelian idea, that heavier objects fall faster than light objects, was disproved. Thus the modern era of science began.

The instant in 1831 when Michael Faraday saw in his experiment with copper coils and magnets that it was *motion* of the magnet and the coil that produced electricity, that instant was the seed of electrical generation.

And the moment in 1928 when Alexander Flemming dis-covered specks of mold in bacteria in petri dishes and, instead of throwing the dishes out, wondered why no bacteria grew close to the mold—from that moment flowed the science and application of antibiotic medicine.

One Principle

The examples are many, not just in science but in sports, war, exploration, travel, and business. You probably can think of many examples from your own business. But the principle is the same. Stretch a moment of decision or action across many connected events, and you have a powerful way to open, structure, and ultimately close your speech.

19. SPOTLIGHT PEOPLE

I once asked a popular philosophy professor, who teaches at a Massachusetts college, the reason for his success. Though he metes out grades with the leniency of Attila the Hun plun-dering a Roman village, his courses are always booked solid. "How do you get students to flock to your course," I asked, "when they know that completing it for credit might screw up their grade average?"

"It's simple," he said. "I make philosophy interesting. Good teaching is *show biz*."

Speeches Are Show Biz

Good speech making is show biz, too. And the speech maker is a performer.

That's why the **Spotlight People** is a particularly good opener. It's show biz! And it's simple.

John A. Schuchart, CEO of MDU Resources Group, says, "In my speeches, I am always talking about people being our most important asset. Our investments don't mean a lot if people don't make things happen."

He says that he concludes most of his speeches by paying tribute to "an individual or a work unit or individuals in a group that have distinguished themselves, be it community service, working on the volunteer fire department, or taking part in company activities. Then I'll use that to end up on a very upbeat note, reinforcing the importance of people to our business."

Show Biz Opener

Schuchart's ending can be your *beginning*. Your show biz beginning. Unless you are creating a laser or fireworks spectacle, there is no show biz without people, without the portrayal of people's hopes, dreams, fears, acts of courage, etc.

So open by spotlighting people. Pack it with dramatic action. And make it short!

Kick Start

Using this opener, you have an opportunity not only to say something dramatic but to *be* dramatic. Be convinced that the individual or group you are describing provides exceptional examples. Communicate your convictions to the audience.

Make sure, though, that you spotlight people that audiences sympathize with.

20. METAPHOR

When Shakespeare wrote, "Those words are razors to my wounded heart!" he was using metaphor—and making words into razors.

So metaphor doesn't compare. It actually transforms, and that transformation can provide a powerful beginning.

There's only one rule for opening with metaphor. Make it strong. What's a stong metaphor? As a supreme court justice said when asked to define obscenity, "I know it when I see it," a powerful metaphor is known when it is experienced.

Sure, that's circular reasoning. But the trouble with understanding metaphor is that it rebuffs reasoning. It derives its power from poetic sensibilities, not from logical cogitation.

Yellow Submarine

I was working with a sales executive whose customers were complaining about the quality of one of his business' products. But key manufacturing and technology people in that business had compiled irrefutable data that the products' quality was exceptional. The customers' complaints were being challenged rather than answered.

The sales executive had to convince the company's management that quality wasn't driven by internal data but by customers' perceptions and that if customers perceived that product quality was deficient, it was deficient, no matter what the data said.

But instead of issuing data sheets to refute data sheets, the executive gave a speech to the business' assembled managers, a speech shaped by a single metaphor: the Beatles' Yellow Submarine.

A Life of Ease

It began with the audio of John Lennon singing about living a life of ease on a Yellow Submarine.

The Land of Disaster

Then the executive spoke:

> *The Beatles rode a Yellow Submarine. And we in this business are riding one too.*
> *It's the Yellow Submarine of Comfort.*
> *The Yellow Submarine of Convenience.*
> *The Yellow Submarine of Self-satisfaction.*
> *Climb aboard. Sit back. Relax. . . . and perish!*
> *Because our Yellow Submarine is a one-way ride to the Land Of Disaster!*

Isolated From the Customer

The point is that many people in the business were comfortable generating their own data about quality, while unsatisfied customers were going elsewhere to get their needs met! So a metaphor, the Yellow Submarine, became the message.

21. ACT OUT A SCENE

A French warship is knifing through night seas. Far ahead of the ship, a single light pierces the dark.

The French warship blinks out a message. *"Make way. I am a French warship."*

The light holds steady.

Again, the French warship blinks a message into the dark. *"I say again, make way. I am a French warship."*

Still, the light holds steady.

The warship drives on relentlessly toward the light through howling wind and tossing seas.

"Make way. Make way. I am a French warship."

Then through the night, the light blinks. It blinks and blinks. It blinks out a message.

"Screw you, French warship . . . I am a lighthouse!"

Be a Performer

It doesn't matter if you've heard that before. The point is, this is the kind of script that you can *act out* as an opener.

Most **Act-Out** openers should be done with one prop.

And they must be acted out with gusto.

For instance, when telling the French warship story (there are scores of other stories you can find to act out), use a captain's hat, with "scrambled eggs" on the bill.

Act out the ship blinking messages by rapidly opening and closing your hands.

When the French ship is finished signaling, whip off the hat, take two or three quick steps, turn and face the ship and hold up both hands together, as if pressing them against glass in front of your face. Those hands will be the light the French ship is approaching.

Tell the story by jumping back and forth from French ship to light.

Is It Crazy Enough?

Don't be concerned about appearing crazy. *Be concerned that you don't appear crazy enough*. This opener is not for the faint of heart. Be dramatic. Roar out the commands. Speak with a French accent. Better yet, a *lousy* French accent.

The **Act-Out** opener is very effective in putting your audience at ease, provoking their laughter and getting them to be more receptive to your message.

It's important that your speech's principle message spring directly from the scene you act out.

The message in the French warship scene: no matter how important you are, you can always get cut down to size.

And when you're acting out the scene, you're communicating a message too: business speeches (and business itself) can be fun.

Watch Out

Be aware of your audience's sensibilities. If your act is construed as an affront to the French (or whatever nation's flag flies from the warship), then get another opener. Or fly another flag. One of the worst ways to begin a speech is to try to be humorous but come off being offensive.

22. "PUT A G ON"

This opener involves giving the audience a challenge that will be met at the end of the speech.

It's been a favorite of those preeminent speech makers, pitchmen.

Years ago, I spent a short period of time with several pitchmen at a state fair, learning their trade to write a magazine article about them. The pitchmen I worked with and interviewed were selling food blenders. Today, I'm still putting into practice lessons they taught me about the craft of the speech.

Mooches and Pork Chops

They don't say that they give a speech, they say that they "pitch." They don't pitch to an audience, they pitch to a "tip." When they attract an audience, they call it "ballying a tip." The place they pitch is a "joint." Customers are "mooches."

A bad pitchman is a "pork chop." Meeting overhead is "making your nut."

Same Tune, Different Lyrics

The lingo may be different from what you, as an executive, may use, but the challenges are the same. Standing in a joint, pitching to mooches in a tip to make your nut is not essentially different than giving a keynote address in the Hilton ballroom to an audience of customers who can help you make your fourth-quarter numbers.

The first lesson I learned from pitchman is an opener. It's called "putting a G on."

Avoid Being a Pork Chop

No, it's not pitchman's striptease. It's a strong, clear challenge that you immediately present to the audience. A challenge meant to rivet the audience.

A pitchman's audience doesn't have to be there. They can walk away any time they wish. The pitchman has to make his audience *want* to be there. If he fails, he's a "pork chop." So the pitch has to have a strong beginning or his audience won't be around at the end when he asks for their money.

That's where **Putting a G on** comes in.

Challenge

The challenge that the pitchman I worked with gave the audience was this: the pitchman would drop a variety of foods in the blender—a banana, an egg (shell and all), strawberries, ice, oranges, and more—and tell "the tip" that when he was finished speaking, he would let them sample the concoction. He declared that it would be one of the most delicious desserts they ever tasted. "Stick around and find out, folks!"

That's "putting a G on."

There are three aspects to that opener: the challenge, the reiteration, and the result.

The challenge started the sell. The reiteration was putting food into the blender as he promoted its features. The result—

his pouring the concoction into little paper cups and having the audience drink the samples—completed the sell.

You Can Do It

Of course, I'm not asking you to stand up there and carry on in the flamboyant manner of carnival pitchmen. Your objective on the podium isn't to be flamboyant but to be *you*. Furthermore, though the pitchmen I worked with were honest practitioners, others have acquired the reputation of using deception to sell goods. Remember, the first thing that an executive speaker has to sell is integrity.

The Executive G

A few tips on making this opener work:

Make the challenge clear and simple.

For example: "At the end of my talk, I want you to have changed your mind about our product—or I've wasted my time up here."

Repeat the challenge throughout the speech. In fact, structure your speech on different aspects of the challenge. "For years, you've thought A and B about our products. Well, let me tell you about C and D. First, C . . . "

Finally, make the result clear. "I told you at the beginning of the speech that you'll have changed your mind about our products. For years, you've been thinking A and B about our products. But this is what I believe you should be thinking now: C and D! And this is what I believe you should do after I'm finished speaking. I haven't wasted my time. You haven't wasted your time. Let's go forward together."

The **Putting a G on** opener can be one of the most effective in your repertoire. Now bally your tip, put a G on, and start pitching.

23. PROBLEM/SOLUTION

You open by describing a problem that your audience faces. The rest of the speech is devoted to providing a solution to that problem.

This opener is most effective when the problem is made as dramatic as possible. If the audience doesn't care about the problem, they won't care about a solution.

You can make the problem dramatic by using other opener techniques we've examined: **Jeopardy; The Hot Knife Fact;** and **Spotlight People,** among others.

24. MAKE YOUR ENDING YOUR OPENING

Write the speech. Take the ending, and use it as the opening. You'll often discover that you have both a fresh opening and a new perspective on the speech.

25. ROAD MAP

Xerox's Joseph Cahalan says: "I find it useful to begin by giving the audience a road map of where the speech is headed. I tell the audience what we are going to talk about. Then, when I get into the middle, I go back to the road map. I tell them that I said I was going to talk about A, B, and C. I've talked about A and B. Now let me talk about C."

Summarize

Arthur Brown, CEO of Hecla Mining Company, says that he uses the **Road Map** opener a great deal in his speeches. "I like to tell people a short summary of what they are going to hear. People tend to remember the points you started with. So as you progress through the speech, they'll search in their memories for those points and relate them to what you are saying."

26. STAGE A SHOW

Samuel Johnson said that if you wish to make people stare, "Make them stare their eyes out!"

A good way to accomplish this is to stage a show!

I was working with an executive whose company had just acquired a competing business. At a meeting in which several hundred managers of both businesses had gathered to get acquainted with each other and learn about the new directions the much larger business was going to be taking, the executive had to give a keynote speech, a speech with several objectives. He had to introduce members of his reorganized business team. He had to make everyone feel at home. (Not an easy task when your former competitors are brought on board.) He had to describe a new vision for their team. And he had to inspire the managers to follow his leadership.

Coach/Players/Team

He opened his speech by staging a show. He donned a sweat shirt with big letters COACH on it, looped a whistle around his neck and had the new members of his staff dress up in football uniforms and come running on stage when he called their names. He transformed the opener into a pep rally in which he vowed that the new team would kick gluteus maximus. A local high school donated the services of cheerleaders and a marching band that came crashing suddenly into the auditorium, playing fight songs.

Nobody there will forget that opener. It served his aims of getting the audience's immediate attention and having people, through humor, spectacle, and participation, start to get to know one another and feel part of a team.

Of course, he followed that opening with serious comments about his values and vision and his hopes for the new business team. But by staging a show at the beginning, he broke the tension and made his audience more receptive to his message.

What You Can Do

His success wasn't assured. He took a large risk. Before the speech, many people were unsure of their roles in the new business. Others were angry and disillusioned. His opener could have come off as an exercise in immaturity and angered, not amused, the audience. But frequently, the more powerful you want the opener to be, the more you have to risk. Never taking a chance is one of the best methods for cultivating monotony. Take counsel from two Roman historians. One is Livy: "In great straights and when hope is small, the boldest counsels are the safest." And the other is Tacitus: "The desire for safety stands in the way of all great enterprises."

Color, Sound, and Excitement

There are many kinds of shows to stage. You can do a magic show, a music show, a light show, an operatic show, a game show. But whatever show it is, make it brief. Make it happen suddenly and unexpectedly. Try to engage the audience in the show. Put a great deal of color, sound, and excitement into it. Then, when it's finished, drop it immediately! Get on with your speech. Move to another part of the podium—preferably where a lectern is—and stand there until everybody becomes quiet.

Complete Quiet Before You Speak

Don't make an instantaneous transition from having fun to delivering a serious message. As in the video-to-real-life opener, make brief humor carry the transition. Finally, the audience should be silent before you begin speaking. The show has enabled them to have fun, but as you stand before the lectern, they should come to understand, not through your words but by your demeanor, that you are in charge, that you have a message to deliver, and that the good time they have just had is a prelude to that message.

27. INTERVIEW OPENER

Open by inviting a person or several persons on stage, briefly interview them, then having them go back to their seats. Use their responses as themes running through your speech.

Bill Cosby does this opener effectively for his one-man comedy show dealing with love and marriage. At the beginning of the show, he brings on stage a young, recently engaged couple and questions them about their feelings regarding each other and their expectations of marriage. He then brings a couple on stage who have been married 40 years and asks them similar questions about their relationship and their views of marriage. The convictions, misunderstandings, foibles, etc., that emerge from these spontaneous interviews are woven by Cosby throughout the rest of his performance.

Warnings

You don't have to call people onto the stage. You can move among the audience and ask questions. Using this opener, you are giving the perception that the audience is beginning the speech. But you have to be in charge. Only use this opener when your knowledge is so comprehensive that you can turn whatever responses you elicit—and be ready for bizarre responses!—to good advantage.

28. FOR YOUR EYES ONLY

This opener hinges on your declaring that your speech is really for only one person in the audience. It's often accomplished by offering a specific challenge. The person is not named. The idea is to craft the challenge in such a way that each person in the audience thinks you are speaking to him or her personally.

Obsessive

I helped work on a speech with an engineering executive who gave the keynote address for a National Engineering Week meeting composed primarily of prospective student engineers. The engineer said:

> *Those of you who know something about engineers and engineering know that our education and training has made us a little obsessive.*
>
> *We are not satisfied unless the project we are working on is 100 percent complete. Not 95 percent. Not 99 percent. One hundred percent complete.*
>
> *I guess that comes from knowing that if you build a bridge across 99 percent of a gorge, you don't have a bridge*

at all. You only have a bridge when you are 100 percent there.

The point is, that engineers are comfortable with absolutes. I want you to understand that before I tell you this:

Though I am an engineer, I'll be satisfied not if 100 percent of you heed my words but . . . one percent.

Turning Point

Just one or two percent. That's enough for me. Then I've succeeded. Succeeded not just as a speaker but . . . more importantly . . . succeeded in this speech as an engineer.

Because . . . for somebody out there in the audience . . . I want this speech to be a turning point in your life. I want you to say . . . five years, ten years from now . . . whoever you are, wherever you are . . . I want you to say in that future time . . . that you were here . . . you heard me . . . and what I said changed your life . . . what I said made you decide to become an engineer.

Strike at the Heart of Their Needs

This can be a strong opener when the majority of the audience thinks you are speaking to each of them personally. If people don't, they may ignore you. So, know their needs, make your challenge clear, and make sure that it applies to nearly all of them as individuals.

29. EXPANSION JOINT

An expansion joint provides an elastic coupling between two points. You can use an **Expansion Joint** opener to great effect. It just takes concentration and courage.

This is a three-stage technique requiring a set-up line, silence, then an opening line. The silence is the **expansion joint** between the set-up and the opener.

Here's how Gibson Greetings' CEO, Benjamin J. Sottile, used an **Expansion Joint** opening before an audience of security analysts:

Tires in Peoria

"It was a two-day meeting involving 15 businesses giving presentations. I was scheduled to speak at four o'clock in the afternoon on the second day as representing the 15th company. When I got to the podium, people in the audience were looking at their watches and wondering if they were going to make their planes or not. On top of that, I had followed a CEO of a truck leasing company. He was talking about the prices of tires in Peoria or something! The room was hot. People had their jackets off, their ties unknotted. When the truck leasing CEO was finished, the lights came on—he had done the presentation with slides in a dark room—the emcee got up and said, 'Let's be patient, we have only one more speaker to go.'

Elizabeth Taylor's Sixth Husband

"I got up there and said, 'Now I know what it feels like to be Elizabeth Taylor's sixth husband. I know what I'm supposed to be doing, I just hope I keep it interesting!'

"Well, the audience started to perk up. There were a few chuckles. Heads were raised. People snapped to. They started looking at me. Then they began to laugh. It was a slow build. I didn't say anything. I just looked at them and waited for the laughter to build. Finally, I said:

" 'I want to talk to you about an exciting business that has to do with Walt Disney and Garfield . . .' I started off on our licensing area. It turned out to be a successful speech. My CFO, who was sitting in the back with the slide projector, didn't know when to start the slides. My preamble was half the talk! I wasn't going to get off that part until everybody was paying attention to me. So a long pause after a setup can be a very effective way to open your talk."

Break-Point

You need two things to make this an effective opener. One is the setup—a strong, brief opening statement. The other is the courage to remain silent for a relatively long period of time. Silence is the key. Don't *expect* anything to happen during it. *Watch* for results. Let the silence go to work for you. Remember the adage of the great pantomimist, Marcel Marceau: "I am silent so I can say more." Let them know that you are not going to speak until you have their complete attention.

But don't let the silence go on too long. If your setup is strong enough, your silence will interest the audience. But there is a point where people stop being interested and start getting bored. It's up to you to begin speaking before this break point is reached.

30. JUJITSU

The jujitsu form of self-defense uses the opponent's strength and weight to disable him. The inspiration for jujitsu came when a man watched a pine bough, bending under a load of snow, spring back to its original position when the snow slid off.

You can use this "spring back" principle as an opener. You simply underpromise and overfulfill. Speaking opportunities have an element of benign combat. Clearly, most audiences are not hostile opponents. But they frequently have erroneous expectations of who you are and what you will say. To give a good speech, you must change these expectations.

Lower Expectations

The Washington Consulting Groups' CEO, Armando C. Chapelli, Jr., suggests that a powerful beginning is to avoid taking expectations head-on by using *psychological* jujitsu.

"First you either reinforce or even lower the expectations the audience has for you," he says. "Then the rest of your speech is devoted to fulfilling those expectations more than the audience ever thought possible. If an audience is expecting 100 and you give them 99, you are in trouble. But if they are expecting 100 and you start off by saying they are only going to get 50—then give them 150—you're in business!"

Correct Spanish

He says he used this technique speaking before an audience of Miami business people. "I came to Miami from Cuba in 1960 then left after four years and had not been back since then," he observes. "I opened by telling the audience that after 30 years of being in the states and 26 years of being away from the Miami micro-culture, I had lost the edge in my ability to speak Spanish. I said this by using a few slang Cuban words to get them laughing. I asked their forbearance with my Spanish. Then I proceeded to make a half-hour speech in perfectly correct Spanish, perfect grammar, and diction. So I got their attention in the opening and kept their attention throughout the rest of the speech; because, if for nothing else, they wanted to catch me off guard. They came up to me afterwards and said how effective that was."

Strong Expectations, Better Opener

The stronger an audience's expectations—even prejudices—the more effective the **Jujitsu** opener. Chapelli will often begin a speech before an audience that may have stereotypical attitudes toward Hispanics by giving the "It's-not-my-job" line. "That line comes from the old television program, 'Chico And the Man,' " he says, "in which a stereotypical Hispanic was always saying, 'It's not my job.' People get a kick out of me saying that. Then I proceed to show them that it *is* my job and that I'm doing it."

31. SPOTLIGHT YOU

This is particularly effective when you want to give an inspirational talk. Start by establishing an aspect of your personality. F. Scott Fitzgerald said that "Character is action." You establish your character through action. That doesn't mean you have to act, though taking a specific action is an option with this opener: saluting the audience, bringing somebody up on stage, falling down on your hands and knees and begging for another record quarter, and on and on.

The CEO of Jack Morton Productions, William I. Morton, says, "In the inspirational talk, the sooner you can get the personality of the individual into it, the better. Don't just say, 'Let me tell you about the rotten year.' Say, 'Wow, that was a *rotten* year!'"

Get Into Character

This opener entails your knowing exactly the character trait you want to communicate, getting into character before you speak, and then speaking forcefully in character.

"Get into character before you speak," advises George L. Pla, CEO of the Cordoba Corporation. "That means getting into a frame of mind that will ensure that you deliver a good speech. A lot of people know their subject, but they are busy or distracted or something, so they go up there and don't give a good speech. Your frame of mind is very important. Before you give your speech, you should visualize how you see yourself up there and how you would like to deliver the speech. In athletics, there is that time in the locker room before you go out on the field. It is quiet. People are thinking about their assignments, whether those assignments are running pass patterns, shooting baskets, or hitting baseballs. You should do that kind of quiet visualization just before you give a speech."

Pre-speech Build Up

"I always have a pre-speech buildup," says James G. Treybig, CEO of Tandem Computers. "Just before I give a speech, I don't sit in a room where speeches are being given. I go to another place and walk around. I want to get positive and build up my body energy. Because you want to create an emotional relationship with the audience, you have to be mentally alert. You have to be physically and emotionally up. I walk around and sell other people on what I'm doing. I make them listen to me. I'll say, 'Great day, isn't it!' or 'Big order!' I might sing a gospel song. I'll talk to anybody. The thing is to get up emotionally, so people say, 'He looks good! He believes what he's saying!'"

Not Jeopardy

Don't mistake this for the **Jeopardy** opener. In **Jeopardy,** the focus is on emotional extremes. In this opener, the focus is on your character and the aspect you want to communicate.

32. THE GRETSKY

Wayne Gretsky said, "I don't skate to where the puck is but where it is *going to be*." This opener gets you not where the audience is, but where you want them to be. It prepares the way for you to deliver a hard-hitting message.

Ryder System's CEO, M. Anthony Burns, uses this opener frequently. It's done in two stages. First, start with humor, usually directed at yourself. Second, communicate that you appreciate them. Then go on to the hard-hitting message.

Be Human. Be Appreciative.

Burns says: "The opening humor shows that I'm human too. It shows that I'm with them. When you follow that up with a 'thank you', then you've started to build a warm rapport with the audience.

"For instance, if I'm addressing a group of our employees, and we've had a tough year, I'd start out, saying, 'Boy, I've just had a tough time with our shareholders.' Then I'd say a couple of humorous things related to that. They'll chuckle. Then I'll say, 'Thank you for everything you've done. But, you know, we—' Note that I'll say 'we,' not 'you'—'We need to do a lot better job.'

"Now if I just started out and said, 'Okay, you've failed!,' it would've been a disaster!"

SUMMARY

"Before passing to the substance of the speech, one ought to pronounce a preamble aimed at winning the audience's goodwill." That advice, given some 2000 years ago by the Roman writer and orator, Lucius Licinius Crassus, holds true today. You can't lead people if you don't have their attention.

And the best way for a leader to get their attention is to obtain their goodwill. These 32 techniques for opening a speech represent a variety of ways to obtain the audience's goodwill in a variety of situations. From now on, in all the speeches you give throughout your career, you should never be at a loss about how to begin.

5

The Middle

You can anger them. (The audience) You can insult them. You can make them despise you. But never, never, my dear, bore the living hell out of them!

NOEL COWARD

The middle of a speech is the toughest part for me to write. I cut and cut and cut—and that cutting is usually from the middle.

CHARLES P. McCORMICK, JR.,
CEO, McCormick & Company, Inc.

I listen to sermons. I am constantly amazed how good the first ten minutes are and how worthless the rest of it is after that. So most speeches, instead of having a beginning, middle, and an end, should just have a beginning, period.

LAWRENCE J. SCHOENBERG,
CEO, AGS Computers, Inc.

Presentations are for teaching, but the purpose of a speech is to make people want to follow you and believe in you. People don't remember the words of a speech. They remember the feeling. In a speech, you are trying to create an emotional relationship with the audience.

JAMES G. TREYBIG,
CEO, Tandem Computers, Inc.

WE MOVE INTO what is often Death Valley for speakers, the middle of the speech, the valley littered with bleached bones of speeches that expired when the droning of tedious speakers switched off the speeches' life-support systems: to wit, the minds of audiences.

Our challenge: get through Death Valley, the audience not switched off but turned on, with us every step of the way, waiting expectantly for our next idea.

After all, they came to hear what you have to say. That's primarily the middle of your talk. Don't waste their time and yours. Tell them something that they won't forget.

THE AUDIENCE IS YOUR RESPONSIBILITY

The Constitution guarantees free speech, but it doesn't guarantee listeners. Even if you do get listeners, there is no guarantee that they will be listening. So your first responsibility as a speaker is to gain and keep the audience's attention. You may be delivering a message that the audience does not want to hear. You may simply be imparting information. You may be trying to change their minds. You may want to persuade them to take a new course of action. Whatever your purpose, you have the best chance for success when you know that their attention is *your* responsibility, yours alone.

As a preacher said: "If you see anybody in my congregation going to sleep, march straight up to the pulpit and wake the preacher!"

Acknowledging your responsibility to the audience is only a first step. The next step is fulfilling it. Here are four ways to do it.

1. BE DRAMATIC

The essence of drama is conflict. There's enough conflict, passion, adventure, fear, ambition, etc., in one day of a Fortune 1000 business to make a Pulitzer Prize-winning drama.

Let just a little of that excitement into your speech, and you'll have a helluva interesting talk!

Cypress Semiconductor Corporation's CEO, T. J. Rodgers, says, "Business speeches are usually about the high cost of capital and where America is going—droning abstractions! People don't want to hear that. If I can't sprinkle my talk with human objectives, emotions, and examples—and frankly I can do it for all my speeches—then I won't bother to give the speech."

Tell Them What You Believe

United Technologies Corporation's speechwriter, Laurence D. Cohen, says: "Speeches often get bogged down because speakers don't realize that speeches are essentially about philosophy. They're not about numbers. They're not about charts. If you want to communicate numbers and charts, then give people numbers and charts. Many books on writing and giving speeches say the middle is where you provide the details. That concept gets speakers in trouble. Maybe you are providing some details, but the speech still has to be philosophy. That's why you're talking to them instead of typing something for them. What you tell them is what you believe, not so much what you know."

Personal Freedom in Sales

Lyphomed's CEO, Gary E. Nei, asserts that weaving philosophy throughout the speech is an important factor in motivating people. He says: "I built an entire speech to my sales organization around the concept of personal freedom. I told them that our business was creating an environment for them that allowed them to have an extensive amount of personal freedom. I know that's true. I know that's true for them. I've been in their shoes before. At the same time, I know the character of the group. So I hit on issues that make them identify with what I'm saying, make them want to get up and go with me."

Examine Convictions

Aristotle said that the difference between men is energy. I'm convinced that the difference between speeches is energy as well, the energy of strongly held convictions. Such convictions create both opportunities and talents.

If communication is transmitting a conviction from one person to another, the communicator must make sure he or she has a passionate conviction to transmit.

General Electric Company's speechwriter, William K. Lâne, Jr., says: "If there is no passion, no personal feelings in speeches, then you just have another business drone speaking. When Jack Welch delivers a speech, the passion has to be there. It is indispensable. A few years ago, at a GE officers meeting, with 130 of the company's top executives in the audience, Jack was up there communicating some point, doing a magnificent job. I saw one of the officers start to pour a glass of water for himself. Ice in the pitcher clinked just a little bit. He put the pitcher back down without pouring the water! The clinking ice was making too much noise! Jack Welch doesn't have that passion because he is reading what some speechwriter wrote. He feels so strongly about what he is saying that he practically comes over the stage into the audience."

Believe in What You Say

The first step in making your speech dramatic is to analyze and draw on your convictions.

The CNA Insurance Companies' CEO, Edward J. Noha, says:

"The most important thing in any speech I give is that I must absolutely believe in what I am saying. No matter how statistically credible you make your points, no matter how much you support your points with facts, no matter how well you develop your theme, you have to have a visceral aspect to the speech. I'm not afraid to appeal to emotions. Ultimately, people are driven by an emotional appeal, not a factual appeal. Though, clearly, you have to stay clear of demagogery."

Find What You Believe in

BellSouth's Director of Corporate Planning and Development, Mylle H. Bell, says, "When you speak, you have to believe in what you are saying, and people have to believe that you believe it. So you find in your speech the thing you really believe in. And you talk from there. If you don't believe in what you say, then don't deliver the speech. Success lies in getting people excited."

Hecla Mining Company's CEO, Arthur Brown, says, "You'd better be a believer, believe in what you are saying. That holds an audience. If the individual doesn't feel passionately about what he or she is saying, the speech is boring."

"You've Got Them!"

Lyphomed's CEO, Gary Nei, observes that he relies on emotions to advance many of his speeches. "If you are doing a really good job, and you are in control of your emotions and you are using them effectively, you can actually feel them in your voice, and it's communicated to the entire room. You know when you have that crowd. There is a stillness. There is something in the air, and you know you've got them."

Critique the Emotion

"Words are important in a speech, but you must structure the flow of humor and emotion," says Tandem's CEO, James Treybig. "When you review the speech, ask yourself are you involving the audience, are you creating emotion throughout, do you have humor, are you making the speech personal? Most people critique the words of a speech, but they don't critique the feelings. You have to critique the feelings in a speech."

The Crucible of Experience

Passionate conviction is formed in the crucible of experience. It is, as Yeats said, "born out of pain. It is the fire shut up in the flint." Remember the times when you faced significant challenges. What lessons did you learn from your experiences? Try to boil those lessons down to a phrase or even a word.

For instance, in writing important speeches for executives under deadline, I learned that it is vital to do what you say you are going to do when you say you are going to do it.

Trust

That boils down to trust, trust between you and the customer. Establishing trust is not easy to do. You have to earn your way every day. But in doing it, you establish the foundations of a business relationship that can grow and become richer over the years.

So the need to establish trust in a business relationship is a conviction that I have used many times in many ways in many speeches.

Stockpile

You can use this technique of remembering the experience, drawing the lesson and describing the conviction to establish a list of your personal convictions.

You'll probably find that you're not creating new ideas. W. Somerset Maugham said that "the great truths are too important to be new." Experience teaches the old verities. "Poverty is violence." "A good example is the best sermon." "The only time you mustn't fail is the last time you try." "Always at it wins the day." "Honesty is exact to a penny."

The difference between merely saying those things and being passionate about them is energy, the energy created by your having experienced them under pressure.

Stock up with three or four convictions. No more! Because they can be described in many ways, just a few of those convictions are enough to fill a career's worth of speeches.

Put Into Action

Now put those convictions in your speeches. One way to do that is to reveal personal aspects of yourself.

The trouble is, many executives are uncomfortable revealing private feelings. Pepsico's speechwriter Steven Provost says, "Corporate people dread revealing personal anecdotes as much as they dread putting humor in their speeches."

That's because people often mistake revealing for exposing. Revealing yourself is not *exposing* things about yourself. Inherent in the act of exposing is the act of exhibiting, disclosing embarrassing secrets. That unmasking might sell on the talk show circuit but clearly not in business. But when you reveal yourself, you become more human, and you reveal the audience to themselves.

Open Up

"If you want the audience to relate to you," says Tandem Computers' James Treybig, "you have to make them understand that you care about them. If you stand up, and never open up, it's unlikely they'll think you care. So you want to share something about yourself so people will feel that you are one of them."

The Bronx Connection

AGS Computers' CEO, Lawrence J. Schoenberg, says:

"My style is to reveal myself in my speeches. At one large corporate management meeting, I had to follow two speakers. One was a man who gave a wonderfully prepared speech, beautiful slides, sophisticated content, a three-ring circus. The second speaker gave a wonderfully smooth presentation. Very slick. Then I came on. I didn't have the sophisticated slides of the first speaker nor the smoothness of the second. So I said, 'It's very difficult for me to follow these two people, but I have grown up with adversity. You see, I grew up in the Bronx.' Well, a very large percentage of the senior officers in the audience had grown up in the Bronx. They stood and cheered! I got a better response from the audience than two sophisticated presentations. And all because I revealed just a little about myself. Revealing yourself shows the audience that you care."

Do Your Homework

Sure, Schoenberg's revelation wasn't profound. Sure, it was fortunate people in the audience were from the Bronx. But the point is, revelations don't have to be profound. They don't have to be—in fact, they'd better not be—detailed examinations of your past. They can be as simple and short as just saying where you grew up. But they can be telling if you have done your homework; if you have found out, for instance, that where you grew up is important to your audience.

A Man, a Rolodex, an Idea

"It's surprising how interested people are in you as a speaker," says the Cordoba Corporation's CEO, George L. Pla. "You may have the greatest speech in the world, but the audience really wants to know about you, how you got there, why you're there, what moves you, what you personally think. The Cordoba Corporation is an Hispanic-owned business. Up till today, some Hispanic businesses in the United States have not done well. So people are very interested about why Cordoba has done so well. They want to know what it takes for an Hispanic-owned company to reach the success level that we have. I don't have partners. I own one hundred percent of the stock. That's unusual for a company our size. People want to know why and how I can get that done. I'm active politically, and they want to know why I'm active. What relevance it has for the business. When I start with any of these subjects, I really grab their attention. For instance, I recently addressed students in the University of Southern California Entrepreneur's Program. I started out by telling them about George Pla. How I started a business with just me, a Rolodex, and an idea."

Culture of Change

I helped an executive put together a crucial speech for some 400 managers in his division. Like so many executives in today's changing businesses, he is shaping a new culture in the division, a culture guided by the principle that power with people is better than power over people. To enable people to be more responsive, he is spreading responsibility through all layers of the organization. (*Responsive* and *responsibility* come from the same Latin root.) Having some managers relinquish power is like asking them to line up for body tattoos. The speech was his first opportunity to address all of his managers about these matters. He did not talk in generalities but instead focused on his own personal experiences and feelings.

Managerial Power

He said:

> *A few weeks ago, I was spending a lot of time on the road, visiting the sites and holding reviews and round tables. Coming back to the office after being on the road for two weeks, I was resigned to facing the mountain of mail and that six-inch high folder of papers, labeled "To Be Signed," waiting for my approval.*
>
> *That's what managerial power is all about . . . right? You sign your name to decisions that have to be made. In effect, you're saying that this thing has to happen, but it's not going to happen until I say it happens and I don't say it happens until I sign my name. Power!*
>
> *Let's admit it . . . power has been one of the most potent driving forces of our careers.*
>
> *But when I got back in the office and opened that "power folder," I didn't see what I expected. I didn't see scores of papers waiting to be signed.*
>
> *There were only two pieces of paper in the folder. Two lousy pieces of paper!*

Empowerment Is Working

> *My first thought . . . on an intellectual level . . . was, "Empowerment is working! We're changing the way we get things done in this division."*
>
> *But my second thought . . . on a gut level . . . was, "Wait a minute, what's going on here? Nobody's asking for my approval. They're doing things on their own. What if I don't like what they're doing? What if they're doing the wrong things? What's happening to my power to control this organization?"*

My world was becoming very different. I realized the most important thing of all in regard to the changes taking place in the division. Not that the marketplace is changing. Or that customers are changing. Or that the division is changing. Clearly, all these changes are taking place. But that I had better change. Change my fundamental beliefs about who I am as an executive in this business.

Poking Fun

Be careful when making personal revelations. Charles E. Rice, CEO of Barnett Banks, says that it is very important that "You don't sound as if you are bragging or have accomplished something others haven't."

One way to advance your message through personal revelations is to poke fun at yourself. Delmarva Power's CEO, Nevius M. Curtis, says:

"You often can relate to people by telling some funny stories about yourself. I make mistakes, and I'm willing to share that. For instance, when speaking, I often tell the story about when an employee marched into my office and told me that something I had written in a company publication was awful and how I handled that. My sharing things like that makes people more comfortable. But I am also mindful that there is a clear line between making fun of myself and not lessening people's respect for the office of the CEO."

Use Judgment

Be judicious in making revelations. Make them brief. Don't tell the audience more about yourself than they are interested in knowing. Tie the revelations to your message. Avoid even the hint that you may be boasting. Be sure they are grounded in your convictions.

People Convictions

Another way to make your speeches dramatic is to reveal other people to the audience. Link one of your convictions to actions one or more people took.

Maybe a member of your team worked hard to establish trust with a customer. Talk about that person. Show that you are inspired by what he or she did. Be eloquent by being passionate.

You Won't Look Foolish

Don't be concerned that your emotional commitment to the subject might make you look foolish on the podium. Throughout my writing career, in interviewing more than 2,000 people from every walk of life, I've learned that passion is eloquence. People who have a deep inner enthusiasm about a subject—no matter what their educational level, their background or their position—are compelling and persuasive.

2. BE A COACH

There is another way to maintain that attention through your speech, and that's by being a coach.

Average coaches simply coach players. But the best coaches enable players to coach themselves. They get their players involved.

John Wooden's UCLA basketball teams won more national championships than any other college team. Yet, Wooden maintains that he never told his players to win. Instead, he told them to concentrate on always playing at their highest level of excellence. Winning would take care of itself. Wooden didn't superimpose a winning attitude on his players but instead enabled that attitude to grow from within.

When speaking, you are often a coach to an audience, giving them new information, getting them to think and act in new ways. Don't be average by just simply coaching (speaking), speak so that your audience becomes involved.

Involve your audience and you don't have to worry if you have their attention.

Self Assurance

Involve the audience by looking self-assured. You can't lead a cavalry charge if you look funny sitting on a horse. When speaking, it's not only who you are but *who the audience thinks you are* that counts. If your audience suspects that you are unsure of your data or your convictions, they'll be unsure about giving you their whole-hearted attention. So from the first moment the audience sees you to when you leave the podium, communicate by words and gestures that you know what you are doing and what you are talking about. You wouldn't have accepted the invitation to speak if you didn't.

Enthusiasm

Involve the audience by being enthusiastic. The word comes from a Greek root meaning "having a god within." An enthusiastic person has a special, almost spiritual quality of excited involvement in things. Enthusiasm not only stems from having strong convictions but from a kind of joy for living. Ralph Waldo Emerson said that "Every great and commanding moment in the annals of the world is the triumph of enthusiasm." And enthusiasm is for free! It's within every one of us. For an executive, enthusiasm is particularly important: sure, you should have it, but don't keep it to yourself, arouse it in others.

The Dexter Corporation's CEO, David L. Coffin, says, "I'm patient, reasonable, even-tempered. But once my patience runs out, I give my best talks. Your best speeches come when you are entirely engulfed in the subject, dedicated, and fully informed about it. Something has to be done. You want to get it done!"

Action

Involve the audience by getting them to act. Having an audience listen to you is one thing. Having an audience learn from you is another. But having an audience act on what they learn from you is what matters most in speeches.

The end of a speech isn't to have the audience say, "That was a nice speech," but to say, "I want to do something about that!"

Keep people involved while you talk by having them act while you talk. Challenge them with questions. Get people in the audience to answer the questions. Bring members to the stage and let them assist with the demonstrations. Interrupt your speech by having the audience form small conference groups to discuss points you are making, then report back. Ask them to supply material for demonstrations. Distribute handouts (never a copy of your speech!) that are related to the slides or, if you're not using visual aids, to the main points you want to make. Pass out visual aids that they can construct or write on while you speak. (Danger: don't lose control. Be precise about when the audience should be working on the aids and when they should be listening to you. Pier 1 Imports CEO, Clark A. Johnson, says he will tell an audience, "Anyone I catch working on the handouts when I'm talking, has to come up and finish the presentation.") Finally, get people to engage in interpersonal assessments with people around them, then report to the audience on the results of those assessments, keying the results to your message.

Notebook Bullets

Delmarva Power's CEO, Nevius Curtis, uses a special audience-involvement technique during his annual employee meetings.

"At this meeting, we have some 600 employees in the room, from vice presidents to janitors. Only one third of our work force attend these meetings on a rotating basis. It's difficult for linemen who spend a lot of time outdoors to sit in a tutorial environment and listen to speeches. So before I speak, I give them a booklet that has six bullet headings in it. Their job is to write down a key idea from my speech beside each bullet. Then they take that booklet back to their jobs and share those ideas with other workers."

Appreciation

Involve the audience by telling them that they are appreciated. For one thing, praise does wonders for people's sense of hearing. For another, as Voltaire said, when we voice appreciation for excellence in others, we share a little in that excellence. The trouble is that most speakers don't go far enough in their expressions of appreciation. They don't speak effectively about what is excellent in others. Not that they should pour on the praise. It's just that they speak the way an inept lawyer once did when addressing a jury: "And these, ladies and gentlemen, are the conclusions on which I base my facts."

Expressions of appreciation such as "It's great to talk before such an important audience," "You're doing wonderful work," and "You're the leaders in your industry" are as substantive as rumors hidden behind a wall of mirrors.

Homework

Do your homework. Has the audience done something as a group that they are proud of? What exactly did they do? Be specific. Tell them. Be as proud of it as they are. Showing that you know, shows that you care. And people don't care how much you know until they know how much you care. Keep the middle continually interesting by headlining each major point with a specific dose of appreciation. And when you care for and appreciate them, you'll share some of their excellence.

Empowerment

Involve the audience by giving them choices. Find out what's at stake for the audience. Tell them what's at stake. What's their most pressing challenge? Give them the choices to meet that challenge. Think of choices they haven't considered. Enrich the choices they already know about. Weave those choices throughout the middle of your talk. Their awareness of choices is empowering. When they are being empowered, they'll most often be with you every step of the way.

Simplicity

Involve the audience by keeping things simple. Winston Churchill said, "If you have an important point to make, don't try to be subtle or clever. Use a pile driver. Hit the point once. Then come back and hit it again. Then hit it a third time—a tremendous whack!"

Make sure that the point you make is important to the audience's needs. If it is, they'll appreciate the whacks.

What's In It for Them

Involve the audience by showing continually what's in it for them. Ask not what the audience can do for you. Ask what you can do for the audience. The true test of a good speech lies in the opportunities it gives an audience. The audience isn't there for you. They are there for themselves. They want to know how you will inform them, inspire them, convince them, make them laugh, and make them vigilant. So keep telling them. Make the middle of your speech ring out again and again about what your concepts, your challenges, your advice, and your vision are doing for them. Then there will be few stragglers on your march through the Valley.

3. BE KNOWLEDGEABLE

Every CEO interviewed for this book said that knowing your subject is vital to keeping the audience interested. Nevada Power Company's CEO, Charles A. Lenzie, says, "Don't ever get into subjects you don't know a thing about. There is always some expert in the audience who will challenge you."

Your knowledge-acquiring machine should be of the perpetual motion variety. Harry Truman said that the only things worth learning are the things you learn after you know it all. Keep learning—not just about the things of your business but about current events, the latest scientific and medical discoveries, sports, travel, etc. (See Chapter 3.) Infusing your speeches with a constant stream of fresh facts and insights, many that are often far afield from your business' knowledge base, will help make those speeches constantly interesting.

Clippings and Shifting Gears

Square D Company's CEO, Jerre L. Stead, actually brings clippings of what he read to the podium. "I don't read speeches. I write an outline in bullet form and speak from that. But when I'm in the middle of the speech, I am working hard at trying to read excerpts from an article or book that ties into my subject. That way I can better drive a point home and at the same time shift gears a little."

4. BE ORGANIZED

The way many speakers organize their talks, you'd think they got their training from the great abstract painter Kandinsky, who said, "Form is what happens."

"Form is what happens" may work for artists, but speeches must be more tightly organized. A speech lacking organization will most likely wind up DOA with a tag on its toe.

Old Kent Financial Corporation's CEO, John C. Canepa, says, "Organization is the key to the middle of the speech. If you don't organize, you tend to ramble. You have to drive home your points one by one, making sure each point is keyed to your message."

Logical Flow

Organization might not be apparent to the audience, but it has to be there. At the simplest level, an organized speech is a logical speech.

Central Maine Power Company's CEO, Joe C. Collier, Jr., says he spends a lot of time making sure that his speeches progress logically. "If your message doesn't flow logically, you have to find out why. You have to find out what you are doing wrong. So I always work from a logic flow."

Organization Not Enough

But merely organizing your speech is not enough. Beware that your logic flow doesn't navigate into the corporate doldrums. Aetna Life & Casualty speechwriter, Stephen R. Maloney, says, "Too often, business speeches are very predictable. They start with 'I'm pleased to be here' move to 'Point number one, point number two, point number three," then move to, 'What do we do?' then move to, 'First, we do this. Then we do that.' then, 'Thank you very much.' "

Avoiding the doldrums isn't hard. There are many ways to organize speeches. You can do a problem/solution speech; a cause/effect speech; a goal/plan speech; a macro view/micro view speech; a geographically structured speech; a time-structured speech; a speech structured in three acts, like a play;

a dialectical speech: thesis/antithesis/synthesis; a scientific method speech: hypothesis/experiment/result; and on and on.

Maloney's Law

Whatever organization you choose, don't expect that it alone will carry you through the middle.

Aetna's Stephen Maloney says, "When one of our executives first started giving important speeches, he felt that if he laid out points one through twenty, people would go out and put them into practice. So he laid the points out. But people did nothing! So people started to misunderstand his message. He wanted to give a tough speech, and people thought he was saying they were no good. So I told him that there is *Maloney's Law. The first time you give a message, everybody misunderstands it. The second time, they misinterpret it. And the third time, they claim it was their idea in the first place!*

Keep Summarizing

Bell Atlantic's Director Of Executive Communications, Joellen Brown, says that constant summary is an effective organizational tool. "Keep summarizing as the speech develops. Keep recapitulating the argument as the speech progresses. Since the audience can't go back and read what you've already said, the speaker has to keep reminding them of his or her logic train."

Blue Pencil

Finally, wield a persistent, bold, and ruthless blue pencil.

General Electric speechwriter, William Lane, Jr., says: "You can't lose focus when writing the middle of the speech. When I get a pretty good draft written, the hardest part for me is to take a pen and start hacking stuff out. You have to take out things you might find personally interesting or that the company finds interesting but that the audience has no use for. That's very difficult to do. I remember helping Jack Welch write a speech when I spent the greater part of a day working a passage that was only a page and a half. I loved it. Still, it was nagging me. It didn't contribute to the central point that Jack wanted to make. It was so damned good I couldn't take it out. Jack said, 'Why don't you read it to me?' I started reading the speech. When I came to the passage, I felt my face getting red. I sensed that Jack was fidgeting. I knew why. He knew that the passage didn't belong in the speech. So, out it came. You have to stay focused on the speech and what the audience will get from it and have the discipline to throw out stuff you have spent a lot of time working on."

SUMMARY

Though Thomas Edison was deaf, he refused to wear a hearing aid. "The things I've needed to hear," he said, "I have heard." The middle of the speech is what the audience came to hear. Don't whip them into a stupor. Keep their attention by making sure that what they listen to is what they want and need to hear. There are four basic ways to keep their attention. Be dramatic. Be a coach. Be knowledgeable. Be organized. Study those techniques and put them into practice, so that your audience will hear what you want them to hear when they should hear it.

6

The Ending

I'm an unabashed believer in emotional conclusions. Many business people deny it, but businesses are really run on emotion.

STEPHEN R. MALONEY,
Ætna Life & Casualty

Now the close of the pitch is like making love. You've got to be gentle but stick to the point.

STATE FAIR PITCHMAN

Always leave them wanting more.

HELEN HAYES

Speeches should always end on an upbeat. I have never given a talk in which I didn't end in that way.

DAVID S. TAPPAN, JR.
CEO, Fluor Corporation

M Y INTRODUCTION TO THE ENDINGS of executive speeches started nearly two decades ago with the beginning of my first pitch. That's when I was researching a magazine article about pitchmen by working with them at a state fair, pitching blenders to crowds myself to understand selling first hand.

I didn't do too badly, but what I learned about the art of the pitch—and the art of the speech—was much more valuable than the profits on blenders I sold.

BAPTISM OF IRE

I remember that when I started that first pitch and switched on the blender, pineapple juice and emulsified carrots suddenly shot out and splattered my shirt. Laughter broke out in the crowd of some 30 people sitting on folding chairs under the big tent in front of me. One woman was angry. "You're making a mess!"

I tried to rescue myself. "Now that shows you the dynamo power of this machine!"

But she persisted. "I want my food on a plate. Not on the ceiling!" She jumped up and huffed up the aisle, past Duby whose hand covered his eyes.

GOOP

Al Dubach, pitchman and mentor, had told me to cover the bowl before I switched on the motor-reverse so that I could complete the liquefying action. "Cover the bowl," he said, "so goop won't hit the fan."

I had forgotten. I hadn't covered the bowl. The blender's blades, suddenly reversing, had hurricaned the liquid into the air. The goop had—literally—hit the fan.

But I muddled through and actually sold a few blenders—and triggered a career crises: pitching blenders paid a helluva lot better than writing magazine articles! Afterwards, I approached Dubach for a critique with the cheerfulness of a place kicker who blew the game in the last seconds shanking an extra point. I said, "Screwed up that beginning royally, didn't I?"

ENDINGS COUNT

But he merely shrugged. "Beginnings, shmaginnings. *Endings* are what count. Because that's the close. In the close you ask for their money. If you can't ask, you don't get. And if you don't get, what good is a beginning?"

Doesn't matter if you're a pitchman or an executive inspiring your team or a CEO speaking before security analysts, you've got to "get their money" in the end, however you define the "getting": marketing your services; gaining goodwill; or rousing them to bust out of there and set sales records. If you've interested them in the beginning and kept their attention through the middle, don't blow the end. Make it count.

TINKER BELL CLAPPING

Good endings just don't happen. They're not like Tinker Bell clapping and saying, "I believe!"—and suddenly they materialize. They may *appear* to be spontaneous and almost magical. But they're most often the result of study, reflection, and effort.

The ending is so important that you should be thinking of it when you are determining whether or not to give the speech in the first place. It's so important that you often write it before you begin developing the rest of your speech.

CICERO'S PERORATION

The importance of a good ending has been recognized for thousands of years. In Cicero's first essay on the orator, he termed the ending the "peroration to amplify and reinforce all the points which support one's own arguments, while invalidating and demolishing those that favor the other side."

You yourself don't necessarily have to provide a classical recapitulation. There are many ways to end the speech. But whatever ending you choose, it must possess four criteria.

COMMUNICATE IT'S THE END

First, the audience must know it's the ending.

"I hear so many talks that have seem to have ended, and they start up again," says Barnett Banks' CEO, Charles E. Rice.

Or—a speaker stops talking, and the audience is left hanging, waiting for more. Then they catch on that the speech has ended, and break into applause. In that moment of confusion, those still awake in the audience are probably wondering what the speech was about in the first place—or worse, wondering if the speaker himself knows what the speech was about.

"I always end my speeches with something provocative," says Gibson Greetings' CEO, Benjamin J. Sottile. "Whether I am ending with the main point of the message or a story or anecdote, I want people in the audience to know I have finished and turn and look at each other and nod, smile, or do something to show that what I said made an impact on them. You need the audience to react to your ending rather than simply applaud politely."

ASK FOR THE ORDER

Second: ask for the order.

Take a tip from pitchmen: always ask for the order. The order can be defined in many ways: a call to action, asking for support, an expression of appreciation, and so on.

That means you have to know your role, the audience's role, then do something about it. Doing something about it is getting the order. Clearly, you're not trying to sell products in every speech. Still, every speech is a sell. You must understand what the sell is in each situation and what asking for the order is actually going to entail.

Know Why You're There

Speechwriter for United Technologies Corporation, Laurence D. Cohen, says: "You have to tell them (the audience) why they are there. Many speakers have a difficult time wiggling out of the speech. One of the reasons is that they go in not knowing what they want people to do. If you don't know what you want to say, you are communicating that you don't want to modify the audience's behavior. You talk to them because you want them to do what you want them to do. Not necessarily what they want to do. So in the end, you have to say, 'This is what I want!' It has to be very clear. In most cases, when speakers have trouble with the ending, they are not sure why they are there."

BE BRIEF

Third, the ending must be brief. An actor who played the lead in a play I wrote for New York's Third World Theater said, "I've got acting down to very simple things. I come on stage. Plant my feet. Say my lines. Then get the hell off!"

A good ending entails getting off in a hurry. Don't drag it on lest you want the audience to wish that you be dragged off.

Cincinnati Financial Corporation's CEO, John J. Schiff, says, "The quicker a speech is ended, the better people like the speech."

BE OPTIMISTIC

Fourth: It must be optimistic. A sure way to kill a good speech is to end pessimistically. You can have a pessimistic conclusion to an essay, a novel, a movie, a newspaper editorial. But never, never to a speech.

MDU Resources Group CEO John A. Schuchart says, "No matter how dire or foreboding a message I might bring, I always end on an upbeat note."

"There's always a positive highlight in every speech," says Nevada Power Company's CEO, Charles A. Lenzie. "I end on that highlight."

After all, leadership is just another word for inspiration. Optimism and inspiration go hand-in-hand. Nobody gets inspired by a leader who doesn't think the job can get done. Leaders must try to increase the sum of freedom and responsibility in every person they lead. They cannot suppress those qualities, even temporarily. I'm not advocating that you constantly give don't-worry-be-happy speeches. Executive leadership entails looking reality square in the eye and insisting that the people you lead do the same. So, if need be, talk about things dire and foreboding—just don't end on them.

MANY ENDINGS

Here are a number of ways to end your speech.

For one thing, most of the 32 openers can be changed slightly to provide effective endings.

Tying the beginning and ending together gives a dynamic framework to your ideas; it advances the talk, and it gives the audience an opportunity to understand both your opening and closing concepts in new ways.

The following are openers that can be transformed into endings. You might want to go back to Chapter 4 and analyze the opener from which you are developing your ending.

TELL THEM WHAT THEY DON'T KNOW

Your speech can end by closing with a twist on that beginning. For instance, you could open a speech by talking about how Cyrus McCormick's reaper, invented in 1831, actually helped bring on the Civil War by reducing the need for extensive hand labor on farms—then end by saying that though his reaper caused great changes in society, he invented something along with it that would ultimately cause even deeper and more widespread changes: the installment plan, a revolutionary idea for selling machines to farmers.

CREATE A SHARED RELATIONSHIP

End your speech by making the shared relationship you described in the beginning a springboard for shared action.

Xerox Corporation's CEO, David T. Kearns, addressed a Minnesota educational group on the need to bolster U.S. economic competitiveness through enhanced education. The shared relationship he established in the beginning by acknowledging the state's comprehensive commitment was echoed in his ending.

> *Two centuries ago, Thomas Jefferson said, "If a nation expects to be ignorant and free, it expects what never was and never will be."*
>
> *It is our task—those of us assembled here today—to make sure that all Americans understand that Jefferson's words are as true today as when he uttered them.*

JEOPARDY

Use the opening's jeopardy as a call to action to end your speech.

In a speech to the Dartmouth College Thayer School of Engineering, in which Cypress Semiconductor Corporation's CEO, T. J. Rodgers, dealt with the relationship between entrepreneurship and U.S. competitiveness, he began the speech by describing a time when he was in jeopardy.

It was a time when he had been accepted at Stanford graduate school to study applied physics but, having become interested in computers, had decided instead to change fields. He said:

> *I called Stanford admissions and asked to change over to electrical engineering. They told me that I could not jump from discipline to discipline so easily. They also told me that my fellowship would probably be canceled if I changed disciplines. With that firm guarantee, I took everything I owned, shoved it into the smallest U-Haul trailer rentable, and drove three thousand miles West .... a "U-Haul pioneer" ... and had to sell my coin collection to pay for groceries.*

Ending the speech, in which he talked about how he started up a successful semiconductor business in Silicone Valley, he said:

> *Entrepreneurs have been attacked. We have been blamed for the American competitiveness problem. I do not believe it. I do not think that the data support the claims of the attackers. Cypress is run by a Darmouth graduate, just like you . . . . . I invite you graduates—and I mean it—to join me in the competitiveness war at Cypress, or any one of the other hundreds of Cypress's in Silicon Valley.*

FROM VIDEO TO REAL LIFE

End your speech by going from real life back to video, for example, the speaker in khakis and pith helmet winds up his speech, runs off the stage behind the screen, and on the screen appears the video of a figure, similarly dressed, running away in the jungle, pursued by natives.

THE HOT KNIFE FACT

End your speech by using that fact to trigger audience action. For instance, open with the fact that a recent study of top corporations ranked public relations higher than advertising in regard to return on investment. Close with a call to action regarding better communications in your business.

SPOTLIGHT PEOPLE

End your speech by describing people's actions as exemplifying your business's values. You've begun by talking about an individual or group of individuals who are doing exceptional work, so your ending can describe how they are making plans to continuously improve their efforts—and continuously advance the business' values.

THE METAPHOR

Expanding the dimensions of your metaphor can be an effective ending to your speech.

Let's say that you began your speech by remarking, "A good speech is a human lens . . . enabling the audience not only to look *at* the speaker but *into* the qualities of her leadership and her business." You can close your talk on the importance of speeches to executive success by observing, "I started by saying a good speech is a lens. But now you should understand that the lens is not a static thing. It's not an instrument for simply seeing into things. It's an instrument for actually *changing* things. Sure, let it clearly show you and your business's many facets. But let it also change peoples' minds and attitudes and actions. Let it be a tool to communicate and advance your vision, your leadership, your enthusiasm . . . with power and precision . . . now and tomorrow!"

Fact. Fact. Fact.

Cypress Semiconductor's Rodgers says that he expands the dimensions of his metaphor with facts. "I often end by saying FACT, FACT, FACT, then appeal to emotion, by bringing back for the second, third, or fourth time a positive analogy or metaphor that I have been carrying through the talk."

PROBLEM/SOLUTION

A speech can end by slaying the dragon (the problem) you created in the beginning.

You should have created a fearsome dragon! But the solution you've developed is the dragon-slaying sword. At the end, the audience understands that what seemed like an invincible problem can become, with a slash of sword (the solutions), quite tame, or even quite dead.

Endings like these, coupled with powerful openers and middle sections, can make heroes of speakers.

FOR YOUR EYES ONLY

You have begun by saying that the speech is for one or two people in the audience. At the end, tell them the exact action you want taken. The action should be uplifting. In the speech the engineer gave to students, he concluded by saying,

"Don't be an audience in the great events that are shaping our world today. Be an author of those events. Be an engineer."

If possible, provide a contrast to the beginning. If you started by talking about somebody being lost, end with a rescue. If you began by describing a failure, end with a triumph and a call to action. And on and on.

Those are nine ways to end your speech by tying them to the beginning. Here are eight other ways to end a speech.

1. SHARE YOUR COURAGE

Cato the Elder said that oratory is "a good man skilled in speaking." Speaking skill is necessary but not sufficient in oratory. You also have to be a good person, or for the purposes of this book a good executive, a good leader. A quality every good leader must have is courage: the ability to face difficulties and danger with firmness and flexibility.

The **Share-your-courage** ending is particularly effective when the audience may be apprehensive about something. Business often grows or shrinks in proportion to our courage. Show that you have courage in the face of adversity by telling them that they themselves are brave. When you tell them they are brave, you help make them—and you—brave.

I helped an executive write a speech that he delivered before a national association of design engineers who were concerned about the overseas flight of U.S. manufacturing jobs.

Design Creates Product Success
The executive ended this way:

> *Designers must stand up and be counted. We must be advocates of product advancement in business. We can no longer be viewed as back-seat passengers but as primary*

drivers of product success. We ourselves must understand . . . and we must make management understand . . . that its we who give products value . . . we who meet customers' needs . . . we who enable a business to adapt to change . . . and to drive change."

Vision and Strategy

A CEO of a publishing firm gave a speech I helped him write to his salesforce after the business had just gone through radical restructuring. He said:

> *We need each other. We need each other's help. We need each other's courage. Our organization is coming together. It's new. It's challenging. It's bold. It's fast moving. It's going to be a leader.*
> *We have a vision.*
> *We have a strategy.*
> *We have the people to make it happen!*
> *I'm not asking for what's easy.*
> *I'm not asking for what's convenient.*
> *Instead, I'm saying that starting here . . . starting now . . . starting with each and every one of you who wants to go forward in this business, we are going to work hard . . . we are going to risk . . . we are not going to predict the future . . . we're going to make it. We're going to make it happen together!*

Follow Through

Sharing courage with the audience can stamp you clearly as a leader, but it's important that after the speech is over, you follow through on the action you inspired. It's not good enough to tell people that you want to share with them. You have to do it as well. And keep on doing it.

2. PRIMAL SHOUT

Get the audience to shout a phrase or slogan in unison at key points throughout the speech. Then make the ending be a primal shout. Edward Kennedy used this jab-and-riposte technique through the middle of his 1988 Democratic convention speech when he kept asking the rhetorical question: "Where was George?"—though he didn't use it for his ending.

This primal shout ending is effective only in pep rally-like situations, such as the beginning and endings of sales meetings. Don't make it your trademark unless your leadership style runs to the P. T. Barnum kind.

3. THE VISION

In the Bible, Solomon said that "The people perish without a vision." Businesses, too, can perish without a vision. And so can speeches. End by giving a vision to the audience, and you give your speech vision as well.

I helped an executive for a engineering plastics business put together a speech that he delivered before a federal trade association in Washington, D.C. His objective: to convince the association members that his polymers were not cheap stuff but high-performance materials that enhance manufacturing productivity.

He ended with a vision:

> *Indeed, no other materials match the productivity and performance of engineering thermoplastics.*
>
> *They can help make this nation's manufacturing competitive, its environment safe and clean, and its consumers rich in high-quality goods.*
>
> *Clearly, the U.S. is no longer an agricultural nation. It's a nation of industrial mass production. We cannot go back to the old days. Fifty years ago, we proved that we could not lead the world and be an agricultural nation. Yet we are on the way to proving that we can't survive as an industrialized nation either. We have come to believe that the price we pay for industrialization is smoke, dirt, toxic spills, choked landfills, and poisoned waters.*
>
> *But it doesn't have to be that way! There's another way. It's the materials way. We have the materials to make our dreams of a productive nation supported by clean, productive environment come true.*
>
> *A new common ground is being established in this nation, a common ground based on the uses and re-uses of*

engineering thermoplastics. Let's meet there. Let's use these materials to bring a new age of productivity, prosperity and environmental quality to this nation.

Goal and Vision

Knowing the difference between a vision and a goal and when to use each in your ending is valuable. A goal is often an objective reality. "Our goal is to reach $100 million in sales." Vision, however, is the power of anticipating a particular *quality* of reality. "Our vision is for this business to be the world's leading innovator in surgical laser technology."

The language of goals is the language of logic. You persuade people to attain a goal. The language of vision is the language of emotions and motivation. You motivate by tapping into deep beliefs.

4. CALL TO ACTION

Leading isn't what you think, it's what you do. Of course, getting people to act is the goal of many speeches. Most speakers know it. Every CEO interviewed for this book acknowledges it. Trouble is, though the call to action is the most well-known of endings, it's also one of the least understood.

That's because if the call isn't effective enough, it's usually not specific enough.

Hecla Mining Company's CEO, Arthur Brown, has had some effective calls to action in his speeches. He attributes his success to "getting people to do something very specific. I stress the need for improving our educational system in many of my speeches. So at the end of a speech, I'll tell the audience to call on the principal of their local school, ask about the dropout rate, and how they might be invited to talk to dropouts or potential dropouts. Or if my audience is a technical one, I'll ask them to offer their services to help a teacher for several months. I challenge audiences to get involved, and I tell them exact ways they can do that. After giving speeches with those specific calls to action, I've received more positive correspondence than from any other speeches I have given."

Be in Sync with Audience's Needs

In thinking about what kind of call to action you want to communicate, go back to Chapter 2 and reread the audience analyzers. If your call is not in sync with the audience's capabilities and needs, its clarity and power will be diminished.

5. HIGH STAKES

You must know what an audience wants and what's at stake for them. When you raise the stakes at the end, i.e., make the audience's personal involvement in what you are saying very high, then you have a good chance of making a powerful impact on their thoughts and emotions.

Often, raising the stakes precedes a call to action. But the high stakes technique can be used effectively by itself. In fact, in many cases, a call to action is inherent in a high stakes ending. If the audience knows what must get done, and if it is of tremendous importance that it gets done, then they don't have to be told to do it.

A Different Course

An effective closing technique is to raise the stakes, getting the audience to think a certain course of action is needed, and then recommend a different course.

In a television appeal to support the Children's AIDS Foundation, Ronald Reagan concluded: "I'm not asking for your money. I'm asking for something much more important: your understanding."

Caveats

Always raise the stakes as high as they can go — but no higher than what is reasonable. If you tell a gathering of salespeople that missing next quarter's numbers will trigger the fall of Western civilization, you might have trouble getting them to believe in your reasoning, if not your sanity.

6. SOBER ENDING

New England Electric System's CEO, John W. Rowe, says: "I try to have a sober ending designed to remind people that I wasn't there just to be amusing."

We know that humor can be an effective tool in most speeches. But just as you should end on an optimistic note, you should avoid ending on a *humorous* note—especially if you have used a great deal of humor throughout your talk.

Remember, as an executive speaker, you're not an entertainer. Entertainment must never be the primary purpose for the executive speech. Certainly, aspects of your speech can be entertaining. You can support your main points with humor (See Chapter 7), and you can use humor to set up the ending. "I like to loosen the audience up one more time with humor, before making the turn for home," says Pepsico's speechwriter, Steven Provost. But leave them not with a laugh but a message.

7. HIGHLIGHT SUMMARY

The summary ending is at least as old as Cicero. Trouble is, when a speaker says, "In summary, these are the five points I just made . . ." the audience, if not already afflicted, gets a severe case of MEGO (My Eyes Glaze Over).

An effective antidote is the highlight summary.

Bob Evans Farms' CEO, Daniel E. Evans, uses this often. He says, "At the end, I will tell them that I want them to remember A, B, and C. Then I'll say, 'If you don't remember anything else, I want you to remember this . . . ' Bang! I'll hammer home the one thing that I want them to accomplish."

This technique is like a sudden application of flame to the speech, burning away the dross, leaving the pure gold of a single, condensed message.

8. RAISE YOUR VOICE

Whatever your ending, raise your voice. Be dramatic. A rising voice can infuse your words with drama and passion.

"Often at the end of the speech," says the Cordoba Corporation's CEO, George L. Pla, "I literally begin to raise my voice to hammer home that final message. I go for that standing ovation, raising my voice, sometimes pounding the lectern or ending abruptly for effect."

SUMMARY

The end is where you ask for their money, but it's important that you define what "getting the money" means. Endings just don't happen. They take study, preparation, and practice. Make sure in preparing your ending that you follow the four rules:

1. Communicate that it is the end.
2. Ask for the order.
3. Be brief.
4. Be optimistic.

There are many ways to end a speech. You can find well over 30 in this book. But whatever way you end it, make sure that your words are grounded in passionate conviction. Your ending is just a new beginning.

7

Humor

Dying is easy. Comedy is hard.
ENGLISH ACTOR EDMUND KEAN,
ON HIS DEATHBED IN 1833

A speech without humor shouldn't be given.
ROBERT E. MERCER,
Retired CEO, The Goodyear Tire & Rubber, Inc.

If you don't laugh at yourself, they'll do it for you.
MARIO CUOMO,
Governor of New York

Part of being successful is to have a lot of fun in business.
CHARLES P. McCORMICK, JR.,
CEO, McCormick & Company, Inc.

I don't start with a joke. I've seen too many inexperienced speakers fall flat.
C. JIM STEWART II,
CEO, Stewart & Stevenson Services, Inc.

When a thing is funny, search for the hidden truth.
GEORGE BERNARD SHAW

C. JIM STEWART has a point. If you can't be humorous in your talks, don't try to be funny. Speakers that live by the joke can die by the joke. It's not pleasant to witness a speaker bomb. You feel sorry for him and begin to question his judgment.

Hecla Mining Company's CEO, Arthur Brown, says: "I've seen more speeches flop when people tried to force-feed humor into their talk."

Yet, Robert Mercer is right, too. Every speech should have humor. Humor is essential to good communication: It helps obtain the audience's goodwill and it is a distinguishing characteristic of a good leader.

You *can* be humorous. There is no mystery to it. You'll find out how in this chapter.

First, let's understand why humor can make you a better executive communicator.

1. LAUGHTER IS AUDIENCE PARTICIPATION

"Laughter from an audience," says Syntex Corporation's CEO, Paul E. Freiman, "is audience participation. When they laugh, they become part of the speech."

2. CREATES A BOND

"Humor is the shortest distance between two people," said comedian Victor Borge. In sharing laughter with people, we share a similar understanding, which draws us closer. When the audience laughs with you, they will be, in most cases, for you.

3. INCREASES INTEREST

Humor makes your talk more interesting. The philosophy professor I talked about in Chapter 4 said that good teaching is show biz. He understood that education begins with getting people's attention. When you make them laugh, you've got their attention. Then you're ready to give them the message.

"Seeing myself as a kind of Herb Shriner at the podium is a style I can handle," says New England Electric System's CEO, John W. Rowe.

"It's a style that works well for my kind of speeches. Many executives tend to give speeches that have equal measures of self-righteousness and boredom. The late U.S. Senator Everett Dirksen said that few souls are saved after the first ten minutes of a sermon. What portion of after-dinner speeches do you remember? Very little. You have to be ready to deliver humor to keep the speech interesting."

4. DISARMS HOSTILITY

H. L. Mencken wrote that "Every normal man must be tempted at times to spit on his hands, hoist the black flag, and begin slitting throats."

You've gotten people angry at you on the job, haven't you? As a leader, you better have. You may not be doing your job well if you haven't. The function of a leader isn't to make people happy but to get them to take a course of action, and often that action cuts across what they consider their best interests. Sure, you want to inspire them. But you can't do it all the time. Often, you have to pull rank and say in effect, "This is what we have to do whether you like it or not!"—and, of course, pay the price for your decisions by facing irritated people.

The First Rule of Diplomacy

But humor often disarms hostility. I saw one executive, rebuked by a questioner after he had delivered a controversial speech, stare at the questioner for a few moments, without speaking. Then he said, "I'm practicing the first rule of good diplomacy. Think twice before saying nothing!" Everyone laughed, including the hostile questioner, and a potentially unpleasant interaction was turned around.

"When I'm smart enough to do it," says Delmarva Power's CEO, Nevius M. Curtis, "using humor when somebody is angry with you is a wonderful technique. Most often, you disarm anger by using humor directed against yourself."

Gadflies

Fireman's Fund Insurance Company's CEO, John J. Byrne, says he has used humor against people who disrupt stockholder meetings. He calls them "professional gadflies."

"They are apt to be disruptive in meetings by hogging the time. I've watched all kinds of chairmen try to handle those situations. I started doing something six or seven years ago that works terrifically. That is, I react with exquisite courtesy for the first 15 or 20 minutes. What happens is that the audience gets very mad at these gadflies. They are wasting time. You have to wait for that. You don't dare get snappy early because then the audience turns against you. Because they sense you are snapping out at them.

Humor: The Best Technique

"You show exquisite courtesy until you sense that the audience is mad as hell at them. You'll know it. They'll tell you in their body language and start glaring or somebody will yell, 'Sit down!' Once that happens, you can really do anything you want. You can tell them to stop. You can bring in the gendarmes and have them led away. But the key to the thing is you have to wait. You must wait until the audience gets mad at them. At that point, humor is absolutely the best technique. Your humor is saying to the audience, 'We're not taking these people seriously, are we?' "

5. SHORT-CIRCUITS ANGER

Using humor not only keeps others from getting angry, but it can keep you, the speaker, from getting angry, too.

"The worst thing is to have an angry speaker," says Syntex's Paul Freiman. "Being angry, you may stimulate people in the audience. But you are not selling your ideas. You have to always be up there pitching."

6. ASSISTS MEMORY

Humor sticks in people's minds. We remember jokes—both good and bad. We remember pratfalls—especially ours. We remember practical jokes and how people reacted to them. (Though, to many people, those aren't humorous.) We remember funny scenes in movies. We remember funny things said at the office.

Setup/Punch Line

There are two reasons why. First, humor is often based on the unexpected. The classic comedy structure of setup/punch line is easy to remember.

Your Money Or Your Life

Second, humor is communicated primarily through the eye. Psychological studies demonstrate that things seen are more effectively remembered than things heard. That's why most systems devoted to improving memory are based on visual cues. Often, when a speaker is being humorous, he is using words that show a kind of film clip in the minds of the audience.

One of the funniest gags of all occurred on a Jack Benny radio show. It's become so popular that you have probably heard it or heard of it. It's keyed to the premise that Jack Benny was a tightwad, "So tight that when he winks his knee caps move." We hear Benny's footsteps walking on pavement. A gruff voice orders, "Your money or your life." There is a long silence. Then the voice orders once more, "Your money or your life." Benny impatiently replies, "I'm thinking! I'm thinking!"

A Radio Gag We See

Being a radio gag, we hear it happening; but, more importantly, we *see* it in our mind's eye: We *see* Benny walking, *see* the robber approaching him, *see* Benny with his hands up, *see* the look of pained thoughtfulness on Benny's face and his genuine exasperation when he says, "I'm thinking!" We see it because it's funny, and it's also funny because we see it. In seeing it and laughing, we don't forget it.

Tie the humor to your message, and your audience will remember that message because they remember the humor.

7. GROUNDS ENTHUSIASM

I told you about the importance of speaking with passionate conviction (See Chapter 5). The Boston Brahmin bank executive who said that "Self-control is the most exquisite of emotions" would make a poor Henry V on a horse trying to rouse the troops to battle the French at Agincourt.

But an executive who doesn't spice his enthusiasms with humor may come across less as an inspiring leader and more as a fanatic.

8. REDUCES STRESS

Most highly successful executives that I have worked with and interviewed tackle their occupations with an infectious joy. Sure, they've failed many times. If they hadn't, they wouldn't be so successful. But despite the ups and downs of their careers, they've had fun working. And they've communicated that fun to people they lead—even through the worst of times.

Abraham Lincoln said, "With the fearful strain that is on me night and day, if I did not laugh, I should die."

9. TURNS WEAKNESSES INTO STRENGTHS

"When you're not afraid to be self-effacing in a humorous way," says The Washington Consulting Group's CEO, Armando C. Chapelli, Jr., "you can turn your weaknesses into assets. I came to the United States from Cuba when I was thirteen, so Spanish is my first language. But I've been able to turn my language challenges into assets by being humorous. It's in people's minds anyway, so why not get it out of their minds by laughing about it?"

SUMMARY

Humor is the air cavalry of speeches. It strikes quickly and unexpectedly. It adds versatility and punch to your talks. But you win wars with regular troops, not air cavalry, and the regular troops of speeches are knowledge of yourself, your subject, and the audience—and your ability to put that knowledge into action when speaking.

Still, when used in combination with your regulars, the air cavalry of wit can make your speeches fresh and interesting.

Let's see how you can create humor and put it to work for you.

HUMOR IS MADE, NOT BORN

Many executives make the mistake of believing that humor is like blue eyes: You either have them or you don't; you're either humorous or not. Thinking they themselves are not the humorous type, they aren't—trapping themselves in a self-fulfilling prophecy.

But most great comedians struggled for years learning their craft before finally succeeding.

Thomas Edison described genius as 90 percent sweat and 10 percent inspiration. Being consistently humorous in speeches entails the same sweat/inspiration ratio, the sweat involving your constantly practicing proven techniques and putting them to work in your talks.

"When I put humor in a speech, I know it's going to work," says J. Bruce Llewellyn, CEO of the Philadelphia Coca-Cola Bottling Company. "It's humor that I've tested many times in speeches."

Don't Mingle With Guests

Before we begin to examine these techniques and how to apply them, it's important to understand what podium humor is by understanding what it is *not*.

It is not entertainment.

When the great violinist Fritz Kreisler was invited to play at a social gathering, he was asked what his fee would be.

"One thousand dollars," he said.

"That's awfully high," the host said. "We'll pay it, but remember that you're there as an entertainer, so please don't mingle with the guests."

"If I don't have to do that," Kreisler said, "My fee will be only *five hundred* dollars."

Become Acquainted With the Audience

The host was validating the old show biz commandment: *entertainers do not mingle with the audience*! That's because the entertainer's job is to divert and amuse, not become acquainted with an audience. Kreisler wanted to play, not get acquainted with people. But as an executive speaker, you are not there to amuse but to become acquainted with the audience and to acquaint the audience with you and your goals.

Your Opportunity

With that in mind, you are free to be humorous. If a comedian doesn't get laughs, he flops. But if you don't get laughs, that's okay.

Pepsico's speechwriter, Steven Provost, says, "Audiences don't think executive speakers have to be Robin Williams. Just get the punch line out, and people are going to chuckle."

Not only is your humor not expected to provoke uproars of laughter, but there may be something wrong with your speech if it does.

"Humor is critical in a speech," says Lyphomed's CEO, Gary E. Nei, "but you also have to remember to avoid excessive humor."

Here are techniques for making humor work in your speeches.

TIE HUMOR TO YOUR MESSAGE

"An executive speaker shouldn't try to be a comedian," says Worthington Industries' CEO, John H. McConnell.

"Don't use humor where it doesn't apply. Humor is only good if it is tied to what you are trying to convey. A lot of speakers get up there and throw out one-liners, and you think you are listening to Bob Hope. That's bad. You're not an entertainer. People might laugh, but you also can get side-tracked from your message."

So knowing that you don't have to get a laugh to send the message, relax and be humorous! If people don't laugh at your humor, don't wait for the laughter to come. "You will die up there, if you look around after trying to be humorous, waiting for laughter and it isn't there," says Steven Provost.

Just move confidently into the point that the humor set up.

SAVE UP ONE-LINERS

Stock up on a number of one-liners that can be used after a joke falls flat, such as: "That's the last time I buy a joke from . . ." or "I haven't got silence like that since the last time I asked for an 8 percent mortgage." Then move into your message.

Finally, you can take comedian Robert Orben's advice: "If they don't laugh two minutes after the punch line—to hell with them. They had their chance."

CREATE A GRAB BAG

"The best way to introduce humor," says Old Kent Financial Corporation's CEO John C. Canepa, "is through examples."

Keep a grab bag of humorous things that happen in and out of your business. Your grab bag is a notebook. Write about humorous incidents and insights.

Bob Evans Farms' CEO, Daniel E. Evans, uses this kind of note taking. He says:

"Humor is very important in my speeches, especially in the first 75 percent of each speech. Some of it is spontaneous. But much of it is planned. For instance, I'm going to be giving a talk to employees. I've been compiling humorous stories about employees for some time. I'm going to use those stories in that talk. I probably have half a dozen of them in my shirt pocket right now. I won't decide which one or two to use until the day before the talk. But everybody expects me to tell humorous stories when I give talks to employees."

Book Humor

Syntex's Paul Freiman says he gets much of his humor from books. "I must have 20 books in my home that contain humorous anecdotes, quotes, quips, and such. I go through them thoroughly. They must be the most well-thumbed books in my house."

No Put Downs

Be careful about the humor you use. I said in Chapter 4 that there is enough drama in most Fortune 1000 businesses to have a Pulitzer Prize-winning play written about each one. Likewise, you can find enough comedy in one day of the life of a Fortune 1000 business to make a sitcom pilot. You should not lack humorous material. Your challenge will be to use it properly.

Florida Progress Corporation's CEO, Andrew H. Hines, Jr., says, "I keep my eyes and ears open for jokes and stories. But I'm careful not to use humor in a demeaning way. Humor should always be on a high level. It should never put people down."

Shave Tail

This is especially important when you are telling anecdotes about people who report to you. Leadership is both stimulus and response: providing direction for people but also being grounded in the needs and experiences of those people. Don't make fun of people who report to you.

I learned this lesson as a shave-tail platoon commander in the Marine Corps. I gave a talk to the platoon, trying to make a point about some tactical issue by making fun of an awkward PFC. I said something about his leading the way in the "March of the Two Left Feet." The platoon laughed—but not my platoon sergeant. He told me later, "Don't make fun of somebody who can't make fun back. You're a lieutenant. He's a PFC. What you did was unfair."

Be Fair

It's okay to poke fun at people and describe humorous situations. But be circumspect. Be fair. Don't embarrass people just to get a laugh—especially people you lead.

Make Fun of Yourself

Instead, make fun of yourself. Your grab bag notebook should include a section for you alone.

Many CEOs I interviewed use humor in their talks by poking fun at themselves. Fitness, Inc.'s CEO, Sheila T. Cluff, says: "I have to have humor in my talks. My humor is based on anecdotal jokes against myself. For instance, I'll tell them that back in the 1950s, when I used to jog for exercise, people would stop and ask if I wanted a ride. Now they don't stop and ask anymore, and I haven't decided whether it is changing times or that I was 19 then and am in my mid-fifties now! If you spoof yourself, it relaxes the audience."

Getting Away With Murder

"When you use humor," says Fireman's Fund CEO, John Byrne, "make yourself the butt of your jokes first. Once you've done that, you can get away with murder. For instance, when people stand up and say something, you can say, 'Boy, that is the dumbest question!' But you can't do that first. You have to make yourself the butt of the humor first."

"I've lived my business most of my life," Alan G. Hassenfeld, CEO of Hasbro, observes. "I've probably made more mistakes than most. I have no problem telling people with humor the pitfalls I've encountered."

Two Dollar Haircut

"Use yourself as the butt of your jokes," advises Worthington Industries' John McConnell. "For instance, we have had company barbers here since 1961. Back then, haircuts cost a dollar. Then they went up to two dollars. Then a couple of years ago, we raised them to three dollars. And if you want your hair styled, it'll cost you four dollars. I'm totally bald. So, I say I seldom get the styling. Then I'll say, 'On the other hand, what you see here is 28 years of two dollar haircuts. That's what happens to you!'"

Best Weapon In the Arsenal

"Humor is the best weapon in the speaker's arsenal," says Benjamin J. Sottile, CEO of Gibson Greetings. "Sometimes people use humor within the context of the message, and they often come off as not being serious or responsible about their tasks. I am very serious about my tasks. I tend to use humor against myself. If there is a foil in anything I am going to communicate, I am the foil. When you are in a position of power, and you make somebody look foolish, that hurts. When you turn it around and say, 'I felt foolish' or 'I was the fool because the other person was the bright guy,' people accept you better."

Altar Bells

Some executives are not comfortable poking fun at themselves. If you're sensitive about that, you can still be humorous about yourself—your *younger* self.

For instance, Xerox Corporation's Director of Corporate Communications, Joseph M. Cahalan, gives many speeches and often talks about the time he was an altar boy in a Manhattan church when, during one particular service attended by hundreds of parishioners, he thought he was supposed to ring altar bells on cue.

Fear and Trembling

Cahalan says: "I was a very nervous six-year-old, and it came close to when the priest was supposed to say, 'Sanctus,

Sanctus, Sanctus,' and I was supposed to ring the bells three times. I looked down where I was kneeling and where the bells should be, and they weren't there! Unbeknownst to me, the bells weren't supposed to be there. During this particular service, bells were not supposed to be rung. But I didn't know that. There was no doubt in my mind that I was supposed to ring the bells. Now I was trained in the ritual by Jesuits, very rigorous training in which I was told that if I became confused I was not to let on that I was confused but was to do something decisive. Following this advice, I got up and before the packed church went very deliberately with a great show of confidence to the side altars. The bells weren't there. I went deliberately to the sacristy, but they weren't there either. Then I went back to my place and knelt down. My mind was in a whirl. I knew that the priest was soon going to say, 'Sanctus. Sanctus. Sanctus.' If I didn't ring those bells, we were all going to hell or something terrible was going to happen. Finally the priest intoned, 'Sanctus. Sanctus. Sanctus.' And I yelled out as loud as I could, 'Dinga-ling! Dinga-ling! Dinga-ling!' "

Advantages

Just as you should have a stock of strongly held beliefs acquired by remembering challenging experiences (See Chapter 4), you should also have a stock of humorous anecdotes, created from stressful experiences.

Stock Up, Rework, Then Practice

Select four or five experiences, rework them over and over. Make them short. Make them dramatic.

Practice relating them aloud, first when you are alone, then later in front of others.

You are not telling the anecdotes simply to get a laugh. If laughter comes, so much the better. But the anecdotes' primary objective is to make a point or draw a lesson. For instance, many lessons can be drawn from Cahalan's anecdote: adapting to change; grace under pressure; taking responsibility; etc. Tying your experience to lessons can provide dynamic echoes throughout the speech.

DEVELOP IMPROMPTU TECHNIQUES

Often the best humor is impromptu. It's fresh; it springs directly from the occasion; and it imbues the humorist with warmth and likeableness—that is, if the humor is done right and doesn't offend or distract.

The great German actor, Karl Unzelmann, a contemporary of Mozart and Beethoven, was notorious for distracting his fellow players with impromptu remarks. The management forbade him to improvise. Shortly afterwards, he appeared in a play on a Berlin stage riding a horse, which raised its tail and dropped manure on the boards. As the audience laughed, Unzelmann shook his finger at the horse and scolded, "Don't you know, it's forbidden to ad lib!"

Prepared Improv

Most likely, you don't have the gift of an Unzelmann, but you can, nonetheless, do an adequate job of improvising humor, as long as you adhere to what I call "prepared improv."

No Pain Is Gain

The first step in mastering the art of "prepared improv" is to conduct basic research. Becoming adept at ad libbing is much like getting into physical shape. It takes daily effort. Not much effort. Maybe 15 minutes a day. But the effort has to be consistent.

You've heard of "no pain, no gain" in regard to physical conditioning. But in regard to developing improv techniques, the rule is, if there is pain, you *don't* gain. In other words, if you are not having fun, you're not doing it right.

First, don't read theoretical discussions on humor. Just immerse yourself in humorous things—and laugh.

Comedy 101

Set out for a month to read only humorous books, read comedy newsletters, watch only humorous movies. Have a good time! This is Comedy 101. You don't get academic credit, but you'll get something much more: the beginnings of a new and powerful dimension of leadership.

Write down what makes you laugh. Pay particular attention to compressed humor: one-liners, puns, short anecdotes, and sight gags.

Dropped Dishes

Ad lib humor is a condensed, immediate response. For instance, you're speaking at the podium, behind which is a closed door that leads to the kitchen. Behind that door, somebody drops a load of dishes. You heard it. Your audience heard it. You have to do something about it. You're the speaker, and are in charge. You can't lose control of the situation. When noise interrupts you, acknowledge it. But you won't get back in charge by saying that those dishes being dropped and broken remind you of a joke—and then tell a long joke. Improvised humor is the sharp, quick retort. So, you'll say: "Did you hear somebody just make a prediction about our first-quarter earnings?" or "That's the last time we get our chairman to clear away the dishes."

Career Investment

When the list gets longer, divide your material into categories. Every week or so review it. Think of situations in your business where these bits of humor would fit.

You might say, "I don't have time to spend on something as frivolous as humor." For one thing, 15 minutes a day is not much time. And for another, it's not a frivolous exercise. The payoff is your becoming a more effective leader. So look at those 15 minutes of having a good time as an ongoing investment in your career.

Impromptu Takes Practice

Mark Twain said, "It usually takes me more than three weeks to prepare a good impromptu speech."

Improvised humor takes diligent preparation, too. Plan ahead. Analyze the situation you will be in. Anticipate being called on to speak. Think of one-liners you may use.

For instance, Lyphomed's Gary Nei says that he often scouts out the environment where he may be called on to speak. "I find it's important to get there an hour or so ahead of the time I may be speaking, listen to what is going on. I can usually pick up two or three little tidbits that can add impromptu humor to whatever humor I already have planned for the speech."

Do It

Practice, of course, isn't enough. You've got to put your impromptu ideas into action.

Just as the humor you build into your speeches doesn't have to provoke gales of laughter to be effective, so your ad libs don't have to be show-stoppers either. They just have to be mildly amusing.

Generally, there are three types of ad lib situations, and most of them derive from something unexpected happening: the glitch.

- ☐ Your glitch
- ☐ Somebody else's glitch
- ☐ A glitch in the environment

Your Glitch

When you make a mistake, mispronounce a word, or forget your train of thought, you have a great opportunity. It's an opportunity for you to use humor against yourself and thus show that you can take a joke and think quickly on your feet.

Now that you are building a repertoire of one-liners to fit different occasions, make sure a great number of those one-liners can apply to mistakes you may make: mistakes in flubbing words ("Did you ever get the feeling your lips forgot to pay the electric bill?"); mistakes in proposing an idea that your audience doesn't like ("I thought I had a brainstorm, but I guess it was just a light drizzle"); mistakes in operating audio visual equipment ("Right now, the little I know, I owe to my ignorance" or "Never let reality get the upper hand").

Nobody likes to make mistakes, especially a leader who is in front of people he leads. But mistakes are inevitable. Turn them to your advantage through "prepared improv."

Others' Glitches

The foibles of other people can provide an opportunity for ad libs. New England Electric's CEO, John Rowe says: "Just the other day I went to give awards. Three people were there on the podium. One group of engineers had a nifty gizmo that flashed and buzzed. Another group had a personal computer illustrating their product. This other poor guy just had a single chart. Well, there's your situation for a joke!"

But Rowe advises that you make sure your humor doesn't insult others. The very essence of executive humor is that it must be kindly. You can make it kindly by doing two things: Immediately praise the individual. Or immediately turn the joke back on yourself with self-deprecating humor.

Glitches in the Environment

Glitches taking place in the environment that you and your audience share are a rich source of ad lib humor. They are usually linked to four factors: light, temperature, sound, audience.

Build up a repertoire of one-liners that can be applied in each different situation.

Be Natural

Don't pull out one-liners on cue like a magician pulling handkerchiefs from his fist. You're not a one-liner robot. Ad lib remarks must come naturally. They must fit you, the occasion, and the moment. That's why you have to prepare so diligently before you are ready to go into action in front of a live audience. With many one-liners at your disposal, you can use the one that fits, and if it doesn't exactly fit, tailor it on the spot. However, if you can't tailor it, don't ad lib.

INTEGRATE TECHNIQUES

I've talked about developing humor to put in a prepared text and developing "prepared improv." Now it's time to weave the two together. Clearly, humor should be embedded in the structure of your speech to interest the audience and help them remember your main points. But you can give your speech added interest if you stop now and then to deliver some ad lib humor. Of course, it can be "prepared improv" humor. Before coming to the podium, you should have a good idea of the kind of ad libbing you want to do, and when you want to do it in your speech.

SUMMARY

Don't avoid trying to be humorous. Humor helps bond the speaker with the audience, creates interest and a change of pace, relieves tension, disarms hostility, and makes your points more easily remembered.

The primary purposes of executive speeches are to persuade, inform, and inspire. The use of humor must be seen as only a means to achieve those ends. You don't have to get people laughing hard. You don't have to get them laughing at all. As Charlie Chaplin said, "If you've got something funny to do, you don't have to be funny doing it." Just make sure that your humor leads directly into the points you are making.

The ability to be humorous isn't a gift, it's a skill you acquire through constant practice and application. Build a repertoire of quips, quotes, gags, and anecdotes. Be creative in weaving these through your speeches. Look for opportunities to use them spontaneously when giving speeches.

Humor won't come to you unless you go to it.

8

Writing the Speech

Writing when properly managed is but a different name for conversation.

LAWRENCE STERN

The last and greatest art, the art to blot.

ALEXANDER POPE

Any good speech is going to gore some oxes.

JOHN O'BRIEN,
CEO, Grumman Corporation

Most speeches are very dull. That's because the speakers are presenting a lot of statistics and graphs—dry, dull numbers. There is no fun in that. It just wears out the mind.

BENJAMIN J. SOTTILE,
CEO, Gibson Greetings, Inc.

Now that we're more than half way through the book, we are ready to talk about writing the speech. That's because at least half of writing entails preparation.

"I like people," said Lillian Hellman, "who refuse to speak until they are ready to speak."

We know that the preparation in getting ready to speak involves knowing your needs, the audience's needs, a core idea and how you may begin and end the speech. This preparation might take weeks—or, if you know the audience and your material well, only a few minutes. Still, you should go through every stage of the preparation (Chapters 2 through 6) before writing the speech.

Speech Building

---

1. WRITE IT THROUGH

Grumman's CEO, John O'Brien, says:

"A weakness in many executives is that they agree to give a speech, walk into the room with no preparation and try to ad lib for twenty minutes. Repeat themselves again and again. That will not happen in our business. If you are going to give a presentation, show the audience the courtesy of preparing well.

"That's why I insist on the written speech because I believe that unless you sit down and write out your thoughts and put them in a cogent order, you can't deliver a cogent speech. Maybe some people have mastered that art. But I have seen too many people give speeches that they really haven't thought out."

Our Words Shape Us

Our ideas don't come into our minds marching in lock-step, ready for our bidding. Instead, they come sailing at us like covies of clay pigeons triggered at a skeet shoot. Snatching what ideas we can and putting them on paper, giving them structure, coherence, and continuity is a rigorous discipline.

Yet it is a discipline that, if patiently adhered to, can be liberating and transforming. When we shape words, the words often shape us. I have never written anything to be read or spoken that has not been, in small or large ways, transformed into something I hadn't expected—transformed for the better.

Writing Is Discovery

Innovation often works best when it surprises. Often, I write a letter, speech, article, or book one time through before I truly understand it. When I come to understand it, I some-times see that it is not the piece that should be written. Maybe its beginning is the ending of the speech. Or maybe its ending is really the beginning. In any case, primed by the first draft, I can write the real piece.

Don't Get It Right, Get It Written

So begin writing your speech by simply writing it, word for word, beginning to end. Some speech-writing experts recommend writing the ending first then returning to the beginning and finishing up. This can be an effective technique. But if writing is truly discovery, then we frequently don't know what the ending will be until we get there.

This doesn't mean that when it's time to deliver, you read from prepared text. You write the speech to understand it and improve it, not necessarily to read it. Later on, you can decide whether to read it or not.

Meaning Comes Later

My writing this book is an example of this write-to-discover concept. I've broken the text into many headings so that you don't have to read the book cover to cover. You can turn to what technique you think might help, read it, think about it, put it into action, then put the book back on your reference shelf until you need another technique.

The point is, I have no idea what the name of each heading will be until after I write the section it introduces. I generally know what the section will cover, but the act of writing uncovers its true significance—and its heading.

Make Writing Dynamic

For me, the image of the writer isn't one of a lonely soul hunched over pen and paper or typewriter or word processor, carving prose word by careful word. Instead, it's the image of the abstract expressionist painter, Jackson Pollock—Pollock standing with a bucket in one hand, a brush in the other, flinging paint madly across a canvas.

I don't pretend to understand Jackson Pollock's paintings. From my viewpoint, his importance isn't only in his product but in his process. He made the act of painting dynamic — and thus offers a lesson both to artists and writers: Make the act of writing dynamic.

Gagged and Hog-tied

Like Jackson Pollock before a canvas, scatter your ideas across the pages. Don't think about structure and continuity. Go from start to finish with the critic in you gagged and hogtied. You're not trying to obtain finished results but a kind of balloon release of ideas. Then, if you have time, pigeonhole the draft for a few days.

Subconscious

Don't underestimate the importance of your subconscious. Allow it to reflect on what you've written. The subconscious is a treasure trove of fresh ideas and analysis. Many of our most important ideas come when we're not thinking consciously about trying to create them.

"I believe that your subconscious can work for you on speeches," says Florida Progress Corporation's CEO, Andrew

H. Hines, Jr. "A week to ten days before I'm to give a speech, I start feeding material into my subconscious. You know you are going to be in front of a group and need to say things they need to hear and want to hear. So I begin looking at newspapers and magazines with a different eye, just feeding my subconscious."

The Rewrite

A sage once said that good writing is "Clear as light, clean as bone, firm as stone." Most often you fulfill those requirements not through writing but rewriting.

Dorothy Parker said that she couldn't write five words without changing seven.

General Electric Company's speechwriter, William K. Lane, Jr., says that a recent speech he and Jack Welch wrote went through 60 drafts. "It's a very important speech," Lane says. "It's Welch's view of business in the 1990s. Of those 60 drafts, eight or nine are major."

Don't just make fine adjustments. Make the first rewrite a complete rewrite. With the first draft on paper, you now can be more deliberate. You can choose the right ideas, the right words to express those ideas. You don't have to be a Jackson Pollock now. You can be more like a skilled baseball batter, swinging only at good pitches, laying off bad ones.

Make It a Speech

A strict English teacher would probably give you an F for grammar if you submitted a written speech for a grade. If you didn't get an F, there would be something wrong with the speech. A good speech should have sentence fragments, dots, and dashes. If the speech will be published, then you can rework it into standard English form.

Avoid Businesspeak

Avoid the trite, the stereotyped, and the overblown of businesspeak.

In Aetna Life and Casualty's *Style Booklet: The Bare Bones of Writing*, speechwriter Stephen R. Maloney writes that businesspeak is "the sound of one hand clapping. We should eliminate businesspeak in all our communications, unless compelled by a truly irresistible force. 'Businesspeak' includes words and phrases that have had their moment in the sun — and will have their eternity in the shade."

Avoid the Worn-Out

He continues: "Examples abound: *implement* (Does this mean 'begin,' 'manage,' 'write,' 'give directions'?), *coordinate* (What specific actions does this word conceal?), *prioritize* (Does this mean 'set priorities'?), *finalize* (Does this mean 'complete'?), *component* (a big word that means 'part'), *bottom line*, *unique* (most things aren't; and if they are, they can't be 'very unique,' 'rather unique,' or 'somewhat unique'), *process* (especially as a verb), *impacted* (and, even worse, 'favorably impacted,' which sounds something like an enjoyable auto accident).

Avoid the Over-Used

"Run a red pencil through the following words that are either worn out from over-use or designed to hide reality rather than illuminate it; *innovative*, *maximize*, *quality* (used as an adjective), *market-oriented*, *facilitate*, *indicative*, *aggressively managed*. Take a stand against 'cutesy' words like *touch base*, *connectedness*, and *comfort level*. Avoid technical terms (including 'computerese') that serve to make the world seem a dark, cold, mechanical place: examples, *input*, *output*, *throughput*, *feedback*.

"Finally, let us never return to *square one*. Let us make our last visit to *re-visit*; let us recognize *win/win* situations as losers. Let us acknowledge that *cutting edge* has lost its sharpness; let us say, 'Down with *rachet up*'; let us affirm the artlessness of *state-of-the-art*."

Enthusiasms Prevail

Don't be concerned, however, if your speech is sprinkled with a few businesspeak terms; you won't crash and burn on the podium. Casual English can never been cleaned of all cliches. (The style booklet's "Bare Bones" title proves that.) Nor should the language be so sanitized. English is vernacular, having for centuries been invigorated by new expressions. Knowing your audience, knowing and being passionate about your subject (See Chapter 4), being humorous—these determine, to a large extent, your ability to get the audience on the edge of their chairs—*not* having a low cliche-count. I have witnessed many inspiring speeches that, when transformed to black ink on white paper, looked as commonplace as the Wizard of Oz operating levers after the curtain was pulled away: the speaker and her enthusiasms having been what worked magic with the words. "Everything bows to success," said Victor Hugo, though in another tongue. "Even grammar."

Buy Our Products

Still, scraping away the detritus of businessspeak and building your speech on the stone arch of standard prose gives you the best chance to communicate clearly, crisply, and forcefully. After all, when you tell your customer he can *maximize* his *bottomline* by *getting in bed* with you to be *proactive* in *pinpointing viable options* that have been *blue-skyed* and *finalized* into *meaningful, in-depth breakthroughs* that *zero in* on *marketplace-oriented, fall-back positions*, why not just say, "Buy our products"?

Your Best Lick

Hall of fame tackle Merlin Olson said, "There are so many moves you can make in football, so many stunts. But the best philosophy is simply keep hitting them with your best lick."

That's also the best philosophy in regard to writing speeches. Keep hitting them with your best lick. You do that by keeping your speeches simple, short, and direct.

Most speeches, ultimately, have a simple end in mind. For the politician, it's, "Vote for me!" For the businessperson, it's, "Buy my product!" For the capital campaign chairperson, it's, "Give us money!"

The Throat of the Issue

"Many speeches are awful," says AGS Computers' CEO, Lawrence J. Schoenberg, "Because speakers talk around issues or merely spout platitudes. They think that's what a speech is for. They're so afraid of saying something wrong, they won't say anything right."

Don't make your speech the equivalent of a four-corner basketball stall. Instead, take Napoleon's advice: "If you start to take Vienna, *take Vienna!*" Go for the throat of the issue. One way to do that is to replace mutterings with simple, muscular words.

Mutterings and Muscles

Mutterings	Muscles
so for that reason	so
but at the same time	but
are in agreement with	agree
In my opinion	(Just state the opinion)
at present time	now
but in any case	but
due to the fact	because
in the course of	during
and all that	(delete)
when all is said and done	(delete)
to the tune of	(just provide the number)
you take it from there	(delete)
in the final analysis	finally
in close proximity to	near
consensus of opinion	agreement
as a matter of fact	(delete)
in a matter of minutes	minutes
is a matter of	involves or depends on
overwhelming (or vast) majority	most people or nearly everyone
but on the contrary	but
to come to the realization	to realize

to reach an agreement   to agree
under the necessity of (or to)   must or have to

Courage to Cut

Producer Sam Goldwyn, a stickler for producing movies within budgets he set, visited the director John Ford on location.

"You're a day behind schedule," he demanded of Ford. "You're going to run over budget. What're you going to do about it?"

Ford opened the script. "I shoot five pages a day," he said. He ripped five pages from the script. "Now I'm within budget."

Writing a good speech involves being creative in putting things in, but also being ruthless in taking things out.

Too many speakers try hard to expand the greatest number of words to cover the smallest amount of thought.

If the end of speechifying is, as Demosthenes said, action, action, action—then a primary means to that end is cut, cut, cut.

Boil and Polish

In advice to writers for the daily press, the 19th century American folk humorist Joel Chandler Harris said:

> When you've got a thing to say,
> Say it! Don't take half a day . . . .
> Life is short—a fleeting vapor —
> Don't you fill the whole blamed paper
> With a tale which, at a pinch,
> Could be cornered in an inch.
> Boil her down until she simmers.
> Polish her until she glimmers.

So let me offer what may be one of the most important techniques of all in this book: *you can never cut enough from any speech you write.*

How To Do It

Leaving out is hard to do, but here are ways you can do it. For one thing, make those cuts arbitrary.

Cut the first three minutes of your speech. Often in simply taking out the beginning, you have made your speech a lot more effective. If your cutting doesn't advance the speech, you can always put the material back.

Cut the End and the Middle

Cut the last three minutes. If possible, don't assess the damage until the next day. Do you really need that ending? Can it be made shorter? Or can it be eliminated altogether?

Cut the middle. Wait a day. During that interval, put your subconscious to work again. Don't think about the cuts you made. Then go back to the speech and assess it. Put the middle back if you want. Or just put parts of it back. Or keep it out altogether.

The Q & A Speech

If there is going to be a question and answer session at the end of your speech, cut half of your speech. Make sure you give the half you cut as answers to questions. It doesn't matter what questions are asked, you can always make a transition into what you want to say.

Line-By-Line/Word-By-Word

Go over the speech line-by-line. Make each sentence justify its existence. If it can't, throw it out.

When a sentence passes muster, don't be done with it. Compress it to a critical mass. Like sun rays, words burn more deeply the more intensely they are focused. Make sure the sentence hinges on active verbs. (For instance, change: "The product is the kind we want" to "We want this product.") Making your verbs active often eliminates many unnecessary words. Cut out most adjectives. Transform a sentence into a phrase; a phrase into a word; a word, if possible, into a deleted word. A carpenter is known by his chips, a mason by his joints, and a writer often by the words she leaves out.

Get Criticized

After you have written, cut, compressed, and polished the speech to the best of your ability, then take it on the road. Get it criticized. Read it to people who not only can tell you what may be wrong—but how they think you can set it right.

"I give a lot of speeches," says Delmarva Power's CEO, Nevius M. Curtis, "but I only write one a year. That's the speech I give before the stockholders meeting. I write it out, actually present it to the the senior executives. If they don't like it, we change it."

2. WRITE IT WITH A WHEEL AND SPOKES

Often you may not have time to write it down. Or writing it word for word may not be, for you, an effective way of preparing a speech. Being essentially a conversation, a speech must be written in conversational style and form. Many people don't have the knack for doing that. It's not that they have been educated badly. It's that they have been educated too well, educated that writing must follow rules of composition. But the rules of conversation are different. In fact, conversation has only one rule: do what works.

Topic-Spoking

Here's what can work for you. Don't write it word for word. Prepare your speech by simply writing ideas that will work for that audience. But don't make a long list of ideas. Go about it systematically.

Draw a topic-spoking diagram. Put the speech's single idea in the center (See Chapter 3). You'll note that coming up with a single idea for your speech is a systematic process in itself. Make sure you go through every step of the process. Though you are not writing the speech, don't take a shortcut. Develop that single idea by assessing your needs and the audience's needs (See Chapter 2).

Spokes

Each spoke radiates to a specific idea. Write down three to five ideas. They should be ideas that you feel strongly about. Let's say that you are active in community affairs. You've become a trustee of your town's library, and you want to inspire an audience of local business leaders to support a capital campaign to expand the library.

Your central idea is "Support The Campaign."

The spokes radiate to reasons why the campaign should be supported. One spoke points to Children. Another spoke points to Staff. Another spoke points to Stacks.

Don't try to make a logical sequence of these ideas. That's why they are around the spoke. You shape this speech the way a sculpture shapes a block of stone, moving *around* the idea.

Establish a Strongly Felt Commitment

Analyze each idea (See Chapter 5). Establish a strongly felt commitment to each one. Clearly, you must have strong convictions about why children, staff, and stack facilities must be enhanced. Cluster your convictions around each idea. For instance, around children you may write *education, broaden interests,* and *personal remembrances.* Your cluster of convictions support the idea, which in turn is tied to the single idea of the speech.

Talk About

Talk about the spoke ideas. Talk about the importance of expanded library facilities for enhancing children's education and interests. Talk about your personal remembrances of the library. Use a tape recorder, if you wish. Go to the Staff and Stacks ideas and the thoughts you clustered around them. Talk about each one. Write down key words.

Sequence

Put your ideas in sequence. Write a transition between each one, and: *voilà,* you have a speech!

3. WRITE IT WHILE YOU GIVE IT

Finally, there is one more way to write it. Write it while you are speaking to the audience. That is, let the stimulus of the moment give substance to your speech.

New England Electric System's CEO, John W. Rowe, says that often his most memorable speeches are the ones he gives from notes. He says:

"My suggestion is don't write them if you don't have to. I find the speeches with the most significant impact are done from fairly sparse outlines. The problem is that sometimes you make mistakes. If you are giving a speech in which you can't afford to make a misstep, then the price is too high. It depends what you want to do. If you want to get on and off the stage without getting hurt then write your speech. If you want to communicate with people, sell them something, want them to trust you, then don't read a speech. Be live! Any fool can see that you are reading a canned speech. My training in the law helped me this way. I spent so much time in one bankruptcy courtroom with the same judge and the same lawyers that I started to depart from text, to crack jokes, and soon found out that my departures were getting a good response. When I made the transition to being a CEO, I was already comfortable with the thought that I generally do well when I take a little gamble in front of an audience, as long as I didn't get too hamish, erring a little bit on the folksy side. So I prefer to invent the humor, the color, the context while looking at the audience and feeling their response. Sometimes you have to change from being too humorous to being more sober, or vice versa. Sometimes you see that what you are excited about, the audience isn't. So reduce the emphasis on that and add it somewhere else. Sometimes you get there with your outline and the fellow before you just gave the speech. Of course, there are times I am not going to give the spontaneous speech. If I am doing something that I think will affect my company's stock the next day, then I'm damned careful and give a prepared talk."

Flip Chart Speech

Fireman's Fund Insurance Company's CEO, John J. Byrne, creates his speech using a flip chart and audience participation.

"I started using this technique several years ago. And I've grown fond of it. My audiences like it, too. I've been invited back many times after using it. It doesn't sound like much. You really have to see it. On the floor, I set up a big flip chart. It's blank. I walk down to the floor with a lavaliere microphone. Don't stand on the stage with this. Be down on the same level as the audience. Hopefully, there will be an aisle in the center that you can walk up and down while you speak. I start off by saying, 'I have a lot of terrific things I want to talk about.' Sometimes I have slides with me. I flash those slides, giving them the impression that I have a wonderfully prepared speech. Then I say, 'My experience is that when I talk about what you want to have me talk about, you are much more interested in what I have to say. So what I'd like is for you to tell me what subjects you like me to talk about.'

Long Silence

"There is usually a long silence. I say, 'Come on somebody!' Finally, somebody will say, 'Will you talk about underwriting casualty business in California?' So I go to the flip chart and put up 'Underwriting in California' in brown pencil. As soon as somebody breaks the ice, then the hands are up all around. Now be careful not to answer those subjects. You are trying to get a list of subjects. The moment you start giving answers, you stifle the whole thing. As you are writing the subjects down, try to be very careful not by body language or anything else to suggest that there is such a thing as a good or bad subject, or a subject that you want to talk about or not talk about. Stay neutral.

Color Patterns

"I keep going until there are perhaps eight or nine subjects up there. Sometimes I use different colors. I'll put one subject in black. Another in green. The audience starts to think there is some kind of mysterious color pattern to this thing. The truth is, there really isn't.

Five Dollar Kitchen Timer

"I have a five dollar kitchen timer with a loud bell on it. I say to the program director, 'How much time do we have here?' He'll tell me. I ask for somebody to be a time keeper. I hand the timer to the person. I say, 'When the timer goes off, your job is to stand up and give me the code word. That code word means that *it is time to stop talking, Mr. Byrne.* You know what the code word is? Well, the code word is *bullshit!* Can you handle that? When the timer goes off, your job is to stand up and say *bullshit!*'

Relaxed Audience

"Now the audience is relaxed. We've had a little fun with a list of subjects. Those are their subjects up on the flip chart. Then I start talking about the subjects. Very, very seldom do I find that there is a subject that they put up that I don't know enough about at least to say something about. So I keep talking. People will stand up and say, 'You don't know what you're talking about!' I encourage that. I walk up and down the aisles and try to have as much fun with people as I can. The next thing you know the alarm goes off.

The Perfect Way To Leave the Audience

"We are usually only half way through the subjects. I'm having a great time, the audience is having a great time. The alarm goes off and stops me. Which is a perfect way to leave the audience. They want this to go on another hour. The beauty of this is that here is the chairman of the board of a major company who doesn't take himself very seriously, who is obviously having a good time. That works fine for an audience of less than a hundred people. They walk out thinking that you talked about what they wanted to hear. So many times, in the insurance business anyway, the CEO really thinks that the audience wants to hear what is on his mind. That is seldom so. The audience is not a bit interested in what he does with his day, or economics, or taxation in Congress, or all these sort of poetic subjects. The audience has its own idea of what they want to hear. If you ferret those ideas out first, you have a much bigger impact on the audience."

Not Impromptu

Creating the speech while delivering the speech is not an exercise in impromptu speaking. Instead, this technique requires the same systematic preparation as a written talk. Go to the podium knowing your subject and the audience's needs cold, knowing the exact points you want to make, knowing examples and humor that will support those points. You may use notes. Or like Gibson Greetings' CEO, Benjamin J. Sottile, you may go up there without notes. He says, "Too often I find myself using notes that I have taken to the podium as a crutch. They get in my way. In many cases, I can be more effective without notes."

Work Hard

Often the notes that good speakers make are not hastily scribbled. Old Kent Financial Corporation's CEO, John C. Canepa, says that though he does not write speeches word for word, he still works diligently to create good outlines.

"I develop three outlines," he says. "The first outline is from 12 to 14 pages on a half hour speech. I reduce that to a second outline, which is 8 pages. Then, the day before I am ready to deliver the speech, I've reduced that 8-page outline to an outline on a single page."

Facial Expressions and Body Language

When creating your speech while you talk, remember these techniques: Look members of the audience in the eye. Speak directly to each individual. Read their facial expressions. Read their body language. Pay particular attention to people in the back of the room. If your message is not interesting the audience, people in the back and at the sides will most likely be the first to begin registering negative reactions. Speak more slowly than you normally would. Pause a great deal. Be deliberate in your presentation. Feel that you are holding an informal conversation in your living room. Be in charge. Be enthusiastic about your ideas. And (as always) be brief. Don't take forever to go nowhere. The longer you talk before the audience, the greater the danger that you will start talking about more than you know.

SUMMARY

The test of the speech is in the speaking. But when you write what you will later come to speak, you frequently discover new ideas and ensure that your words are appropriate and concise. You don't have to get the first draft right, just get it written. In subsequent drafts, you can polish your ideas, integrate your single idea, and give structure to the talk. If you don't wish or don't have time to write the speech, you can use topic-spoking diagrams as an aid in jotting down your main ideas. Finally, if you know your subject well and are confident on the podium, you may actually develop your speech while you are speaking, letting the immediate feedback from the audience help you shape your concepts.

9

Delivery

My first rule of giving speeches is that the audience doesn't remember what you say, they remember the general impression you leave.

> JOHN J. BYRNE,
> *CEO, Fireman's Fund Insurance Company*

About 10 seconds before I stand up to speak, I feel a burst of panic. That's good. It gets the adrenaline flowing. That panic goes away fast, but it's always there.

> PAUL E. FREIMAN,
> *CEO, Syntex Corporation*

I always remember Bob Hope saying that for the first 20 seconds, he is nervous. That has always kept me from being nervous.

> JOHN J. SCHIFF,
> *CEO, Cincinnati Financial Corporation*

Many people judge executives on their ability to think quickly on their feet.

> GEORGE L. PLA,
> *CEO, Cordoba Corporation*

D ELIVERY IS THOUGHT IN ACTION. Let's not view delivery in terms of how to use your hands, how to stand or how to use your voice. Those things can't be taught because you already know them: They are you. Your objective in writing, rehearsing, and giving speeches is to be you—without gimmicks. You are the only you that ever was or will be. Don't mess with quality. Sure, eliminate distracting mannerisms: a nervous tick, the fig-leaf or reverse fig-leaf pose, rubbing your hands, jangling change in your pocket, holding onto the lectern, fiddling with the microphone, keeping hands in pockets, leaning on the lectern, etc. You can discover such mannerisms by having people analyze you and by using a video recorder.

CONSULTANTS

"Delivering good speeches takes a lot of practice," says Martha S. Hicks, CEO of Harwell Hicks Real Estate Research. "If you haven't done so before, I recommend that you get a communication consultant. Women speakers should make a special effort to take on an air of command and take control on the podium."

But don't eliminate the unteachable you from your delivery. Anneal it in the heat of constant speechmaking.

DELIVERY IS INSIDE OUT

Work on your delivery not from outside in—using gestures, etc., to help communicate—but from inside out. Delivery isn't in the hands or face or stance but in your heart and mind. Deal with challenges associated with that attitude, i.e., nervousness, reading versus giving impromptu speeches, and doing well in Q & A sessions, and the outside aspects of delivery will take care of themselves.

JITTERS AND OTHER NERVOUS CONDITIONS

A Kentucky politician, a contemporary of Andrew Jackson, was such a crack shot that he could cut a string in two at 20 paces with a single bullet. Once he was challenged to fight a duel, but his pistol hand began to shake. He couldn't aim the weapon properly. He and his opponent missed each other. Afterward, somebody asked how come he could miss a man but hit a string.

"That damned string never shot back!" he said.

PULL THE TRIGGER

You can write and rewrite speeches, practice them repeatedly, but the time will come when you have to get up in front of an audience and pull the trigger. You have to open your mouth, work your larynx and tongue, and speak words that inform, motivate, and sell. The audience doesn't shoot back, but the fear a live audience often invokes in a speaker can be akin to the anticipation of mortal combat.

QUEASINESS AND TERROR

Pascal said that if you wish people to speak well of you, don't speak. But an executive *must* speak—often when people are not thinking well of you—and, in speaking, must conquer emotions that can run from queasiness to outright terror.

Prespeech nervousness is a fact of life. The authors of the *Book Of Lists* found that 41 percent of surveyed people rated speaking in public as their worst fear, while only 19 percent rated their worst fear as death. Rare is the speaker, even the most experienced and skilled, who does not feel nervous before speaking.

TUMMY TICKLERS

Rare, too, is the successful speaker who does not recognize the importance of being a little nervous. Delmarva Power's CEO, Nevius M. Curtis, says, "Sure, I get the 'tummy ticklers.' The bigger the speech, the bigger the tummy ticklers. If I don't get them, it's a lousy speech."

DOUBLE RISK

Woody Allen said, "Just because I'm paranoid doesn't mean that somebody isn't out to get me."

Because you're nervous doesn't mean there aren't good reasons to be nervous. Executive speakers are confronted by several challenges: Often, they must entertain, inform, and inspire, all in one speech.

Pier 1 Imports' CEO, Clark A. Johnson, says:

"As a leader you are required to stand up and talk about the future, talk about action steps that, if everybody follows, will get them to a golden mountain. So you are taking a double risk: speaking in public and risking that you will look bad, that you will stand up and communicate your vision of the future, and if that vision turns out to be wrong, people will say, 'Do you remember when that dummy said *that*, and he was wrong?'"

MAKE ENEMIES, FRIENDS

Abraham Lincoln said that the best way to defeat an enemy is to make him a friend. The best way to conquer speakers' nerves is to acknowledge that there is a lot at stake when you speak, that nervousness is justified, and that you deal with that nervousness not by fighting or ignoring it but by using it, making it your friend.

"When you first start to speak before people, it's normal to be nervous," says Carolyn B. Elman, CEO of the American Business Women's Association. "You've got to know where that nervousness shows up. Some people's hands shake. So they shouldn't use notes that are on paper but instead on cards. Other people's knees shake. So they should stand behind a lectern. My anxiety showed in my voice. I overcame that through experience, by speaking again and again. Often, I'll write on my first note card, "Think . . . low." (Meaning speak low) "Speak slow."

13 Techniques to Deal with Nervousness

1. PREPARATION

Every CEO interviewed subscribed to the classic antidote for speaker's nerves: preparation. "In order to be relaxed," says Central Maine Power Company's CEO, Joe C. Collier, Jr., "you need to be well prepared. It's a terrible thing to go into a speech not knowing what you're saying."

"Major flops occur," says Lyphomed's CEO, Gary E. Nei, "when you are to speak before an important occasion and are not prepared to do your best."

Make the Strange, Familiar

We frequently get nervous when confronting a strange environment. But we can help make the strange, familiar, and reduce our nervousness, by knowing that we have a message that meets the deepest needs of the audience.

"Always speak directly to the audience's needs," says Joseph W. Marshall, CEO of Idaho Power Company. "You have to establish a need for what you are going to say."

"Make sure you always have a strong message for that audience," says Barnett Banks, CEO, Charles E. Rice, "whether that message is congratulatory, inspirational, or appreciative."

Laser Shot, Not Scattershot

Many speakers make the mistake of working hard in preparing a speech, not working smart. Their preparation often consists of time-consuming scatter shots—researching a number of topics related to the speech—not a laser shot that identifies that exact point where audience needs and speaker's knowledge and abilities meet—then hitting it dead center.

To create your laser shot, review Audience Analyzer #10 and answer the two questions: What does the audience want? What's at stake for the audience? (See Chapter 3.)

2. MEMORIZE THE OPENER

Ryne Duren was a fireballing righthander for the New York Yankees in the 1950s. His fastball could almost puncture armor-plating. The trouble was, Duren was notoriously near-sighted. He wore bottle-bottom-thick glasses. Many times, during his warmups, he seemed to lose his bearings, and fired pitches not into the catcher's glove but up into the press box high behind the batter. Afterwards, many a batter would come to the plate wishing that he would rather be testing bullet-proof vests.

An Attack of the 'Maybe's'

Sometimes, no matter how well you prepare, how experienced and confident you are as a speaker, you will, like the batters who faced Duren, find yourself in a pickle. Maybe you are speaking for the first time to hundreds of people. Or maybe you are speaking to new customers who will be scrutinizing every gesture, every word. Maybe an attack of hyper-nervousness rolls over you, and suddenly your mouth gets dry as sofa stuffing, your fingers play a tattoo on your notes, and you feel as if your face has gotten that stricken look of a deer caught in headlights.

Adrenaline Rush

A technique to get through those first nervous moments looking confident and in control is to memorize your opener.

Cypress Semiconductor Corporation's CEO, T.J. Rodgers, does this often. He says:

"When you've prepared well, you have enough confidence that you don't worry about getting nervous. Once you get into your cadence and through your introduction, your speaker's fright is gone, and you're just going. The more you prepare, the less you have to worry about being nervous."

Washington Testimony

Recently, Rodgers spoke before a congressional subcommittee in Washington, opposing the formation of a government consortium of semiconductor manufacturers on grounds that the consortium would stifle competition in the industry. He says:

"When I went to Washington, I had my speech down cold. But trust me, in that hearing room, when the guy next to me slid the microphone in front of my face and I was staring at a house committee, and they're looking at me, and it's my turn to talk, it didn't matter how cold I had it, I got a rush of adrenaline that you couldn't believe! That can be a big problem. It can cause you to lose your cadence, talk fast, huff and puff, and lose your voice quality. So one thing I did was to get my first few lines down rote cold. By the time I work my way through that, I'm usually in the groove."

Be Spontaneous

Memorization must not replace spontaneity. Take another tip from pitchmen. (See Chapter 4.) The pitchmen I worked with repeated essentially the same pitch—often talking five hours a day up to 30 straight days at a time; but they always appeared to be speaking the words for the first time. Don't drone on like Hal the computer up there. You might have said those lines a hundred times in your sleep, but when you repeat them to your audience, make it appear as if you are making them up on the spot.

3. CARE FOR THE AUDIENCE

Nervousness is often self-inflicted pain. Before we give a talk, we torture ourselves with questions: "What will they think of me?" "What if my mind goes blank?" "What if they think my ideas are stupid?" "What if they don't laugh at my humor?"

Be easy on yourself. Refocus your thoughts. Don't think, *me, me, me*. Think *them, them, them*. We say we *give* a speech, i.e., transfer a possession from us to the audience. Speaking, we give a gift that they need. To understand what they need, care for the audience. See not your predicament, but theirs. Every audience, just like every person, is facing a challenge. What is that challenge? Are their sales falling? Are their markets becoming more competitive? Are their products losing their technological advantage? What help do they need? How can you provide that help through your speech?

By sharpening the focus on them and their needs, you dim the focus on you and your fears. You stop sweating and start helping.

Negative Versus Positive Nervousness

Fitness' CEO, Sheila T. Cluff, observes that though she is always a little nervous before giving a speech, she recognizes that there is a difference between negative nervousness, the kind stemming from your not being prepared, and positive nervousness, the kind deriving from your being genuinely concerned for your audience's welfare. She says:

"I feel strongly that if a company is paying me a handsome amount to give a speech, I'm obligated that their employees listen to me. That's a tremendous responsibility, and that makes me nervous. My nervousness comes from making sure that they get information that's meaningful, that they have a good time, and finally, that they get information about my products without thinking that I am being commercial."

4. BE AWARE

Many fears are born from fevers of the imagination. Mark Twain said, "I've known a lot of troubles in my life, but most of them never happened." I'm not saying your worst fears *won't* come true. You really might walk to the podium with three hundred pairs of eyes locked on you, set your notes down, stare out at the sea of faces, open your mouth, realize that your mind is blank, and begin sweating bullets. You really might begin speaking, and nothing comes out of your mouth but an hysterical giggle. There really might be somebody in the wings with the proverbial hook on a long pole and that person might pull you off the stage, to the accompaniment of loud laughter.

Lock Onto the Present

Then again, these fevers may never materialize. Worry gives small things big shadows. It does us no good, and often some harm, to let our minds and emotions take flight.

The remedy: Lock your thoughts on the present. Before you rise to give the speech, be aware of reality: the water glass in front of you, the way your suit fits across your shoulders, the feel of your toes in your shoes. Those things, insignificant as they seem, are far more important than the stuff of your imagination.

5. REDUCE BARRIERS

"Good fences," Robert Frost said, "make good neighbors;" but, for my money, good fences make lousy speeches.

I'm talking about those fences or boundaries that stand before the speaker and his audience.

Sometimes, they are real boundaries, like a stage, a podium, lectern, or teleprompter screen. Sometimes, they are imaginary boundaries of pride, anger, or confusion.

Whatever the boundaries, removing them can help calm the nervous speaker.

Speeches Involve Separation

Clearly, there has to be some separation between you and the audience. Though a speech is conversational, it is not, in most cases, a conversation. That dynamic alone establishes some separation.

But there is a difference between necessary and unnecessary boundaries. If you are especially nervous before giving a speech, you may be afflicted by an unnecessary boundary condition.

Inspiration, Not Intimidation

Gibson Greetings' CEO, Benjamin J. Sottile, warns about the dangers of placing fences between you and the audience. He declares:

"Gear your message to the level of the audience. A platform is not the place to show people how smart you are. A mistake many speakers make is that they talk down to the audience. I believe that if you talk down to the audience, you turn them off. If your goal is to communicate to them, give them something they like. On the other hand, I don't want to patronize them. I just want to make them feel comfortable that what I am about to communicate to them isn't going to be painful.

Get Off the Pedestal

"A lot of times, the way we set up a talk is very intimidating to an audience. The type of chairs and equipment and size of the podium can be intimidating. I try to do away with all that. I try to get away from the podium and face the group. When I'm trying to communicate, I'm trying to teach, trying to make it as informal as possible. I've been told that some people think it may be a come-down for a CEO to speak so informally. But my overwhelming conclusion from experience is that it is quite the opposite. People get far more comfortable and receptive when they recognize that you are just a regular guy as opposed to some blue serge suit person on a pedestal that only has time to make his comments and leave. Whatever you're speaking about, whatever your responsibilities are, whatever your position is . . . take them very seriously—but don't make the mistake of taking yourself seriously."

Psychology, Not Physiology

If nervousness is preventing you from giving your best performance, analyze your relationships with your audiences. Your problem may not be one of physiology but of psychology.

Have you broken down all the unnecessary barriers between you and the audience? Do you talk to them not as a know-it-all, but as a person interested in communicating to them on an equal basis? Do you speak their language? Do you make fun of yourself, not them? In question and answer sessions, are you willing to be told you are wrong, and accept criticism with an open mind? (The person who argues with you at least has been listening.)

If your only point of reference is yourself, you've lost your compass. Lower your ego, and you may find that you become more comfortable with your audience.

6. KEEP DOING IT

Many athletes contend that the best way to handle pressure is to have been there before. High-tension championship games are often won by players who have consistently competed in championship games. One of the best cures for speaker's jitters is to bathe yourself in them. Stand up before audiences again and again. Don't expect to emerge as a confident speaker until you have paid your dues by being there many times before.

New England Electric System's CEO, John W. Rowe, says, "The answer to stage fright is to get on stage again. So you've won a few and lost a few. Just have enough confidence that you're batting average is okay."

How Can I Do It Better?

Don't dodge speaking invitations. But keep two things in mind: One, accept only those invitations for which you know more than the audience and are prepared to speak mainly on that knowledge. (See Chapter 2.) Two, don't stint. Even if you are giving a speech to your neighborhood block committee of six people, you should still go through the process of analyzing your needs, your audience's needs, tying the speech to a single idea, giving it a good opener, supporting your points with humor, and providing a strong closing.

An executive I work with has a challenging philosophy. No matter how well he and I prepare a speech, he always asks: "How can we do it better?"

Making continuous improvement as a speaker involves trying to make every speech your best speech. And then asking, "How can I do it better?"

7. GET EXCITED

Think of something that excites you at the moment you speak. Maybe your wife just got an MBA degree. Maybe your children won an award in school. Maybe your business broke a sales record. Maybe your favorite sports team won an important ballgame.

Then tell the audience about it. Use it as your opener. Talk about your excitement. Feel your excitement as you talk.

Get Your Audience Excited

"Everybody has a little bit of stage fright," says AGS Computers' CEO, Lawrence J. Schoenberg. "You just have to learn to go out and deal with it. What helps me is to get up and say something right away that I'm excited about and that can get the audience excited."

It doesn't matter what you talk about, just as long as it excites you. You can always provide a transition into your speech. Your excitement will reduce your nervousness, communicate your enthusiasm, and make the audience more receptive to what you will say.

8. APPEAR TO BE CALM

In June of 1940, when the Germans had just broken through the French lines, and the fall of France looked inevitable, Winston Churchill flew to Paris and met with the French war cabinet, displaying, he said, "In those times when it was just as good to live or die . . . the smiling countenance and confident air thought suitable when things are bad."

If Churchill could put on a show of confidence in those dark hours of Western civilization, certainly we who stand before an audience today can give a similar appearance, no matter how nervous we may be.

The Audience Hasn't a Clue

Many inexperienced speakers believe that the audience is as finely tuned to their agitation as a radio telescope to the faintest of deep space signals. The fact is, the audience hasn't a clue to what you are thinking and feeling — if you don't give them a clue. It's up to you. Projecting an air of calmness and confidence, no matter what is going on with your heart, sweat glands, fingers, bowels, mouth, stomach, no matter if the butterflies in your stomach are twin engine jobs—requires discipline and practice. Frequently, when you make yourself look calm, you actually calm down a little.

NASA Johnson Space Center Equal Opportunity employment manager, Lupita Armendariz, says that, though she gives scores of speeches a year, she still gets nervous before many of them. "My stomach has butterflies and my knees knock so hard I think everybody can hear me. But I *appear* to be calm. People tell me afterwards that I look so calm up there. If you hear my first thirty seconds, you may not have noticed the change in my voice. But I know it."

To Have and To Have Not

If your nervousness runs to shaky fingers, think of Lauren Bacall in the movie "To Have and To Have Not." On the screen, she comes across as cool and confident. But she claims that she was actually so nervous during filming that her fingers were constantly trembling. Once, lighting a cigarette in close-up, she found that she could get control of her hands only if she very deliberately lowered her head when she brought the match to the cigarette. That gesture became a kind of trademark of Lauren Bacall sophistication and was copied by fans around the world. The irony is that the gesture was born of great anxiety.

9. RAISE A HIGHER PURPOSE

When astronauts first went to the moon, the Earth they looked on was one of swirling white clouds and spectacularly blue waters, framed by infinite space. Earth appeared not as a jumble of isolated oceans and continents but as it actually is, an integrated unit, a small, fragile, and miraculously beautiful water planet.

Seen within the true context of our world, our lives and endeavors are not isolated either but part of an integrated biosphere. Every speaking opportunity is connected to a higher purpose. You may be talking about getting better sales results, but there is also the higher purpose of establishing trust among ourselves and with our customers. You may be informing them of your vision of the job you're doing, but there is also the vision of your job within the business and the industry, and how that job, business, and industry fit into worldwide human and environmental dynamics.

Serenity and New Perspectives

There is no subject that is not in some way connected with the web of more important issues facing our world today.

Think of those issues. See how they relate to your speech. You may or may not raise them with the audience, but in connecting what you want to say with higher purposes, you'll obtain a new awareness that may provide you with a measure of serenity.

10. PICK OUT FRIENDLY FACES

Unless everybody is ready to run you out of town on a rail ("In which case," said Will Rodgers, "look like you're leading the parade"), there will always be friendly faces in the audience. "Most of the time, we are speaking to people who are a lot like us," says New England Electric System's John Rowe, "more or less bright, more or less decent." Pick out several friendly faces (if possible in separate parts of the audience), and speak directly to those people, one at a time. Block out everything but the person you are talking to. Make it a one-to-one conversation. Then turn to another friendly face. Speak to that person, one-to-one. Talking to friendly faces helps change your environment to a friendly one.

11. BE ENTHUSIASTIC ABOUT YOUR MESSAGE

An earlier technique advocates taking anything that you are excited about at the moment and making it your opener. This technique involves your becoming enthusiastic about your message (See Chapter 5). Put its advice into action. Come out slugging for what you care about. Jockey Angelo Cordero said, "When the gate opens, you have no mind, no family, no fear; you just want to win." Speak through your fears with passionate conviction, and they will generally fade away.

12. THEY'RE GLAD IT'S YOU

Pier 1 Imports' CEO, Clark A. Johnson, says: "When I stand up in front of a large group of people, rather than feeling nervous, I know in my heart of hearts that 99 percent of the people I'm speaking to are damned glad that I'm up there, not them."

13. WHEN ALL ELSE FAILS

Finally, when all else fails and you are still nervous, Clark Johnson advises that you should tell the audience, "Look, I'm very nervous. I hate the idea of standing up and speaking in public. But what I have to tell you is so important and so needs saying that I am going to go right ahead and do the best I can." Then charge ahead.

SUMMARY

A Persian proverb says that you catch a snake with your enemy's hand. You deal with nervousness by using it to your advantage. Face that nervousness. Don't let it face you down. Make your nervousness not a weakness but a strength. Adrenaline doesn't have to be paralyzing poison. Today, in business, danger can drop out of an envelope; it doesn't pounce from a bush. But the adrenaline that courses through our blood is the same that coursed through the blood of our cave-dwelling forebears. It's meant to help us rally our mental and physical resources. When you put this chapter's techniques to work, you can make nervousness boost your performance.

READING VERSUS IMPROMPTU

You're sitting in an audience. A speaker comes to the podium, plops a document on the lectern, and begins reading word for word, hardly bothering to look up.

You're ready to reach for the tomatoes.

Most audiences resent having a speech read to them. For good reason. The speaker is wasting their time. It would be better to give everybody a copy of the speech and let them read it at their leisure.

Don't Read a Written Speech

Sometimes prepared scripts are necessary—when, for instance, the subject may be so important and need such vigorous analysis that you don't want to take the chance of rambling or misspeaking.

The answer: *Don't read a speech—even if you have to talk from a written speech.*

Nobody Wings It

Diligent rehearsing is the key, according to United Technologies Corporation's Director of Editorial Services, Laurence D. Cohen:

"I don't believe executives should wing it. Nobody actually wings it. Nobody should wing it. To be good with a script, you need training. Somewhere along the line, many executives have learned that reading from scripts is no good. But that's simply not true. You can be very good with a script. It takes a little training and practice to learn how to do it.

Tennis Lesson

"I used to teach tennis, and I would tell beginners that I would give them a tip that would change their lives. I said, 'If you don't learn anything else about playing tennis, learn that you never hit the ball when it's in front of you. Step to one side. There. You are a 40 percent better tennis player than when you started.' Now I tell people when they read the script, 'Don't talk until you're looking at the audience. That'll improve your script reading 40 percent.' Because reading a script doesn't mean reading. The speaker is instead looking down, seeing what comes next then looking up and saying it."

Choreography

"I prefer to read a speech," says Grumman's CEO John O'Brien. "But when I deliver it before an audience, I have read that speech probably 15 times in rehearsal. The speech I deliver is all marked up in red pen. It has emphasis points. Words are underlined. It's choreography! I can tell by scanning the page where the emphasis is going. You can't do that unless you have a fully prepared script."

Rehearse and Rehearse

"The extemporaneous speaker frustrates me," says John F. Budd, Jr., vice chairman of Carl Byoir & Associates, "because it's difficult to get multiple uses out of speeches unless they are written down." He asserts that segments of a written speech can be sent to the media and other public relations channels to publicize the speech *before* it is given. But that can't be done with a speech that will be given extemporaneously. He says, "If the speaker is really good, you can write the speech down then he or she can give it using extensive notes on cards."

"I don't like to read a speech," says John Schiff, CEO of Cincinnati Financial. "I just don't think it's good business. But there are times I do have to read them, and when I do, I rehearse and rehearse, 12 to 15 times. I do it at home before a mirror. I rehearse the movements, the motions, so it becomes a kind of act."

Format

- ☐ Use large letters and wide margins.
- ☐ Triple space between lines. Four spaces between paragraphs.
- ☐ Make each sentence a paragraph.
- ☐ Put full stops (three or more) and dashes between words and phrases to enable you to pause and achieve rhythm.
- ☐ Complete each sentence on the page—don't have a sentence run onto the next page.
- ☐ Stop your text two-thirds of the way down the page so you don't feel like you are hurrying from one page to the next.
- ☐ Rehearse with the script. When you speak the script out loud, you'll make changes so that the text conforms to a conversational style.
- ☐ Use a speech box—a device that allows you to slide your pages inobtrusively one on top of the other rather than lifting them up and turning them over.
- ☐ Don't give the press the script you read from. Transform your script into standard essay style and provide that as a handout.

IMPROMPTU SPEECHES

Despite rapid changes occurring in business today—markets becoming global; technology spreading around the world at the speed of electronic impulses; highly specialized products and services proliferating—some things remain the same: Executive success is largely determined by how well you persuade and inspire people.

The impromptu speech is vital to that success. Doing it well can demonstrate your convictions, validate your ideas, and stamp your message with sincerity. Doing it poorly can brand you as ineffective.

Don't Go Off Half Cocked

Many executives make the mistake of having not a Ready-Aim-Fire! approach to impromptu speaking—but a Ready-Fire-Aim!

Ready and Aim are 90 percent of impromptu speaking. Do them first. The "Fire!"—the speaking—will then come naturally.

GETTING READY

To be done well, an impromptu speech can't be impromptu. The term *impromptu* implies making or doing things without previous preparation. But the definition applies to the perception of the speech, not the reality. The reality is that you never talk unless you know what you are talking about (See Chapter 7).

"I am the most spontaneous speaker in the world," said George Bernard Shaw, "because every word, every gesture, and every retort has been carefully rehearsed."

"I always prepare ahead of time for an impromptu speech," says NYNEX Corporation's CEO, William C. Ferguson.

Make Notes, Don't Use Them

So does American Business Women CEO, Carolyn B. Elman. She makes her prepared talks seem impromptu. "A speech is more effective if you can do it in a conversational way," she asserts. "I try as much as possible not to use notes. I think it's a matter of pushing yourself to feel comfortable not using notes." She says that as she gained more experience as a speaker, she made herself rely on less detailed notes. "You need to move from detailed notes to single words that trigger your thoughts. Then, when you know your speech well, you are ready to step away from the lectern and give your speech without the use of notes."

Preparation

It's the same preparation that you would do for a prepared speech.

First, think about what you know in relationship to what the audience knows and what they need to find out from you (See Chapter 2).

Do this before you enter the environment in which you may be called on to give impromptu remarks.

You may already have a general knowledge of the subject or you may have to bone up.

Pier 1 Imports' CEO, Clark A. Johnson, says that whenever he goes to an event in which he might be called on to speak, "I have my thoughts well placed in my mind, and I am always ready to speak up to 20 minutes. When I stand up in front of a group, whether its five or five thousand, it is just like I switch into automatic pilot."

Save Up Impromptu Speeches

"I give all my speeches to our employees impromptu," says Paul E. Freiman, CEO of Syntex Corporation. "But I never begin an impromptu speech without knowing what I am going to talk about."

Arthur Brown, Hecla Mining Company's CEO, says he has a number of impromptu speeches saved up for different occasions. He doesn't give the speeches verbatim but adjusts them according to his immediate speaking objectives.

He says, "I've been lucky enough to have traveled a lot and have an array of experiences and a background of information when making impromptu speeches. I can talk about interesting people I've met, our business, current events, and other topics."

Rehearse

Demosthenes said that good delivery comes from diligent rehearsal. You can only go so far in emulating the great Greek orator. (He rehearsed keeping himself locked up in an underground chamber, speaking with pebbles in his mouth to improve his diction and shaving one side of his head so he wouldn't be tempted to go out into society.) Still, you can rehearse diligently, giving speeches in your mind: in airports, when going to and from work, when mowing your lawn—so that when you actually deliver them "impromptu", they are honed and polished.

AIMING

Let's say that you've been called on to speak impromptu. It may be before a hurriedly called staff meeting, a banquet to acknowledge being given an award, or a Q & A session after you have given a speech. You shouldn't have been caught off guard. You should have been prepared for this moment.

Frame the Issue

Frame the immediate issue. Tell the audience why you are going to talk. Explain the reason for the meeting. Reiterate what the award is about. Or repeat or paraphrase the question.

By framing the issue, you buy time to collect your thoughts. You clarify the situation or the question. And you make sure everybody has heard the question.

Organize

Organization is the key.

"I give impromptu speeches around the office all the time," says Armando C. Chapelli, Jr., The Washington Consulting Group's CEO. "I have to watch myself because I have a bad habit of saying what's on my mind. Many times I have to pause before I speak and make a conscious effort to rephrase what I was going to say. For example, I might start to say, 'That's a terrible idea!' I'll catch myself, pause and say, 'Have you thought about other ways of looking at that issue?'"

Here are several ways to organize your thoughts.

Beginning and End

Think of a beginning and end to what you will say. "Every impromptu speech should have a beginning, middle, and end," says Armand V. Feigenbaum, CEO of General Systems Company. "Have a clear picture of how it will open and how you will finish, then the middle usually takes care of itself."

Problem/Solution

Sometimes you are called on to give an impromptu speech because a problem has arisen that needs your attention.

"If you don't think through an impromptu speech in a problem-solving situation, you can get into trouble," says Idaho Power Company's CEO, Joseph W. Marshall. "I start by presenting the problem. It's important that we clearly understand the problem first. Clarifying the problem and the situation in which the problem exists better enables you and the people you're speaking with to think through to a solution. Then as we start analyzing the problem, I tend to lean in the direction I think the solution ought to go. But I leave the people I'm talking with plenty of room so they can go where they want to go. Then I close by coming up with a solution. It's important that they get involved in finding a solution."

FIRING

If you have prepared well, speaking should be an exhilarating experience—for you and the audience.

TEFRA's CEO, Linda S. Mathieu, gives mostly impromptu speeches that are largely determined by questions she initially asks the audience (See Chapter 2). She says:

"Since my talk is really decided by my audience, I take individuals there as examples of points I want to make. I'm kind of a small person, about five feet tall. I won't stand behind a podium or sit. I am always moving. First of all, I want them to see me, but I am not comfortable standing still. I carry a lavaliere microphone around. I have a booming voice if I am in a small enough room. I have been stuck behind a podium with bright lights in my eyes, and that makes me uncomfortable. I would rather be a part of the audience. So I go to specific individuals and ask them specific questions. If I see the audience getting bored, I change the subject in a hurry."

Say What's On Your Mind

You may consider taking a different tack by simply telling the audience what is on your mind at that moment. Gibson Greetings' CEO, Benjamin J. Sottile, uses this technique often.

"If you are called on to speak on an impromptu basis, the message is clear: Whoever is asking you to speak wants to know you. Therefore, be yourself. Speak your mind. That is not the time to try and conjure up some image. So when somebody says, 'Get up and say a few words,' I take them literally. They want to know what Ben Sottile has to say about what he's thinking. I tell them. I have no problems talking about what is currently on my mind. People find that refreshing."

Keep Eye Contact

"Eye contact with the audience is always extremely important," says Syntex's CEO, Paul Freiman. "It's as important for me as the speaker as it is for the audience. When you are delivering a good speech, you get people nodding their heads, smiling, winking occasionally. While speaking, I smile and nod and occasionally wink back at them."

Play the Pause

What you *don't* say can be sometimes more effective than what you say. Calvin Coolidge observed, "Don't speak unless you can improve upon the silence." Many speakers hurry through their talk, avoiding pauses that could help them better communicate their message. To be heard, we often have to first be silent. Pauses, and the silence that develops, can work for you. When Benjamin Sottile told the audience of security analysts (See Chapter 4) that, being the last speaker of the day, he knew what it feels like to be Elizabeth Taylor's latest husband: "I know what I'm supposed to be doing, I just hope I keep it interesting!", his subsequent long pause allowed the humor to sink in, and got a build-up of laughter. If he had kept talking, he would have been stepping on his own lines, and the audience might have missed the point.

Perishable Goods

Silence is a powerful but perishable commodity. There is no rule that you have to answer the instant the questioner completes the question. Often, you may want to develop strategic silence. By taking your time, you show that you are in control.

But silence can quickly overripen to disinterest. Calvin Coolidge commended the virtues of silence. But when his death was announced, Dorothy Parker asked, "How do they know?"

Be Brief

Abide by the "stand up, speak up, shut up" rule. Frequently, an audience gets its greatest enjoyment from a speech when the speaker shuts up and sits down.

Be Loose

"Be loose," advises Hibernia Corporation CEO, Martin C. Miler. "If you are giving an impromptu speech and your nose is buried in notes, that puts off the audience. Depending on the physical layout, I try to get away from the podium and walk around when I'm talking."

Be Audible

Miler also says that if you are speaking to a large audience, make sure everybody in the room can understand you. "Make eye contact with the people in the middle and the front, but don't forget the people in the back. It's very frustrating to be the prisoner of a speaker and not hear what he is saying."

Be Aware

"I learned long ago," says Mrs. Evelyn Echols, CEO of The Echols Schools, "that when I'm speaking I always look for a person who is falling asleep. I talk to that person. Wake him up. Then you can be fairly certain that you have your audience's interest."

———

QUESTIONS AND ANSWERS

Q & A is the overtime of public speaking. Regulation play is over. The game can be on the line. Don't let down. In Q & A, you can demonstrate impromptu speaking abilities, provide added dimensions to your message, get feedback on your ideas, and create an intimate bond with the audience.

"When you can engage in an extended period of questions and answers, answering any question," says Edward J. Noha, CEO of The CNA Insurance Companies, "you communicate that you are not only a professional person but that you are a real person, that you have solid values."

24 Techniques for Taking Charge of Q & A

1. PREPARE

In preparing for your speech, you have already done your audience analyzers (See Chapter 2) and come up with a single idea (See Chapter 3). Now play variations on that idea. The Q & A session isn't a new game. It's overtime of the same game. The audience may want to get off on different tangents, but you should stay focused on your speech's message.

When you go into the Q & A session with the conviction that the audience needs to hear more about your message and that you are going to use this opportunity to tell them more, you've probably done the necessary preparations.

Don't Ride for a Fall

"I wouldn't want to talk on anything that I didn't feel totally qualified to discuss," advises David S. Tappan, Jr., CEO of Fluor Corporation. "If you had somebody write a speech for you and didn't really know the subject, you are riding for a fall in the question and answer period. I have been in plenty of audiences when the speaker seemed to really know his subject when he delivered the speech, but then two questions into the Q & A, you realize he didn't know what he was saying. That's a good way to lose credibility. You'd be better off to stay home."

2. DOUBLE BARREL

If Q & A is on the agenda, bring a double-barreled talk with you. Remember the techniques for cutting discussed in Chapter 8. Cut your speech in half and deliver one portion in the Q & A session. It doesn't matter what questions are asked. You can make them a bridge to what you want to say.

Of course, you take the chance that you may not be able to fire the second barrel. If it's important that you communicate a complete, integrated message, then do it during your speech and save Q & A for amplification and clarification.

3. ALERT THE AUDIENCE

At the beginning of your talk, let the audience know that you will welcome questions after your talk is finished. This gives them the opportunity to formulate questions and helps preempt the possibility that someone may ask a question while you are speaking. At the end of your talk, tell your audience again that you welcome their questions, then tell them how much time is left on the agenda.

4. ASK YOURSELF A TOUGH QUESTION

The beginning of Q & A marks an abrupt transition from a speech. You have been talking; now it is time for you to both talk and listen.

Sometimes it's hard to get questions going. An effective technique is to ask yourself a tough question. It alerts the audience that tough questions are wanted, and it usually elicits questions from the audience.

5. LISTEN INTENTLY—AND NEUTRALLY

A good speaker should be a good listener. All we have to do to keep the attention of many people is just listen to them. Listening is caring—caring for who's asking the question and caring for the audience. Be attentive to the question. Don't show by your mannerisms or expressions what you think about the question.

"Never convey that the questioner asked what you thought was a dumb question," suggests William C. Ferguson, NYNEX Corporation's CEO. "If it's a dumb question, the audience knows it's a dumb question. But they don't want you to pick on that person. I saw a speaker say in effect that a question from the audience was dumb. Then the speaker wondered why he didn't get any more questions. Treat the questioner with respect."

Don't make distracting gestures while the question is being asked. If you nod or shake your head while the question is being asked, you're already answering it. You can't clearly understand a question that you're answering while it is still being asked.

6. ANSWER THE QUESTION

You may look ill prepared or insincere or both if you don't answer the question directly. If the question is hostile, disarm the hostility; if the question is irrelevant, say, "We can use this opportunity best if we stay on the subject before us."

"I answer directly every question asked me," says Jerre L. Stead, CEO of Square D Company. "But at the same time, I drive home the points I want to get across."

7. RESTATE

Restating the question helps clarify it and allows the questioner to validate your understanding. It also helps other people in the audience who may not have heard or understood the question. It allows you to keep your receiver on while transmitting. And it enables you to transform an inflammatory question into more positive terms.

"I try to disarm hostile questions with humor," says Hibernia's CEO, Martin Miler. "But you can't stop there. You can't say something funny and ignore the question. At least it takes the tension out of the air if you can make your response humorous but not deprecating."

Be fair to the question and the questioner. Don't restate the question in a hostile or demeaning way. "Life is not so short that there is always time for courtesy," Emerson said. Ask the questioner if you have clearly restated the question. As the speaker, you must be in charge, but don't be unfair or you may turn people against you.

8. BE BRIEF

Your speech is over. During Q & A, don't make another speech. "A simple question deserves a simple answer," says Martin Miler. "Don't elaborate too much. Some people answer questions by going on and on in waves of discourse. I try to keep answers short."

9. USE A BEGINNING, MIDDLE, AND END

No matter how brief your answer, you should try to structure it with a beginning, middle, and end. Even what is considered the shortest poem in the English language, "The Genesis of Germs"

Adam
Had 'em.

has a beginning, middle and end. Remember Armand Feigenbaum's technique of thinking in terms of a beginning and an end and then letting the middle take care of itself.

When you end, always come to a conclusion.

10. DISARM THE HOSTILE QUESTION

Embedded in every hostile question is a great opportunity. Such a question will always perk up an audience. Anybody can give a decent talk to people who agree with you. But the real test of a good speaker is to speak persuasively to people who don't agree with you. You don't have to welcome hostility, but you can face it squarely and make it work for you. Hostility is proof against indifference, the killshot of audience reactions.

Restate

Most hostile questions have emotionally charged words, "You're *blind*;" "Your business is *bulldozing* . . . ;" "The program has *failed*." Extract those words from the question. Examine them. Use the word as the focal point of your answer.

For instance, "You said the program has failed. But if you look at the program in a larger context, we might see that the failure was a necessary first step toward a greater objective. You only fail when you stop. We're not stopping. We're going on until we reach that objective."

Recognize

Recognize the questioner's emotion without being patronizing. For instance, say, "You seem angry about this issue."

Establish common ground. "I can understand your anger if you look at the program as a failure."

Then repeat the question in a more positive way. "Are you asking why the program has not met our original objective?"

Don't put words in the questioner's mouth. Don't make light of his anger. Don't get angry yourself. Speaking angrily to an audience will only cause you to plow up a snake among them. Don't substitute vague expressions for the question's specific expressions. The object is to get the questioner to agree that you understand his anger and his question—then communicate to the audience that your answer benefits their needs.

But don't get into a debate with the questioner about the merits of his question. If he disagrees with the way you have represented the question, have him state it one more time, then try your best to answer it—and go on to other questions.

Focus on the Issues

Most hostile questions come from legitimate concerns. Your objective is to see through the hostility and understand and deal with the concerns. Keep personalities out of the interchange. Focus on the issues. As long as the questioner believes that his concerns are being addressed, he will most likely accept your way of dealing with him and, if he doesn't agree, at least accept your way of answering.

Broaden the Issue

"Even with a hostile audience," says Edward Noha of CNA, "I try to find an issue or application that shows the merit of my position—certainly acknowledging my self-interest but trying to speak to a broader and equally important issue and principle."

Fair Treatment

Sometimes you may be confronted with an angry questioner who will not listen to reason. Usually, such a questioner acts in either of two ways: asks a long-winded question or keeps asking questions after you have finished answering. As for the questioner who repeatedly asks you questions, you can point out to him and the audience that other people want to ask questions. If he still insists on being hostile, you can remind people that you are there not to engage in verbal combat but to communicate, to share your views. When communication becomes combat, you have the option of withdrawing your participation in the Q & A.

11. CURTAIL LONG-WINDED QUESTIONS

This is probably one of the most common challenges of Q & A. If you don't handle it right, you may turn the audience against you.

To understand how to handle it, let's examine commonly acknowledged ground rules of most speaking engagements.

In order to communicate those views, you have to be in charge. You can't hand that responsibility to somebody in the audience. As long as questions enable you to communicate, they're appropriate. They're inappropriate when used for the purpose of communicating the questioner's views. Once the questioner starts making a speech, you must gracefully put a stop to it.

Grace Under Pressure

Be careful how you do it. You don't want to seem hostile. Nor do you want to make the questioner look bad. You must be firm and polite. Make the audience understand that you are interrupting in their interests. Don't appear to be exasperated or angry. Interrupt from the questioner's point of view by saying something like, "I understand your concern over this issue. But what specific question do you have for me in regard to that?" Or, "Is this what you're asking me?" Then briefly ask what you think the question is.

If all fails, and the questioner insists on giving a speech, you can do one of two things: Listen to the speech and let the audience turn against the questioner. Or look at your watch and say, "We only have a few minutes left. In the interests of time, can we move on?"

12. SEPARATE THE MULTIFACETED QUESTION

Confused questions make confused answers. Asking good questions is a skill few people have—or know they should have. So let's not blame the person asking the question. If confusion results, blame the person who answers the question. If it is not a good question, it's your responsibility to first make it a good question—then provide the answer.

The first rule in asking a good question is to ask one thing at a time. The multifaceted question breaks this rule. Recognize the facets. Then restate the question in this way, "The way I understand it, the question has three parts." Name them, then answer each part, one at a time.

13. DON'T ANSWER THE IRRELEVANT QUESTION

Be careful. This is a judgment call. *Your* call. You decide whether the question is irrelevant to the discussion. Big League umpire Bill Klem said of baseball pitches, "They ain't nothing till I call them." When you make the call on this question, you'd better have good reasons for labeling it irrelevant—or else the message you are conveying is "That question ain't nothing" and, by extension, "*You* ain't nothing."

Make your call this way, "I'm sorry, but I don't see how that question pertains to what we're talking about. We don't have much time. Let's stick to the subject at hand."

14. CORRECT ERRONEOUS FACTS

Many questions are based on erroneous facts. Don't answer the question until you get the facts straight. Correct the fact not in the spirit of getting the goods on the questioner but in the spirit of better communication. Imagination should be tied to facts, not facts to imagination. A question that takes a flight of imagination should be grounded right away.

You can correct facts by quoting experts and recent studies, citing your own personal and professional experience, or questioning the questioner about where he got his information. (See point 22.)

15. SLIP BETWEEN THE HORNS OF THE DILEMMA

Some questioners may try to hang you on the horns of a dilemma. They present two choices; both of which can draw blood. For instance, "Is your new productivity strategy designed to enrich the vice presidents or impoverish blue collar workers?" Don't impale yourself on one or both horns. There are more choices in this world than what the questioner pre-sented. Either take on one horn or slip between them. You might say, "Neither . . . the new strategy is designed to make us more competitive. Then we'll all be enriched."

16. SAY YOU DON'T KNOW

To be a consistent leader, you must be what you appear to be. You can't be what you are not. You can't try to appear to know what you don't know. Eventually, you'll be found out. If you don't know—say so. Either throw the question back at the audience to see if somebody else has an answer, or say you'll find out yourself and get the answer to the questioner — or the audience.

17. AVOID HYPOTHETICAL QUESTIONS

Illusion is a vice of many well-intentioned questioners. They want you to travel to the great unexplored continent of What If. Don't go—unless you want to. A question that begins "What if . . ." can only be answered by what you speculate will be—not by what you know to be. You may wish to engage in speculation, to hold forth, for example, a goal or vision that you want the audience to achieve. That's all right, as long as you are aware of what you're doing.

It's one thing to not know something. If you don't know, you find out. But it's worst to *not know that you don't know*. If you answer a "What if" question, you're putting your cred-ibility at risk.

When asked "What if . . .," you can say, "You're asking me to talk about something we don't know will happen. I can talk about what I *do* know. Let's analyze . . ."

18. DON'T SUCCUMB TO MIND READING

Don't let questioners read your mind. Many mind-reading questions begin with, "You think that . . ." and then develop a question based on what the questioner says you are thinking. If you answer such a question, you're acknowledging that the questioner possesses supernormal powers and that you are willing to communicate his or her message, not yours.

Questioners sometimes won't try to read your mind but speak your words. They often begin questions with, "What you're saying is . . ." then load the question with whatever conjectures they wish to make.

Avoid such questions by saying "Your putting thoughts in my head (or words in my mouth). Isn't there a better way to ask that question?"

19. DON'T ANSWER FOR OTHER PEOPLE

Many times you'll be asked what your boss or a worker would do in a certain situation. People aren't characters in a play you're writing. You can't script their actions. Beware of answering a question that presupposes that you do.

20. LOOK. SCAN. LOOK AGAIN

When the questioner is speaking, keep eye contact with her. The question deserves your full attention. Be cordial. Be open. Be patient. Address the first part of your answer to the questioner. Then scan the room as you give your response. Conclude by looking at the questioner again and assessing her reaction. If she does not look satisfied with your answer, you may ask her why. But don't get into a give-and-take with the questioner. Other people have questions. Give them a chance to ask them.

21. BRIDGE TO YOUR MESSAGE

Tough questions, hostile questions, confusing questions, irrelevant questions, hypothetical questions—they can all be used as platforms to build a bridge to your message. It's important that you acknowledge the question. Almost every question has some merit. Verify the merit. Then build the bridge with such phrases as:

"You've got a point. But let's look at it another way."

"That may be true in your case. But let's broaden the context of the issue."

"There are a lot of us in the room who agree with you. But let me also talk about . . ."

There are many more. Always have a stock ready when you begin Q & A.

22. USE HUMOR

Your use of humor can be the glory of Q & A. Just as long as you don't overdo it (See Chapter 7). Of course, it must be impromptu humor; but if you have followed my "prepared improv" techniques (See Chapter 7), you can pull it off with powerful effect.

"Remember to smile when you are being humorous," says Nevius M. Curtis, CEO of Delmarva Power. "I have told some wonderful jokes with a frown, and nobody laughed."

23. QUESTION THE QUESTIONER

If a questioner tries to put you on the spot, reverse things. *You* be the questioner. Socrates proved that any question can be questioned. Probe the questioner about why he or she asked the question, about the reliability of the question's facts, about the question's reasoning.

Be careful how you interrogate the questioner. In general, don't answer a question with a question. This is a special case. You can turn the audience against you if you do it in a nasty way or if you argue. Do it in the spirit of clarification and good communication.

24. ALWAYS SUM UP

There are a number of places in each speech in which opportunity doesn't knock but pounds hard: the introduction, the beginning and ending of the speech—and at the end of Q & A.

Many speakers just say, in effect, "Thanks for listening," and walk off—and keeping the door of opportunity locked as securely as the door to a Manhattan walkup.

"I do a lot of Q & A," says Square D's Jerre Stead. "At the end of that, I always summarize the kind of questions I got and what the most important points are."

Read Chapter 6, and know the kind of wrap-up you want to develop. But be flexible. Your wrap-up should flow from the experience.

Take Advantage

Here's how to take advantage of the wrap-up opportunity.

☐ List the two or three main points you want them to remember after the speech is over.

☐ Use highlights of the Q & A to illustrate those points.

☐ Talk about what you wanted to communicate before you spoke and what you want to communicate now that you have finished speaking.

☐ Say that *you* have been changed by the experience. And tell why you have been changed in relationship to the message you wanted the audience to receive.

☐ Develop a specific call to action growing from what you and the audience learned in your interaction.

☐ Depending on the circumstance, you may want to try to make the event an emotional as well as an informative one.

DRESS

Clearly, the way you dress is an important part of your delivery. But I won't examine the many facets of executive dress. Simply dress for a speech like the executive you are.

Beau Brummell, who set the standard for men's fashion in early 19th century London, was once told that a particular

English gentleman was so well dressed that people turned to stare at him.

"Then, in that case," Brummell said, "he's *not* well-dressed."

When you're speaking, people will have their eyes on you from a few minutes to up to an hour or more. Since dress is in itself a visual statement, what you wear will have some impact on what you say. Don't let your clothes get in the way of your message. Wear what suits you and what suits the occasion and the audience—not what will attract attention.

SUMMARY

Preparation is the key to impromptu speeches. If you know in advance that you may be called to speak impromptu, prepare as diligently as you would a regular speech. Even rehearse. When you begin speaking, first frame the issue, either by repeating the question or briefly describing the occasion in a larger context. Before you get into your subject, make sure you have a strong beginning and ending in mind. Since you wouldn't be speaking if you didn't know your subject well, the middle should take care of itself. Be brief. Be relaxed and informal. And be aware of your audience's attentiveness.

Don't neglect the importance of Q & A. If questions aren't immediately forthcoming from the audience, start by asking yourself a question: a tough question. Be patient, open, warm, and friendly when fielding questions. Don't be anxious about getting hostile questions. They can be your opportunities. Poland's Solidarity leader, Lech Walensa said, "Without people hostile to me, I, a simple electrician, would never have won the Nobel Peace Prize." You won't win the Nobel Prize with your Q & A performance, but by handling hostile questions well, you can win many converts to your cause.

Understand trick questions and be practiced in turning them into answers that can work for you. Make sure everybody in the room hears you. Always be ready to bridge from the question to your message.

At the end, take the opportunity to sum up. Tell the audience what you yourself have gotten out of your interaction with them, what you hope the audience will remember, and what action you want them to take.

10

Visual Aids

If you're thinking of buying an airplane from me that costs fifty million dollars, the least we can do is have the presentations' slides be right.

JOHN O'BRIEN,
CEO, Grumman Corporation

No photographer is as good as the simplest camera.

EDWARD STEICHEN

Any good leader knows the value of a good visual. Otherwise, he wouldn't wear a three-piece suit and have his hair cut a certain way.

LESLIE H. BUCKLAND,
CEO, Caribiner, Inc.

When the audience laughs, I smoke. When they stop laughing, I talk.

GEORGE BURNS
Explaining how he used his cigar to prompt laughter

Visual aids should be made to steer, not to row.

JOHN W. ROWE,
CEO, New England Electric System

T HE BLOODY STRUGGLE FOR A SMALL, uninhabited, volcanic island in the western Pacific is today as famous as any battle in United States history. The battle for Iwo Jima has taken on mythical dimensions, not only because of the bravery of the combatants but because of a single photographic image taken at the height of the battle, an image of Marines hoisting the U.S. flag atop Mount Suribachi.

The grim beauty of that image is so powerful that it transcends that particular battle, transcends even the Marine Corps, and has come to be a national symbol of courage, sacrifice, and patriotism.

Images have the power to change or reinforce perceptions, to motivate, mobilize, educate, and be remembered. Understanding how to use them—and how to avoid misusing them—is essential to becoming an effective executive speaker.

TONIC, NOT OPIATE

Visual aids are tonic, not opiate. The first rule in using them is try not to use them. They are pathways to knowledge and tools for remembering that knowledge, not knowledge themselves. They can't communicate for you, they can only help you communicate.

Furthermore, they can be dangerous substitutes for analysis, allowing people not to think about issues but simply feel good or bad about them.

The best visual aid is often no visual aid. Don't think visuals, then speech; think speech, then visuals.

You have been called on to speak, not to put on a slide show. If your visual aids become more important than you as a speaker, you may be making a statement that you'll regret.

12 Ways To Use Visual Aids

1. VISUALS START WITH YOU

The visuals begin when the introduction ends. When you rise to speak, you are the first visual. You may have had visual aids, such as a video module, to set a mood or provide information before you speak. But the audience is there to see you. They're watching your grooming, comportment, and expressions before you utter your first word.

Learn from comedians. All great stand-up comedians are great speakers. Study your favorites. Every one has a distinctive way of coming on stage and acknowledging applause. Their comportment isn't accidental. It's carefully planned and practiced. It takes them only a few seconds to walk on and get set to do their routine, but those seconds are vital to the success of their act. Make those same seconds vital to the success of your speech.

Show Confidence

"Show confidence when you walk onto that stage," says Mrs. Evelyn Echols, CEO of The Echols Schools. "Let them know you have utter confidence in yourself."

2. ADDS COLOR AND DIMENSION TO YOUR WORDS

Your visual support doesn't have to be on a screen. Einstein said that imagination is more important than knowledge. Images evoked in the mind can be just as important—even more important—than those created by slides and films. Churchill did not project a slide of an iron curtain in his Fulton, Missouri, address. Yet, the image of an iron curtain dividing Europe has shaped Cold War thinking ever since.

Word Picture

Give speeches that stir the imaginations of your audiences. Illustrate your points by telling vivid stories and anecdotes. Here's the beginning of a speech that I helped write with a marketing executive, which was delivered to a national management forum devoted to U.S. manufacturing competitiveness.

Six Gun Justice

He said:

American businesses are committing a monumental blunder. It's a blunder tied to design and designers. If the blunder isn't rectified, the power of American industry will be crippled for years, possibly decades.

This blunder can be viewed through the lens of an American myth.

The hired stranger rides into the Old West town, guns down the quick-draw outlaw, then rides out of town into the sunset.

Justice is served. The townspeople are rescued. The stranger rides off to save other towns. The Great American myth endures.

Justice Deferred

But reality was often much different than the myth. In the Old West, hired gunslingers more often than not didn't ride off into the sunset after dispatching the outlaws. Instead, they plundered the people that hired them.

Today, the reality of the Old West is being repeated in American business. Beset by fierce overseas competition, many American businesses are acting like the townspeople of the Old West. They are hiring outsiders to save them. To cut costs and increase profits, they are having their products designed and produced offshore.

But offshore designers and producers are becoming the very nemesis of the businesses that hire them.

3. ENHANCES QUALITY

Still, visual aids can make an important difference in the effectiveness of your speech.

"If you want your speech to stand out," says Aniforms CEO, Vincent Sottosanti, "have the visuals stand out. I've seen overheads done simply on typewriters, but they work because the speech was well written. Visuals really help the mediocre speaker better than anyone."

Be Professional

Professional visual aids don't necessarily have to be created by professionals outside your business. Football coach Joe Paterno said, "Professionalism has nothing to do with getting paid for your services. Performing at a consistently higher level than your competitors is the mark of a true professional."

Visuals Reflect You

To an audience, visuals aren't simply what they are, they are who you are; they're a reflection of your character and your leadership. Robert E. Lee's schoolmaster said that Lee, as a youth, infused his work with a professional quality. "In my class, he imparted a neatness and freshness to everything he undertook. He drew complicated diagrams on slate, that he rubbed off, with as much accuracy and finish, lettering and all, as if it was to be engraved and printed."

Whether you are using a blackboard, a flip chart, an overlay, an overhead projector, slides or videos, you should always perform at a consistently high level, within the constraints of your budget.

Checklist

So it's not who puts your visual aids together—what's important is that they, and you, are professional. Visuals must be believed before they are truly seen.

That means making sure that:

☐ Your visuals are consistent and properly paced.
☐ Each visual makes a single point.

- ☐ You use only necessary numbers and graphs.
- ☐ Each is legible and accurate.
- ☐ Slides are clean, in the right order, and right side up.
- ☐ Your words coincide with the visual that the audience sees.

In addition, you should:

- ☐ Arrange for somebody to turn the lights on and off.
- ☐ Keep the lights off as briefly as possible.
- ☐ Avoid turning your back on your audience.
- ☐ Avoid standing in front of the visuals.
- ☐ Be able to deliver your remarks if the visual aids fail.
- ☐ Make sure your equipment runs properly and that you have back-up projector light bulbs.

4. SHORTENS COMMUNICATION

Good visual support can often shorten the time needed to communicate ideas. Sottosanti observes: "Visuals tell things in a hurry. For instance, you can visualize many concepts simply with an arrow. If it is not important that sales, say, went up 2.8 percent, but they have been going up for 9 months, then you simply put up an arrow. I have seen hour-long presentations that, when professionally written and visualized, were told in only eight minutes, told in a memorable way; and because it was only eight minutes, people listened."

5. SIMPLIFIES

A good speaker is simply a pizza man: The audience orders, you deliver. Simplicity and naturalness are your ingredients. By simplifying concepts, a telling visual can reduce misunderstandings and reinforce key elements of your ideas.

Cetus Corporation's CEO, Robert A. Fildes, says that he frequently uses visuals to support his speeches for the biotechnology firm.

Strange Ideas

He says: "I was born and grew up in Europe and came to America in the mid-seventies. One of the things I found was that the average American sometimes has strange ideas about Europe. These ideas came to the surface a couple of years ago when we decided to go in a different direction than other businesses in our industry. We decided to build our own European business. I got all sorts of questions from people on this side of the Atlantic. Questions such as, 'Aren't you misusing your resources at a critical time?' 'Why don't you concentrate on your U.S. position first?'

Doubling the Market Potential

"It was clear that they did not understand that the European marketplace was equal in size to the U.S. marketplace. By positioning ourselves to get access to both the U.S. and European markets—after all, American drugs work on Europeans just as well as Americans—we were doubling the potential of any product that we successfully developed. I had to find a way for people to see it.

The U.S. Superimposed

"So I had a slide made up in which I superimposed the outline of the United States in one color, over the outline of Europe in another color. The result was quite startling. Western Europe fits into the United States several times over. On top of each one of those two shades, I put the population figures. One market, the United States, was 250 million people. The other market, Europe, was more than 300 million people. And because the European market concentration is much higher, it is easier to get access. So I was able to communicate in one slide two very important messages."

Simplify to Clarify

Don't simplify things pass the point of understanding. Reducing concepts to images can give your speech power and simplicity, but be sensitive to the image's message. Make sure people understand the image and its message and are not offended by it.

6. CLARIFIES

Know when you are using visuals to simplify and when you are using them to clarify.

You simplify by reducing things to plainer elements. (Simplicity is not stupidity. Picasso said that he spent his whole life learning to draw like a child.)

You clarify by making things intelligible.

Simplification is transformation; clarification is purification.

When an Indianapolis 500 winner said, "There's no secret in winning the 500, just press the accelerator to the floor and steer left," he was simplifying how to win, not clarifying.

State a Problem Clearly

In speeches, you should always be clarifying but not always simplifying.

That doesn't mean that you should be constantly using visuals to clarify your points. When you state a problem clearly, you are half way to solving it. But you should first state it in words. If words can't do the job, only then, with great reluctance and in the name of clarification, use a visual.

Keep Technical Information Off the Screen

But just as a visual can clarify, it can also confuse. In regard to speeches, it's better to be clear about less than confused about more. Executives sometimes think that putting information on a screen automatically makes it clear and interesting. United Technologies' speechwriter, Laurence D. Cohen, disagrees:

"The screen has to be an aid. It can't be what the presentation is about. For instance, in regard to technical information: don't put it on the screen! It can't be absorbed. That's why it's called *technical* information. It's not easy to understand. If you want to do slides with technical information, do slides to your heart's content, then don't put them on the screen, hand them out. That way, they can take them home, mull them over, and figure out what you're talking about."

No Relationship

"I find it particularly bothersome with some technical people," says Grumman Corporation's CEO, John O'Brien, "who think that they know the subject in depth, particularly bothersome where there is a slide or viewgraph, and you see the speech bears no relationship to what's on the screen. That's a disaster!"

7. INCREASES INTEREST/AROUSES ENTHUSIASM

Just as there is a difference between simplification and clarification in regard to using visuals, there is also a difference between increasing interest and arousing enthusiasm.

When you provide information, you want to increase interest. When you want to inspire, you arouse enthusiasm.

William I. Morton, CEO of Jack Morton Productions, says that, in general, "Informational speeches need visualization. Inspirational speeches don't need visualization. Visualization is a detraction from inspirational speeches."

Commercial Interest

"We add interest in speeches at Pepsico," says speechwriter Steven Provost, "by interspersing them with recent television commercials from our businesses. As soon as the commercial is done, it's also very effective to make a transition back to the speech with a brief joke. I call it the 'come down' joke. Don't use it too late. It has to come from the speaker as soon as the commercial is finished on the screen."

Slides Add Color

"Slides are very, very important in my talks," says Daniel E. Evans, CEO of Bob Evans Farms. "My speeches are usually 30 minutes, and I use about 30 slides. They mainly involve financial information. They add interest to the speech by showing pictures."

TV Anchor

"TV news is the perfect example of how to use visuals," observes Leslie H. Buckland, CEO of Caribiner, Inc. "You have the anchor talking, interspersed with charts, graphs, interviews, gutsy film clips. Does the weatherman talk about the weather? No, he shows you the weather. Does the sportscaster talk about sports? He shows you clips."

8. ORGANIZES

Organization is the deep, ballasted keel of your speech, enabling you to venture into deeper and riskier audience waters than if you relied on an unorganized, flat-bottomed speech. Visuals can sometimes help your audience see your organization and thus view your message with fresh insight.

Organize With a Carousel of Slides

Fireman's Fund Insurance Company's CEO, John J. Byrne, uses sets of carrousel slides to organize many of his speeches.

He says, "I've come up with a couple of techniques. They are very simple. They don't sound like much, but they work just fine for me. One is that I have a couple of basic themes. One of my themes is that our business must maintain a disciplined balance sheet. Another theme is that we work for many constituencies and have done a fine job with some of these constituencies but not with others. Another theme centers on Mao Tse-tung, and the way he put Communist China together, and the lessons we can learn from that.

Changing Slides Stimulates Ideas

"For each theme, I have a package of 35mm slides. There is a statistician in the company that brings those statistics up to snuff every couple of months. There are industry statistics about pricing and return on equity and industry trends and so on. I know that I always have on my secretary's desk a carousel of 30 to 35, well-organized slides. I can pick up that carousel and give a decent, informal talk. I don't have to write anything down on paper. I know that when I flip through those slides, they will remind me of a whole range of comments. I did this recently before an audience of 5,000 people in Chicago. I arrived at the hotel with almost nothing written down. I insisted on a lavaliere mike instead of a podium mike.

Talking to the Slides

"I simply walked out to the front of the stage and up the aisles. I started looking at the slides and started talking to the slides. The speech came off very informally. It makes my talk look as if this is all extemporaneous."

9. GIVES CONFIDENCE

Having your main points on the screen for all to see—and not on a lectern, in your hand, or in your head—can often increase your speaking confidence. You don't have to refer to notes. And you don't run the chance of losing your train of thought. You're free to put all your energies into articulation and delivery.

10. ENHANCES PRESENTATIONS

In Chapter 1, I broadened the context of speeches to include presentations. Presentations are special kinds of speeches. Most often, their objective is to persuade and inform. They tend to be given in an intimate, teaching or selling environment. They frequently run longer than a formal speech. And because their primary objective is usually informational, they are supported with sometimes extensive visual aids.

Viva La Différence

Xerox Corporation's Director of Corporate Communication, Joseph M. Cahalan, believes that the differences between a speech and a presentation determine whether or not visual support is needed, and if it is needed, how it is used:

"A speech tends to be about 20 minutes, a half hour at the most. For the most part, I'm against audio visual support for speeches. They tend to distract the audience, making them focus on the screen instead of the speaker. There is a great risk that something will get screwed up in a strange environment. There is the added pressure on the speaker of worrying about punching slides or having somebody else do it.

"On the other hand, if an executive is giving a presentation of 45 minutes to an hour, more of a classroom environment, where a lot of information is being conveyed, visual aids can add a lot."

11. MAKES CONCEPTS MEMORABLE

Images stimulate and improve memory. (See Chapter 7.) A sales executive I worked with had a tough challenge for a speech. He wanted to convince the managers of his manufacturing business that the business was in serious trouble, even though it was the clear leader in the industry and was achieving record profits. The problem was that, over the past year, the rate of sales *growth* had declined dramatically. We used one visual, the growth-rate decline, and showed it only three times during his speech. Every time he showed it, it made a telling point. The audience left with that visual imprinted on their minds as well as the need to support his strategies to reverse the trend.

12. PROVIDES HUMOR

Visual aids are an important way of providing humor. But remember, you're not an entertainer. Your humor must have a message (See Chapter 7). "If I was limited to one source of slides in the entire world," says United Technologies' Laurence Cohen, "I'd pick *New Yorker* cartoons. They tend to say very profound things very simply and humorously."

Humor is the DMZ

Humor can be the demilitarized zone of business. Issues can be aired in this zone that might be distorted, stifled, or ignored in other venues. Visuals are an important way of communicating humor.

Aniforms' CEO Vincent Sottosanti says: "If you know that you are going to give a speech or presentation that is somewhat controversial, put the objections of the audience on the table. Find a way to get them spoken in a humorous way. One way to do that is through an interactive cartoon. The cartoon character is a doubting Thomas.

Reveal the True Issues

"For instance, if you are talking about a new delivery system to ensure that orders get filled on time, the cartoon character can remind everyone in the audience that every delivery system up till now has failed. He says what's on the audience's mind. You don't have to use a cartoon character as a doubting Thomas. You can plant one in the audience. Or you can have a second speaker on the podium play that role. The point is that the doubting Thomas is voicing the very real concerns of people in the audience. Though I suggest that those concerns can be voiced humorously when you have a cartoon character. The live person is better off playing it straight."

Humor Is Powerful

Visual aids can be powerful tools to provide humor. But be careful that in getting laughs, you don't offend people (See Chapter 7).

SUMMARY

Who you are as a leader frequently speaks more persuasively than what you say. People draw conclusions about who you are mainly by what they see. Your visual aids encompass more than putting pictures on a screen. They encompass your grooming, actions, and expressions.

Once you understand how to use these visuals, you are ready to begin using other visuals. The first rule in using them is to try not to use them. The second rule is to use them sparingly. (Though in giving presentations, the liberal use of visual aids is often necessary.) Always have a specific reason for using a visual. Understand what the image means to the audience and be sure that the image ties with the message you are communicating.

When Thomas Edison first invented the movie camera, audiences were not used to seeing visuals on a screen. "When we started out," he said, "it took the average audience a long time to assimilate each image. They weren't trained to visualize more than one thought at a time." Today, however, people's visual taste is highly sophisticated. When they look at your visuals, they look into you—into your character, your professionalism, your commitment to quality. Don't disappoint their sophisticated expectations.

11

The Media

In TV interviews, you have to know who is looking at you. You have to look at the other side of the camera and see those people in their living rooms or dens watching the TV screen.
ANDREW H. HINES, JR.,
CEO, Florida Progress Corporation

To a newspaper man, a human being is an item with skin wrapped around it:
FRED ALLEN,
radio comedian

You can't hide from the camera. Say to yourself, 'I'm talking to one person.' People are wrong to think of the enormous audience watching them. Just think of one person.
EVELYN ECHOLS,
CEO, The Echols Schools

I have found out that the way you fight bad press isn't by writing letters to the editors and so forth. The way you fight bad press is to go out and get good press. Giving speeches is an important part of that. I have gotten myself established as somebody who has something to say and isn't afraid to say it.
EDWARD J NOHA,
CEO, The CNA Insurance Companies

"Who was that masked man?" Wild West townspeople asked when the Lone Ranger had dispatched the bad guys and rode off in a cloud of dust and a hearty "Hi Ho Silver!" Many an executive has probably asked "Who was that reporter?" with the same astonishment after the quotes appear in print or the clips are aired.

"I didn't say that!" or "Out of context!" are frequent reactions of executives who received the journalistic equivalent of a blindside, crackback block.

Many injured executives retreat into a badger hole of embittered silence and refuse to speak to the media.

That's a shame. Because executives who refuse to deal with the media curtail their range of communication opportunities.

PAY NOW

Clearly, the media isn't going to go away. You may shut yourself in your office, ban interviews, communicate with the public only through pretaped talks, canned speeches, and public relations releases, but the media will still be there. And at some point in your career, they could hold you accountable: for your business, your job, your leadership. It's better to learn how to deal with them. If you are not practiced in dealing with them, you may at one point in your career bungle an important interview, damaging your career and your business. When it comes to the media, many executives fall under the jurisdiction of the old preventive maintainence law: Pay now or pay a lot more later.

4 Reasons For Establishing Open Relations With the Media

1. ENHANCES THE PUBLIC'S PERCEPTION OF YOUR BUSINESS

When your company, its strategies, and its people get good play in the media, you're getting public relations benefits that money can't buy (See Chapter 1).

Lee Iacocca wrote in *Talking Straight*:

"More than most businessmen, I know the value of good communication and the importance of the media. There were times in our dark days at Chrysler when we had no weapons left in our arsenal except our ability to communicate. We had to keep our employees together and our dealers on board. We had to persuade the government to help us. We had to get more than four hundred banks to lend us money—when we were losing $6 million a day. We needed special deals from our suppliers. Above all, we had to convince America that we were going to make it: We had to get people to buy our cars when they didn't even know if we'd be around to service them.

"That was our most important communication job, and we couldn't do it face-to-face. We had to go on the tube and we had to use print. I truly don't think we would have survived if our crisis had come along before the media age—we'd have died at the starting post."

2. PREEMPTS THE COMPETITION

When you create good relations with the media, you often make them your allies against your competition. I worked with an executive who understood the importance of positioning his business at the forefront of what was then a beginning trend in recycling.

Became the Industry Leader

He saw the trend before his competition did. He delivered a number of speeches before a variety of forums about recycling and the strategies and programs needed to make it effective throughout his industry. He distributed copies of his speeches to the trade media. He became accessible for interviews. In a short time, the media began acknowledging his business' leadership in recycling and publicized it through editorials and articles—putting his competition on the defensive until they too developed their own recycling programs.

An Effective Strategy

You can use speeches as a bully pulpit. Raise the issues to high levels. Raise the stakes. But be sure you have a clear vision to communicate. Don't make your communication a cult of the personality. Let your audiences understand that your vision isn't coming from you but through you.

3. INSPIRES PEOPLE WHOM YOU LEAD

Media praise can rally the public and your employees to your cause.

Grumman Corporation's CEO, John O'Brien, observes that it's important to have good public speakers in a business so that employees can be inspired and well informed. "I've seen a rise in the morale of the Grumman employees in a time of great change for our business, because I have been out in public talking not just about Grumman, but also its impact on the Long Island community."

4. INCREASES YOUR STATURE

When given the task of facing the media, many executives are seized with what I call "the Arnold von Winkelried complex."

Von Winkelried was a Swiss national hero who fought against the Austrians at the battle of Sempach in 1397. The dismounted, closely packed Austrians held a forest of lances and pikes pointed against the Swiss. The defense seemed impenetrable. The Swiss cause looked hopeless. But von Winkelried formed the Swiss into a flying wedge, he at the point, and charged. He was killed as he grabbed many of the lances, turning them aside. But he enabled the Swiss to smash into the small breach and break the Austrians' ranks.

A Modern Day von Winkelried

Unlike von Winkelried, you are not going to sacrifice your life going up against the sometimes seemingly impregnable media opponent; but like the patriot, you may, in overcoming what seems like formidable odds, become a hero.

Deal effectively with the media—especially in times of crisis—and you raise your stature in your business.

Understanding Before Action

In the 1960s, when Andy Warhol's painting of a Campbell's soup can appeared on the contemporary scene, an artist friend of mine said, "A lot of people say that it's trash, not art. I don't know. I want to think about it. I want to understand it before I reject it."

Before you interact with the media, you should understand them. Here are techniques on making that understanding easier.

Techniques for Interacting With the Media

1. KNOW WHO THEY ARE

I know a little about media people. As a freelance journalist, I have moved among the ranks. Though the people are as different as humans are different, what they want boils down to one thing: a good story.

The one element that most good stories have is conflict (See Chapter 5, "Be Dramatic"). Businesses deal with conflict too—but frequently a different kind of conflict: how to meet customer needs. "Customer needs" is just a way of saying "customer problems." Businesses exist because customers pay them to solve those problems, through services, products, or a combination of both.

Media Conflict

The conflict that drives media stories is news conflict. We know that news conflict may involve business stories—but that it ranges across many other areas as well. The media should not be viewed as an extension of your public relations department. In most cases, the conflicts that advance your business and the conflicts that advance their stories are fundamentally different. Most clashes between business and the media stem from executives either ignoring or misunderstanding these differences.

Do Your Homework

When you understand that the media's fundamental reference points are different from yours, you take the first step in dealing effectively with them. The next step is to understand the particular newspaper, magazine, radio, or television station that is employing the person interviewing you. Analyze the readership. Read the articles. Watch the programs. Do they focus on the family, on muckraking, on the outdoors, or on women's issues? Furthermore, analyze the advertisements. Those ads support the newspaper, magazine, or station and help provide the salary of the person interviewing you.

The Person

Try to get information on the person who will interview you. "See if you can know who the interviewer is before he or she interviews you," says Alan G. Hassenfeld, CEO of Hasbro. "How has that person written articles in the past? The interviewer knows you because you are his or her subject. What do you know about the person who will interview you? Has this person presented both sides fairly in the past? Is this person likely to try and do a hatchet job? Just as you know the members of the audience as a speaker, you also have to know the members of the media too."

2. KNOW WHAT THEY WANT

Knowing who they are enables you to better understand what they want. Clearly, they need information from you concerning the piece they are working on. So before the interview starts, make sure you understand what the piece is and what kind of information you are being asked to provide. If you are giving a speech and media is in the audience, make sure you know what segment of the media they are and what their individual needs are.

3. DEVELOP RELATIONSHIPS

Cypress Semiconductor Corporation's CEO, T. J. Rodgers, says that interacting successfully with the media entails understanding and fulfilling their needs—and being available to establish and nurture relationships:

"Think about it: the poor guy's sitting there trying to write his story. He has to write some grammatically correct, factually correct piece, or he gets zapped by letters-to-the-editor on a topic he doesn't know much about. I would hate to have that job. I can sit around and pontificate all day about semi-conductors. I ought to be able to do that. I've been in the field for 20 years. What about the poor guy who has a BA in journalism and today is writing about semiconductors and tomorrow about monoclonal antibodies. This guy has a problem. He needs a friend, somebody he can call up and get data from and rely on the data. I can help him create a story that is of interest to the general public. I'm available, and I'm accurate, and I give him what he needs, nine times out of ten. What I give him is not available for attribution. I'm not trying to get my name in the article."

4. DON'T HIDE

Don't hamper, cooperate with the media. Executives who hide in corporate badger holes of "no comment" or behind public relations covers frequently incite the media, like terriers, to dig harder.

"It's important to communicate openly and honestly with the press—to the degree that the subject allows," says Meredith Corporation's CEO, Jack D. Rehm. "The press wants you to be accessible. Be accessible. Sometimes, you're not always as accessible as they would like you to be. A good practice is to reveal as much as you can. You need credibility with the press. You don't want them to be suspicious of you or suspect you for hidden reasons or motives. Be as open with them as the subject or issue will allow. There are certain times when I found that I wasn't as open as I wanted to be. I had to tell them that."

No "No Comment"

Fireman's Fund Insurance Company's CEO, John J. Byrne, says that over the years he has established frank relations with most members of the media:

"They are constantly asking to have me talk. I am more candid with the media by about 20 percent than I really should be. I would like to see the executives who report to me talking to the press. I don't like professional public relations people talking to the press. I want the businessman who is closest to the situation doing that talking. All my executives know that I will get furious if I read in the paper the next morning that we said no comment—particularly if somebody is criticizing us or bringing a lawsuit against us. If a journalist calls us, and they always do, and some lawyer says that we haven't read the paper so we have no comment, I get furious! The right answer is that the lawsuit is preposterous. When a journalist calls you and asks for your comment, you only have one shot. You say, 'We have no comment today, call me tomorrow.' Give me a break! No journalist is going to call you the next day. The news is only newsworthy for a very short period of time. You have only one window, and you've got to take advantage of it. If you say that you have no comment, you're automatically guilty."

Open Door Policy

"I have an open door policy with the press," says M. Anthony Burns, CEO of Ryder System. "It's very important to keep open channels of communication with them both in good times and bad. You're not going to agree exactly with what they write. But over the course of time, I feel that the press ultimately gives you a fair shake—if you treat them with dignity and give them a fair shake."

5. TALK THEIR TALK

The media is hungry for vivid speech: "Where's the beef?," "There you go again," "The news of my death has been greatly exaggerated." Feed them tasty morsels.

John Byrne of Fireman's Fund says: "When I'm speaking with members of the media, I often have a piece of paper in front of me with five or six action, power words. I know that if I can work those words into the conversation, they will have a good chance of being in print. For instance, instead of saying something like, 'we don't think that matches the facts,' say instead, 'That's such nonsense!' Every journalist likes words like that. Several years ago when American Express was trying to sell Fireman's Fund, there was a lot of controversy as to how big the asking price should be. A *Wall Street Journal* reporter called and asked me whether I thought the price was right or not. I used the phrase, 'It's a shame to be selling this little beauty to the public.' A colorful power phrase, thought about ahead of time, has a very good chance of being included in the piece."

6. ESTABLISH TRUST

Your relations with the media should be based on trust. I know: Telling some executives to trust the media may be like telling the condemned to trust the knot-tying ability of the hangman. But the cost of distrusting the media is too high. To help establish your integrity as a leader, you must believe in the integrity of others—until they prove otherwise. You cannot expect people to trust you if you don't trust them. When you distrust people, you isolate yourself and diminish your communication powers and range of experience.

Don't Move the Shells

In the long run, it is better for an executive to be the kind of person who plays the street corner shell game than the kind who moves the shells. I'm not advocating that you add gullibility to your list of leadership traits. Just as a touchdown is scored not by talking about it but only when the ball crosses the line and the official's hands are raised, so trust is established not in wishes but in reality. It's established by small things: being on time, keeping appointments, returning calls, keeping promises, and being consistent.

Don't Be a Friend

Trust is also created in other ways: establishing that nothing's off the record, not asking for favors, and not being a friend to reporters. A friend is a confidante. You're being unfair to your position as an executive, and he to his position as a reporter, if you are each other's confidante. Trust the media in the same way that a boxer trusts his conditioning, training, and reflexes when he gets in the ring with a slugger. The boxer is safe as long as he doesn't drop his right when he leads with his left.

We Get What We Deserve

It's been said that when we marry, we get the spouse we deserve. That's true for dealing with reporters. We get the reporters and the stories we, as executives, deserve.

We've analyzed general considerations in dealing with the media. Now let's examine how you can work with and help make specific segments work for you.

1. PRINT

This may seem blindingly obvious, but it's crucial to keep in mind: *Before the piece is read, it has to be written.* The writer has to gather the facts, interpret them, and give them structure, coherence, and interest.

Don't expect that what you say to a reporter will come out the way you want it said. Journalistic objectivity is as real as a disappearing elephant act. Every story in print is filtered through the life experience of the writer.

That doesn't mean the reporter should be outrageously biased. You have the right to be quoted accurately in an article that presents a balanced view of the issues.

Bring Rationality

That might not happen a lot. "It's never easy to talk to the press," says Hasbro's CEO, Alan G. Hassenfeld. "Many reporters come in with an agenda. They often already have the answers to questions they will ask me; they know how they want to write the articles. Let's say they want to do a story on Hasbro. They frequently don't want to do a story on Hasbro, they want to do a story on a segment of Hasbro that they have prejudged. All I can do is bring some rationality to the interview in the sense of communicating that there are two sides to every issue."

Avoid Unprofessional Reporters

Clearly, you should avoid reporters that rig quotes or deliberately entrap you. But in bringing rationality to the interview, don't try to engineer the reporter's story to your satisfaction. You'll invariably be disappointed.

Marcus Aurelius' Wrestler

Don't carp about little wrongs done to you by the press. Roman emperor and philosopher, Marcus Aurelius wrote, "When a wrestling opponent gashes us with his nails or butts us with his head, don't protest or suspect him in the future of dirty tricks. Just keep an eye on him, looking at him not as an enemy, but with good-tempered avoidance. Do this in your life with our fellow contestants: overlooking a great many things they do. Simply keeping away from somebody, without feeling suspicion or hatred, is an option that is always open to us."

Relationships First

The costs of not dealing with the press far outweigh petty wrongs. Ultimately, it's not the results of particular stories that are important to your establishing productive interactions with the press, it's the relationships that count. The print community is relatively small. Word gets around it quickly. If you are known as an executive who deals squarely with reporters, most of them will deal squarely with you — frequently giving you the benefit of the doubt and helping you in unexpected ways.

2. RADIO

Historians may look back on our times not as the golden age of television news but of radio news. In many ways, radio is today a much more flexible and powerful medium than television for reporting events. Since reporters can report live from the scene by just using a telephone with satellite relays, radio broadcasting is flexible, mobile, and relatively inexpensive.

Power and Scope

You need to understand the power and scope of radio. Know that the words you speak into that reporter's tape recorder or into the telephone may be broadcast to millions of people. (Watch out: when you take that phone call, you might be on the air!) Before you begin answering a reporter's questions, ask a few yourself. What station does he or she work for? What's the nature of the story being put together. When will the story air? Who else is being interviewed?

It's only fair that you be filled in as to why and in what context the questions are being asked. That gets back to trust again.

Preparation

If a reporter catches you off guard with a question, it's not her fault, it's more often your fault. Stay abreast of the important events occurring in your business, profession, and industry. Anticipate being called on to comment on those events. Be able to articulate both your personal beliefs and your company policy in brief quotes. Know what you want to say before you speak. On the radio, your words and ideas often carry more weight than words you may speak on TV where the visuals often become the message. Be concise. Be vivid. Make only two or three strong points. Don't let reporters lead you into saying what they want you to say. Rephrase their questions. Don't argue with reporters. Don't get angry. An angry spokesperson for a business makes the business seem angry—and irrational.

3. TELEVISION

Consider these two video clips, taken from real life:

Clip One

A New York City mayoral candidate returned to his campaign headquarters during the thick of the 1989 primary contest. "Good news," he said. "My opponents are being investigated!"

"That's *bad* news!" his advisor said. "You're the only one who *wasn't* on the six o'clock news!"

Clip Two

In a television program "Cops," in which handheld T.V. cameras follow cops on the job, the cameras were on hand when cops stormed a drug dealers hide out. The cops had guns, dogs, tear gas—the works.

The drug dealer was known to be violent. The cameras followed the cops as they rushed the hideout, smashed in the door, barged inside, jumped the dealer with the aid of attack dogs, wrestled him to the floor, cuffed his hands, manacled his feet, read him his rights, and started dragging him to the paddy wagon. As he was being hauled past a camera, the drug dealer said cheerfully to the television crew: "Hi, guys. Did you get me on teevee? How do I look?"

Is Life a TV Show?

The question is: is life becoming a TV show? We know that since the end of World War II, television has radically transformed our culture. The old joke of one person saying, "I don't watch much TV. I like the real world," and the other person saying, "What channel is the 'real world' on?" has come true. The Chinese ambassador to the United States observed during the Filipino revolution, "You didn't have to send in the Marines to overthrow Ferdinand Marcos. You just sent in your TV cameras." And in just a few years it was pictures of Chinese students on Tiananmen Square televised around the world that nearly helped to overthrow the Chinese government.

The Times, They Are a'Changing

Until recently, however, most executives have not included the use of television as one of their communication tools. But that is changing. We're not entering an era in which business executives become media stars. But we are entering a new era of television. The development of the video camera and VCR have made television communication available to almost all businesses. As the use of inhouse, video communication grows, your success as an executive will be increasingly linked to your ability to do well on the tube.

Dubbing Seven Languages

As Jerre L. Stead, CEO of Square D Company, continues to expand his business around the world, his communication challenges multiply. One way he is meeting those challenges is by sending out quarterly videotape reports of the business' progress. The tape is seen by 20,000 employees around the world. "The reports are done in seven languages to all of our people," Stead says. "We dub in the languages over my voice.

We do our own dubbing. We have our own television studio. In this way, we can give the same message worldwide. That's very important to being a global business."

The Media Age

So it's not a question *if* the executive is going to learn to make use of television, it's a matter of *how*.

For instance, an efficient communication tool is closed-circuit television.

NYNEX Corporation's CEO, William C. Ferguson, uses it to great advantage. "It's an efficient way of moving information," he says, adding that it is not a substitute for meeting face-to-face but the next best thing. "For instance, at NYNEX, I will do a live closed-circuit television segment. I'll speak for a short while then open it up for questions."

Set Expectations

"People can call in from 40 or 50 locations. The questions are spontaneous. That's a good vehicle for communication. But it's important that you set their expectations ahead of time. People are used to seeing polished television programs. But I tell them, 'Look, this is much like my sitting in your conference room talking to you. You're not going to see an experienced network anchorman. I might stutter or hesitate or what-have-you.' But telling them not to expect a network-quality performance doesn't mean that I'm not prepared or that I don't rehearse my ad-libs."

Understand It

Frequently, in regard to understanding and using television, disillusionment is the first step toward wisdom.

The executive who understands television sometimes suffers the most from disillusionment—at least in initial encounters. He sees that there is a significant difference between giving a speech to a live audience and talking before the camera's eye. New England Electric System's CEO, John W. Rowe, has undergone such a disillusionment.

Excruciating

He says, "I gave a speech about the principles and objectives of our company. The people in the room liked it. There was a high degree of chemistry between the audience and me. We had it videotaped while I was doing it. Boy, did it die on film! It was excruciating. I dwelt on too many details, too many examples."

Let's examine how you can make television work for you.

1. CONCENTRATION: Baseball pitcher Gaylord Perry said that the only batter who could consistently hit his grease-doctored fastballs was Rod Carew. Perry said, "Carew sees the ball so well, I guess he can pick out the dry side."

It wasn't Carew's great eyesight that did the trick, but his ability to concentrate. To do well on television, you have to concentrate, too. You don't need the kind of superhuman concentration that enables you to see the dry side of a greased fastball, but you still must look calm and focused when things are happening all around you.

□ *Prepare For The Extraneous:*   Hecla Mining Company's CEO, Arthur Brown, recommends that before you do a TV interview, you rehearse in a similar environment. "The first five minutes of my first interview on television were not pleasant," he says. "There were a lot of things going on during the interview: the director, the camera man, the sound person, all doing their work. Lights coming on. All the while you are trying to answer questions. Be prepared for that."

□ *Stay With Your Message:*   "Keep your discipline when interacting with the media," says George L. Pla, CEO of the Cordoba Corporation. "Don't be intimidated by the camera. Don't let the microphone distract you. Don't let the questions of the media reporters get you off on another tangent. You have to be responsive to the questions but keep your discipline by making sure that you deliver your message."

2. TALK TO IMAGINARY PEOPLE: Talk to the camera but *imagine* an audience. Hibernia Corporation's CEO, Martin C. Miler, says, "Emotionally, it's more stark to talk to a camera

than a live audience. So I talk to imaginary people. That keeps me from being too robotic or mechanistic in my delivery."

"I imagine a sprinkling of people are behind the camera," says Florida Progress Corporation's CEO Andrew H. Hines, Jr. "Sometimes, I think they are people who have had an awfully hard row to hoe. Sometimes I think there are politicans or community leaders back there."

"Once, when I received an award before a huge audience, an overflow crowd," says Martha S. Hicks, CEO of Harwell Hicks Real Estate Research, "I walked on stage and couldn't see anyone at all because of the TV cameras and lights. So I had to imagine them and talk to them as if I could see them. You have to *feel* that audience even if you can't see them. You have to feel warmth for them. They see you. They see you very clearly."

3. TAKE YOUR TIME: Be in control. Don't be rushed. You may be questioned by several reporters at one time; there might be a crisis atmosphere—but take your time. Answer the questions one at a time. Pause before answering.

Old Kent Financial Corporation's CEO, John C. Canepa, asserts that he is often more conscious of making a mistake when on television than when addressing a live audience. "When you have the camera looking right at you, you sometimes want to get out of there. I measure my words more than usual. I'm careful not to ramble and garble my words. I force myself to speak a lot slower than I normally do."

4. SPEAK WITH YOUR FACE: When you speak before a live audience, body language is important. When you speak on television, facial language is important.

General Systems Company's CEO, Armand V. Feigenbaum, says that he pays particular attention to facial communication during television interviews. "When speaking on TV, you speak with the face to a considerable extent. Your facial communication has to be more dynamic than it normally would be."

□ *Talk To One Person: The Camera:*   Disraeli said of Gladstone, "He speaks to me as if he's speaking to a room of fifty people." Remember, you are not talking to a room of fifty people. You are talking to one person: the camera.

□ *Warm Fuzzies:* Be relaxed, conversational, crisp, and entertaining. Avoid polemics. Show your passion not by body movements but mainly in a low-key way through your face.

The CEO of Delmarva Power, Nevius M. Curtis, says, "I've learned that when you are on television, as long as you smile and send warm fuzzies, you can communicate well. But if you come across as aggressive and negative, that's a put-down. It's not just what you say that makes you an effective communicator on television; it's acting too."

5. TONE DOWN: "One of the challenges of speaking before TV cameras is not to overdo things," says BellSouth's Director of Corporate Planning & Development, Mylle H. Bell. "I have to consciously stay calm. When you're on TV, you don't have the benefit of getting feedback from the audience. So you have to be very sure of your technique and style. You have to project energy, but it has to be a quieter energy than when you are speaking before a live audience. You have to smile and be warm but not come across as a happy klutz."

But don't tone down too much. McCormick & Company's CEO, Charles P. McCormick, Jr., says, "One lesson I learned on a morning television show. I wanted to relax, but when I looked at the show later on, I saw that I was so relaxed that I was sitting crooked in the chair!"

6. LOOK THE INTERVIEWER IN THE EYE: "Don't look away from the person who is interviewing you," says Cetus Corporation's CEO, Robert A. Fildes. "Keep looking right at him. You can send the wrong messages if you start looking up, down, and around. Little gestures like that can create in the minds of the viewers that (A) you don't know what you are talking about or (B) you're not sincere."

7. TAKE A COURSE: "If you are going to be on a network interview," says David S. Tappan, Jr., CEO of Fluor Corporation, "I recommend that you take one of these 'jungle warfare' courses, which teach you how to defend yourself in a

(media) back alley. In the interview, you are dealing with professionals who know all the tricks of the trade. The chances of you coming out with even half your image intact are not too good. Take a professional course that will at least give you a fighting chance to hold your own in that arena."

8. DRESS: Viewers should perceive you for who you are, not what you wear on television. Don't let your grooming call attention to itself. Avoid striking patterns: stripes, plaids, herringbones. Wear light colors, pastels, beiges, and blues. Unless you have a tan, don't refuse make-up.

SUMMARY

Grasp the nettle of the media. Understand that they are not extensions of your public relations activities and that their reference points and objectives are in most cases different from yours. Analyze their organizations and their sponsors and advertisers. Be accessible to them. Establish open, honest professional relationships with their members. But don't make friends of those members. Know the strengths and weaknesses of print, radio, and television. Be prepared to speak before you are called on to speak. Deal fairly with the media, and, over the long run, taking into consideration that, now and then, you'll be stung, they'll deal fairly with you, providing more nourishment than nettle for your business and career.

12

The International Audience

Many of my clients are from the Middle East and the Orient. When it comes to money, finances and retirement plans, we don't have any cultural differences. Their wives might be in the dress of their culture, but I'm in a business suit.

LINDA S. MATHIEU,
CEO, TEFRA, Inc.

In the United States and some Northern European countries, it is essential to do business first then become friends. In almost all the other countries in the world, it is essential to become friends first then do business.

ARMANDO C. CHAPELLI, JR.,
CEO, The Washington Consulting Group, Inc.

When speaking before an international audience, stick close to the subject of your business. Avoid talking about political issues. If you don't, you put your credibility at risk.

M. ANTHONY BURNS,
CEO, Ryder System, Inc.

S EVERAL YEARS AGO, this chapter would have been a footnote in a book on executive speeches. Today, it may be one of the most important chapters in the book. During the past few years, the business world has become truly a world of business. With markets swiftly becoming global, executive communication and speech challenges have multiplied.

Executive leadership is not just who you are but what you do. It's not position, it's action. Multiple challenges offer multiple opportunities for leadership action. There is one effective way to tackle those challenges: return to the fundamental premise of this book that the speech is the keystone of executive communication. By understanding that you are not doing business in a multinational context but, fundamentally, a multilocal context, you can begin to develop global communication techniques.

THE CHALLENGES OF SIMILARITIES

Culture is the sum of the ways people live as well as their values and beliefs, frequently transmitted from one generation to the next.

Clearly, the challenges of doing business in other cultures focus on differences. Yet, to obtain an understanding of differences, it's important to examine similarities. The fundamental similarity of all cultures is that people want to make a good living, they want their families well cared for, they want to love, they want to laugh, and they want to meet people, to do business face-to-face, not fax-to-fax.

THE ANESTHESIA OF INNOVATION

Differences are proof against conformity, which is the anesthesia of innovation. They aren't problems, but communication opportunities. Welcome speaking to international audiences not in spite of differences between you but because of those differences.

11 Techniques for Speaking Well to International Audiences

1. KNOW THE AUDIENCE'S CULTURE

W. Somerset Maugham said, "You don't have to eat a sheep to know what mutton tastes like." You don't have to get a Ph.D. in Asian or German studies to speak effectively to Japanese or German audiences. But you must have at least a few fundamental insights into their culture.

"The most important thing in international speech giving," says Hecla Mining Company's CEO, Arthur Brown, "is to find out about other cultures."

"You have to research speeches to international audiences very carefully," says Aetna Life & Casualty speechwriter, Stephen R. Maloney. "For instance, if you're speaking to Russians, you often can't go wrong quoting fairy tales or saying nice things about children."

The Long and Short Way

There is a long and short way to finding out about other cultures. The long way is to travel and read widely, building up a reservoir of knowledge over the years. The short way is to use your audience analyzers (See Chapter 2) to get information from the person representing the international audience you will speak to. Of course, the best way is to combine both ways.

2. MAKE THE EFFORT

Generally speaking, U.S. business people don't care about the storms you've encountered, they want to know if you brought the ship in. Clearly, results count in international business relations, too. But relationships and the efforts you make to establish them are a vital part of doing business. It's not important that you understand a person's culture and perspectives inside out. What's important is that you make a sincere effort to learn—and to *accept* what you learn.

When giving speeches to international audiences, communicate primarily through personal, sometimes humorous, anecdotes that you are making that effort. The more you focus on the effort, and not just on the results of that effort, the more effective that communication will be.

3. ESTABLISH RELATIONSHIPS

"There is no question that the most effective way of winning an international audience is to completely avoid communicating the sense that your culture is superior," says The Washington Consulting Group's CEO, Armando C. Chapelli, Jr. "A fundamental difference between North American and North European cultures and the cultures of most of the rest of the world, including Japan and other Asian countries, is that we in the United States are quite capable of doing business first then becoming friends. In those other countries, it is essential to be friends first and then do business.

Business Over Dinner and Wine

"Our wanting to do business first has been the basis for so much misunderstanding and crosscultural conflict inside and outside the States. In the United States, we expect people to be concerned about business and money and success and cars. Then we go home and interact with our friends. In much of the rest of the world, business is frequently done over dinner and a couple of bottles of wine, and maybe later on, if time allows, we'll talk about a deal. So when addressing those audiences, you must talk about symbols of friendships, the fine wines of friends, the exquisite cherry blossoms of Japan. You evoke those symbols of friendship and camaraderie first."

Don't Have All the Answers

"When speaking before an international audience, make sure you don't come across as if you have all the answers," says Nevius M. Curtis, CEO of Delmarva Power. "I gave a talk recently to people in Great Britain, and I said right up front, 'I'm going to tell you about what we do in our shop. If I offend you in anyway, I certainly don't mean to. The way we do things is no better than the way you do things.' "

The Great Hall of the People

BellSouth's Director of Corporate Planning & Development, Mylle H. Bell, has been helping lead that business' expansion into global markets. She says:

"Internationally, businesses are much more relationship-oriented than businesses in the U.S. I spoke to some 300 Chinese at the World Economic Forum in the Great Hall of the People in Beijing. I remember wearing a dress that had little epaulets and the same colors as the Chinese army. They all stood up and saluted me. I saluted back. It was just a fluke, but it turned out to be a wonderful moment.

Doing Well as a Woman

"You try to do things that are important to help those relationships. Being a woman in international business is an advantage, because so very few stand out. You'll do well as long as you are competent and credible."

4. ATTEND TO PROTOCOL

Make the necessary acknowledgments of officials and leaders in the audience. When speaking before an international audience, you, as a U.S. executive, are most likely speaking to people that have been shaped by much older cultures, cultures in which protocol is very important.

"Many United States executives need to be more sensitive to protocol when they're speaking abroad," says the Cordoba Corporation's CEO, George L. Pla. "The audience immediately picks up that you have properly acknowledged the heads of state or the people at the head table. Then you have the audience's attention and goodwill because you have made the appropriate gestures to the dignitaries."

5. USE HUMOR—JUDICIOUSLY

"Humor is as personal as sex," said comedian Jean Shepard. When you use humor before an international audience, you should get personal about *yourself*, direct the humor against yourself—not at the audience or their culture (See Chapter 7).

"Wherever you go in the world, people are usually forgiving about faux pas," says Hecla Mining Company's CEO, Arthur Brown. "But never make the mistake of trying to be funny at the expense of the other person's culture. I have witnessed speeches where people have done that, and it doesn't come off too well. If you are going to be funny, tell them that they are right, and how different *you* are. Make fun of yourself."

Announce the Humor

Sometimes it helps to announce in advance that you will be humorous. "I was giving a speech in Japan," says AGS Computers' CEO, Lawrence J. Schoenberg, "I told something I perceived to be funny. Nobody laughed. I told another joke. Still, nobody laughed. Then I told a third joke. I messed up the punch line—but everybody laughed! I asked my translator, 'Why did everybody laugh at a joke I messed up?" The translator said, 'I told them *first* that you were going to tell a joke— then I told your joke.' "

6. PAY ATTENTION TO BODY LANGUAGE

You may be speaking to an audience that cannot understand every word you utter. Body language then becomes vital to your communicating well.

Paul E. Freiman, CEO of Syntex Corporation, says, "Your own facial gestures, your hand gestures, are very important in those situations. People who may not understand your language will assess you as a human being by what they see of you, as much as what they hear of you through a translator."

Be Natural

Unless you are particularly knowledgeable about the culture, don't be too sensitive about using the wrong body language. All cultures have body language taboos. Unless we were raised or spent a great deal of time in the culture, we can never be cognizant of most body language nuances, let alone be natural in avoiding them.

Remember, a sincere effort is the important thing. Body language starts in the heart. Be warm, friendly, and accepting, and your body language should come through for you.

But if you anticipate talking many times to audiences of a particular culture, it's best to study and put into practice appropriate body language.

7. PREPARE A SCRIPT

Reevaluate your attitude toward using a written speech. Many speakers don't like preparing or using scripts. But in international speaking, scripts can help a lot. A CEO told me, "I have a problem when speaking before international audiences. I don't like having a prepared talk. Not having a prepared talk can be a handicap when speaking to those audiences."

Writing a script helps ensure that you focus on using simple, clear expressions. A written script can be distributed to your audience after you speak. Scripts give simultaneous translators a chance to study your words before you speak them. Confer with your translators about what words or expressions might be difficult to translate.

Censure or Celebration

For instance, in Japan, an entrepreneur may be perceived as a person who leaves the group to pursue selfish ends: action their society censures—whereas in the United States, an entrepreneur is celebrated.

Prepare to be Extemporaneous

Because you prepare a script doesn't mean you have to read it word for word. Talk extemporaneously, if you wish— but within the framework of the script. By preparing a script and analyzing it with your translator, you ensure that value-loaded terms, technical terms, and other potentially confusing or offending terms are eliminated or clarified.

8. SPEAK SLOWLY AND IN STANDARD ENGLISH

Trying to understand some U. S. speakers garbling words is about as easy as drinking coffee with a fork. Think of the poor audience that does not understand English well and gets an earful of garble.

No matter how well members of an international audience may speak English, nearly all of them need help in listening to it. You help by speaking distinctly and by avoiding idiomatic expressions.

Slow Down

"Slow down when speaking to international audiences," says Jerre L. Stead, Square D Company CEO. "Instead of driving home three or four points, drive home just one or two. But don't slow down and make it so simple that you insult the audience."

"Speak English slowly to people whose first language isn't English," says Armando C. Chapelli, Jr. "We Americans have a terrible habit of rumbling right through words and sentences. Be deliberate, slow, methodical."

New Kid on the Block

Though English is an old language and, comprising some 800,000 words, the largest in the world, it's still in many ways the new kid on the linguistic block—continually being renewed and reinvigorated by fresh words and expressions and confounding those who are trying to learn and speak it.

One CEO I interviewed says, "I don't do as well in international speeches as I should. My style is very idiomatic and informal."

Use the Old Words

Speak in standard English. Use the old, Anglo-Saxon words—eat, run, go, etc. Purge your script of jargon and other businessspeak (See Chapter 8); don't use sports terms, such as fleaflickers, the bomb, throwing heat, throwing a brick, etc. (unless your audience is familiar with the sport and those exact terms); reduce long, complex words to short, simple ones; shorten your sentences; avoid puns and other plays on words; and illustrate your points with simple, vivid illustrations and stories.

Simple Not Simplistic

In using shorter words, don't talk to your audience as if they were children. Do that, and, bang, you and your speech are dead. Einstein said that if the laws of physics weren't fundamentally simple, he wouldn't be interested in them. Likewise, a business concept that is not fundamentally simple is not only uninteresting, it's useless. There are *no* business concepts that can't be explained in simple words. In fact, all business concepts *should* be explained in such words, whether you are speaking to a North American audience or an international audience.

9. SPEAK ENGLISH INTO THE CULTURE

General Systems Company's CEO, Armand V. Feigenbaum, says that he avoids having his speeches translated into the language of his audience: "I have a reasonable facility in several languages, but I would be very, very reluctant to deliver a talk other than in English, not because of inability but because of fit." His point is that expressions, when translated into another language, often have unintended meanings. "For instance," he says, "in Paris, the controller is the individual who stamps your ticket in the subway. In Germany, it has a more significant meaning. So speak English into a culture, rather than have the translation of English into that culture's language."

"If you take your time when speaking English," says Lyphomed's CEO, Gary E. Nei, "and use good audio/visuals, you can come across in an effective way to an audience that is not facile in the language."

10. ESTABLISH COMMON GROUND

Communication in international business is made successful by finding, developing, and acting from common ground. Most often, it is the common ground not of things but values and goals.

Before you challenge the audience or even tell something that may be difficult for them to accept, establish common ground that you both share.

I worked with a marketing executive who was establishing a worldwide organization. He wanted to persuade the members of the Pacific team to believe that they had an important stake in the team; but, at the same time, he wanted them to recognize the importance of speaking English well. In a speech to them in Singapore, he said:

One Team

> *We want our business to have record growth in the highest growth area in the world.*
>
> *You have the materials, the technology, the manufacturing plants, and the service and distribution network to make it happen.*
>
> *But it can only happen when we become one team.*
>
> *You speak different languages. You're from different cultures. You're divided by great geographical distances. But they are minor things compared to what unites you.*
>
> *You're a part of our business' culture. It's important that you recognize this and meet the standards of this culture—the standards of language, for instance.*

Every culture needs a common language to develop, and communicate its values. Our common language is English. You can't be a full partner in our culture without mastering English.

Deep Trouble

When staking out common ground, make sure your audience agrees with the examples you give. If they disagree with what constitutes common ground, you've got no ground to stand on.

11. PHONETIC MEMORIZATION

One way to distinguish yourself from other speakers in an international environment is to speak the language of your audience—even though you may not know the language at all.

Hibernia Corporation's CEO, Martin C. Miler, says:

"In Japan, I had translators write out my English speech in phonetic Japanese. I deliver it in Japanese. I don't fully understand what I'm saying, but it works. They appreciated it. Once the Japanese phonetic script is given to me, I practice it over and over. Then I get on the phone with a Japanese person and read it, getting corrections in terms of emphasis. So I get my emphasis and cadence right. The longest speech I gave that way was 15 minutes. The Japanese looked at it as a special effort on my part to be accommodating to their own culture and needs. They tend to admire hard work, so they looked at it as a real effort to pay them honor and courtesy."

Miler says he didn't shape his speech to the cultural sensitivities of the Japanese. "I was just as direct in what I prepared for the Japanese as I would be to an audience in the U.S."

SUMMARY

There's a Spanish saying: "To obtain the wealth of the New World, bring wealth with you." This means the same thing as a New World saying, "There's no such thing as a free lunch." You can be an effective speaker throughout the world as long as you bring your own wealth to the podium, the wealth of your knowledge, your culture, your insights, your enthusiasms—and couple that wealth with knowledge and acceptance of the audience's culture.

It is not necessary that you know the culture like a native executive, but make the effort. Your sincere effort to understand people is your gold currency in international business. Be aware of how your humor may affect your audience. Just as a leader should not be funny at the expense of subordinates, you shouldn't be humorous at the expense of your audience's culture. Pay respect to protocol. Don't be self-conscious about your body language, but, at the same time, have a general idea of what body language may displease others.

Write a script. This helps simplify and clarify your ideas, aids the simultaneous translator, and provides a document that can be translated into the audience's language after you have given the speech. Speak slowly and in standard English. When you offer a challenge or make a controversial point, first establish common ground between you and the audience.

AFTERWORD

A business can't survive without a vision.

CLARK A. JOHNSON,
CEO, Pier 1 Imports, Inc.

Let's face it: We executives are not running for the Presidency. There's not going to be a nuclear war if we take a misstep. Our words aren't beamed to the world. But the audience will like us if they think we are alive to them. They'll trust us. They'll forgive our missteps and remember something that we said that was right.

JOHN W. ROWE,
CEO, New England Electric System

A speech is a reflection of what you know and believe. So in a sense, a speech is a Rorschach of you.

ARMAND V. FEIGENBAUM,
CEO, General Systems Company

If I don't expect the speech to have life after I deliver it, I won't give it.

EDWARD J. NOHA,
CEO, The CNA Insurance Companies

I have my own vision of the company, and I'm anxious to share it. I'm ready to speak at the drop of a hat.

PAUL E. FREIMAN,
CEO, Syntex Corporation

THE GOOD SPEECH SHOULD NEVER be finished. Its vision should live on, not just in the audience's minds but in the audience's actions as well. Like the Chinese concept of *ch'i*, a life force radiating through the cosmos, the speech can be a force for change and renewal. Once it is delivered, it takes on a life of its own and, as it spreads through space and time, lives on its own.

WORK ON IT AFTER IT IS OVER

Work on your speech after you have finished it.

- ☐ Write a thank you note to the person who invited you.
- ☐ Score your performance. Keep a speech journal in which you write the audience, the place, the date, the single idea, the points you made, audience reactions, and other pertinent information. No matter how well you did, always analyze how you could have done better.
- ☐ Get feedback from other people about your performance.
- ☐ File a copy of the delivered speech with its marginalia.

EXTRA MILEAGE

Put your speech to work for you.

- ☐ Issue a news release to the trade and regular media.
- ☐ Send a copy of your speech to whatever groups may be appropriate: customers, associations, educational

institutions, shareholders, clients, security analysts, your business' retirees, legislators, and newsletters.

THE SPEECH IS A JOURNEY

The speech can do a lot for you, but don't ask too much of it. It can convince and inspire people that a job needs to get done. But it cannot substitute for rolling up your sleeves, spitting on your hands, and getting a job done. You're not getting paid to make speeches. You're getting paid to lead, to get results.

When you speak to an audience, you also speak to yourself, and help create yourself. And in that speaking, know that your speech is not a place but a journey, not an end but always a beginning. We should always find what we journey for inside ourselves. In your beginnings, and in your journeys, I hope this book stays with you, and in you; and, through you, makes many people delight in your leadership.

The 51 CEOs

ARTHUR BROWN
Hecla Mining Company
Coeur d'Alene, Idaho

CEO since 1987, he's lowering costs at silver operations to help position this North American mining company to become a leading gold producer in the 1990s. By diversifying into industrial and specialty metals and investing in capital projects and property acquisitions, he's building a broad base for future growth.

M. ANTHONY BURNS
Ryder System
Miami, Florida

CEO since 1979, he is pushing a back-to-basics strategy: reducing capital and overhead costs and focusing on increasing the profitability in core market operations. The strategy is maneuvering Ryder through a period of trucking overcapacity and high operating costs resulting from a downturn in some sectors of the U.S. economy, so the business can remain a leader in highway transportation and aviation services.

LESLIE H. BUCKLAND
Caribiner
New York City

He founded Caribiner in 1969. In just four years, the company grew into one of the largest production houses in New York. Today, Buckland oversees a business that is devoted exclusively to production of major corporate meetings and multimedia events, mounting more than 400 days of meetings a year. An avid marathon runner and mountain climber (he's scaled a 23,000 foot peak in Afghanistan and the Matterhorn), he says: "Balancing creativity with cash flow grabs the stomach more than balancing on a 23,000 foot high ridge."

JOHN J. BYRNE
Fireman's Fund Insurance Company
Novato, California

He has been CEO since 1985. "Watch the cards on the table, don't worry about the ones up my sleeve," he wrote in a recent annual report, asserting that shareholders shouldn't pay much attention to a temporary decrease in earnings when the book value per share was up 25 percent. As the insurance industry continues to be buffeted by price cuts, the litigation explosion, and legislative assaults, Byrne is focusing on adhering to a disciplined management of assets and capital.

JOHN C. CANEPA
Old Kent Financial Corporation
Grand Rapids, Michigan

CEO since 1972, he is an independent, conservative banker who keeps costs down while directing a nose-to-the-grindstone strategy that racks up steady earnings for this bank holding company.

DAVID L. COFFIN
The Dexter Corporation
Windsor Locks, Connecticut

Coffin's strategy is focused: to provide high value, highly tailored specialty materials' products to six world markets: industrial assembly and finishing, electronics, aerospace, automotive, food packaging, and medicine. He insists that those products conform so exactly to customer needs that "it is unusual for any major Dexter customer to purchase a product that is identical to that purchased by another major customer." He is turning over the CEO position to K. Grahame Walker, the first nonfamily CEO in the more than 220-year-old history of the company.

ARMANDO C. CHAPELLI, JR.
The Washington Consulting Group
Washington, D.C.

Chapelli founded the company in 1979. WCG provides technical services to private and public clients in aviation, quantitative studies, computer technologies, and education and training. WCG grew rapidly during the 1980s by serving primarily federal government agencies. But as defense cutbacks cause increased competition for technical service companies in the commercial sectors, Cuban-born Chapelli is broadening his market base and diversifying his services around the world.

JOE C. COLLIER, JR.
Central Maine Power Company
Augusta, Maine

Under Collier, CEO since 1989, the company is once again on sound footing after it freed itself from the financial quagmire associated with the Seabrook nuclear power plant. Joining CMP after a 31-year career with Florida Power & Light, Collier is directing a strategy based on having the company provide a mix of energy resources, such as conservation, energy management, and Canadian power.

SHEILA T. CLUFF
Fitness
Ojai, California

Cluff founded the business in 1969, selling physical fitness programs to corporations. In 1977, she converted a 1920s hotel in the resort town of Ojai into a fitness spa, "The Oaks At Ojai." During the past few years, she has changed the focus of her marketing from weight loss to what she terms *lifestyle wellness.* As spas become more competitive, she is differentiating "The Oaks" through increased advertising and innovative fitness programs while stepping up her marketing through an expanded speaking schedule.

NEVIUS M. CURTIS
Delmarva Power
Wilmington, Delaware

CEO since 1981, and facing increased demand for electricity in the 1990s, Curtis is relying on a strategy of energy-diversification, using coal, oil and gas, conservation, and third-party generation. He is also focusing on owning and operating subsidiary projects such as a wood burning plant in California and a trash-to-power conversion in Pennsylvania. An ex-Navy communications and operations officer who served aboard a destroyer in the Far East, he has an informal, people-oriented style of management.

CAROLYN B. ELMAN
American Business Women's Association
Kansas City, Missouri

Elman has been CEO since 1986. The ABWA provides products and services for some 100,000 members in 2,100 chapters across the nation. The daughter of the ABWA's founder, Hilary Bufton, Jr., Ms. Elman is positioning the organization to help businesswomen tackle the new challenges of 1990s, many of which center on women playing leading roles in businesses.

DANIEL E. EVANS
Bob Evans Farms
Columbus, Ohio

CEO since 1971, Evans doubled the sales of his two complementary lines of business, sausage and restaurant operations, during the last five years. Opening new restaurants in the South and Maryland. Some 230 Bob Evans Restaurants now operate in 13 states. Son of the company's first CEO, Emerson Evans, Dan raises quarter horses on his Ohio ranch and rides in cattle cutting competitions.

EVELYN ECHOLS
Echols Schools
Chicago, Illinois

Echols founded the business in 1962. Using her extensive background in travel, television, and business, this award-winning entrepreneur continues to make her impact on international travel and hotel markets.

ARMAND V. FEIGENBAUM
General Systems Company
Pittsfield, Massachusetts

Company co-founder Feigenbaum built General Systems into a leading international engineering corporation, which helps a variety of businesses use quality control programs and products. Previously, the manager of worldwide manufacturing operations and quality control for General Electric, he views the 1990s as a time of renewal for U.S. manufacturing competitiveness, and quality control as playing a major role in that renewal. His book, *Total Quality Control*, has been published in more than a score of languages.

WILLIAM C. FERGUSON
NYNEX Corporation
New York City

CEO since 1989, Ferguson is streamlining the business through early retirement and capital improvement programs. He is using the company's strong position in one of the largest information markets in the world as a base from which to diversify into foreign markets. His strategy for growth involves the need to have public policies governing telecommunications changes.

ROBERT A. FILDES
Cetus Corporation
Emeryville, California

CEO since 1985. Fildes' strategy for this biotechnology company specializing in cancer and infectious disease fighting drugs is to build a fully integrated pharmaceutical business throughout the world. His drive to avoid concentrating on the U.S. exclusively and to open up markets in Europe for Cetus' products has doubled the market potential.

PAUL E. FREIMAN
Syntex Corporation
Palo Alto, California

Freiman has been CEO since 1989. With the patent on Syntex's enormously successful pain-relieving drug, Naprosyn, due to expire, Freiman is making significant investments to develop and market new products for this pharmaceutical and healthcare business so that its record of strong growth and profitability can continue through the 1990s. These products include a variety of drugs that can treat heart disease, stroke, pain, gynecological conditions, and the complications of AIDS. He is also expanding the size and profitability of the company's international pharmaceutical and diagnostics businesses.

ALAN G. HASSENFELD
Hasbro
Pawtucket, Rhode Island

Hassenfeld became CEO of this world leading toy company in 1989 following the death of his brother, Stephan. Alan is building on his success in Hasbro's international business to continue the company's growth in the face of increasingly intense competition.

MARTHA S. HICKS
Harwell Hicks Real Estate Research
San Antonio, Texas

CEO since 1989. She leads a research firm focused on commercial data base management and urban planning and consulting in South Texas real estate. Her products range from analyzing inventory and simple trends to creating comprehensive land plans and feasibility studies. She says, "This is the age of 'nichemanship.' Before entering the business world, a woman must do her homework . . . . Women have to be better than their male counterparts."

W. AUGUST HILLENBRAND
Hillenbrand Industries
Batesville, Indiana

CEO since 1989, Hillenbrand continually repeats his "continuous improvement," "total customer satisfaction" themes to keep the company competitive in highly competitive markets. Originally a casket manufacturer, the business has diversified into hospital beds and patient handling equipment, door locks, American Tourister luggage, and wound care and other therapy units and services. Hillenbrand's strategy focuses on making the industries' six wholly owned operating companies remain market leaders.

ANDREW H. HINES, JR.
Florida Progress Corporation
St. Petersburg, Florida

CEO since 1973, Hines is handing over the CEO reins to Dr. Jack Critchfield and retiring to his 62-foot yacht. But he leaves his diversification strategy for this holding company firmly in place. During the 1980s, as the utility faced construction costs for new plants, increased competition, and continued regulation, Hines chose to make diversified investments, from Florida real estate and building products to financial services insurance.

CLARK A. JOHNSON
Pier 1 Imports
Fort Worth, Texas

Johnson has been CEO since 1985, and his strategy of marketing imported wicker furniture and other home merchandise to affluent baby boomers is paying off. He keeps the strategy on target by paying attention to the changing needs of his market through the use of comprehensive research, including a 1,000-member customer advisory panel, exit interviews, focus groups, and consumer studies. He fullfills those needs by offering unique products in unique store environments in more than 450 nationwide locations.

CHARLES A. LENZIE
Nevada Power Company
Las Vegas, Nevada

CEO since 1989, Lenzie's strategy entails a powerful element of growth. As the demand for electricity grows in booming Las -Vegas, Lenzie, formerly a certified public accountant with Arthur Andersen & Co., must ensure that his utility stays ahead of demand while providing shareholder value.

J. BRUCE LLEWELLYN
Philadelphia Coca-Cola Bottling Company
New York City

Llewellyn has been CEO since 1985 when he and Julius ("Dr. J.") Erving acquired the business. Since then, "Philly Coke" has grown to be one of the largest Coca-Cola bottlers—as well as one of the largest black-owned corporations—in the United States. Serving the metropolitan Philadelphia area, the southern half of New Jersey, and the greater Wilmington Delaware area, the business subscribes to what Llewellyn calls a "giving back to the community" ethic. Each year, Philly Coke provides fund raisers, scholarships, minority supply contracts, and training and educational programs for the communities it serves.

JOSEPH W. MARSHALL
Idaho Power Company
Boise, Idaho

CEO since 1989, Marshall is directing a utility that is rich in hydropower linked to Snake River drainage basin. With growing electrical demands in his area (20,000 square miles in southern Idaho, eastern Oregon and northern Nevada), he is expanding existing hydro facilities. A graduate of the Naval Academy and former Marine combat engineer in Vietnam, he leads a business that is committed to conservation and whose employees own the single largest block of shareholder stock.

LINDA S. MATHIEU
TEFRA
Annapolis, Maryland

Mathieu founded Tefra (Total Employee Fringes & Retirement Administration) in 1984 and is presently a consultant to banks, brokerage firms, insurance companies, and accounting firms. A certified public accountant, she currently administers several hundred pension, profit-sharing, 401K, health and welfare, cafeteria, and voluntary employee benefit association plans.

JOHN H. McCONNELL
Worthington Industries
Columbus, Ohio

McConnell founded the business in 1955 when he borrowed $600 on his Oldsmobile and purchased his first load of steel. During that first year, he and five employees made a net profit of $11,000 on $342,000 in sales. Since then McConnell hasn't looked back. His strategy of tailoring specialized, finished steel products, plastic products, and cast products to customers' individual needs has paid off in consistent growth. He says: "A simple, basic philosophy can serve as a springboard for growth and success. It shows that by dedicating oneself to customers and their needs, the sky is the limit."

CHARLES P. McCORMICK, JR.
McCormick & Company
Hunt Valley, Maryland

CEO since 1988, McCormick has a clear vision for the company, which was founded in 1889: to expand its worldwide leadership in the spice, seasoning, and flavoring markets. To help make this happen, he has sold the business' successful real estate subsidiary, revitalized product lines and enhanced distribution, begun a search for acquisitions compatible with his strategy, and is in the process of disposing of those business components that don't fit the objectives of his strategy.

ROBERT E. MERCER
The Goodyear Tire & Rubber Company
Akron, Ohio

Mercer advanced from sales and marketing ranks of Goodyear to become CEO from 1982 to 1989. His global marketing perspective enhanced the company's position as a major international business in the tire and rubber industry.

MARTIN C. MILER
Hibernia Corporation
New Orleans, Louisiana

CEO since 1973, Miler unleashed "people power" at his bank by linking pay to performance. His $7.2 billion bank holding company continues to thrive in a depressed state economy.

WILLIAM I. MORTON
Jack Morton Productions
New York City

He is positioning the business, which specializes in the design and production of corporate meetings, training programs, entertainment, videoconferencing, and exhibits, for growth in the 1990s. He says, "As corporate America realizes the ever increasing importance of developing its internal culture and of effectively communicating its philosophy, products and services to its internal audience . . . we expect to keep helping companies serve their most important constituency . . . their own people."

GARY E. NEI
Lyphomed
Rosemont, Illinois

CEO since 1988, Nei led a successful turnaround of this pharmaceutical company from a low point when product recalls and plant closings had helped create a 70 percent decrease in the price of the stock to a high point when a Japanese business bought Lyphomed for $1 billion—more than six times its annual sales.

EDWARD J. NOHA
The CNA Insurance Companies
Chicago, Illinois

The business was on the brink of insolvency when Noha became CEO in 1975. Aided by an infusion of cash from parent company, Loews Corp., he reorganized and pumped new life into CNA. Today, he is recognized as one of the most effective executives in the industry, and CNA as one of the most well-managed insurance organizations in the United States. An outspoken advocate of the free enterprise system and of tort reform, he is in demand as a speaker among agency associations and other industry groups.

JOHN O'BRIEN
Grumman Corporation
Bethpage, New York

O'Brien has been CEO since 1988. In a time of change and challenge in the defense industry, O'Brien is directing a fundamental overhaul of the business. His strategy of renewal involves a program that encourages all employees to organize themselves into self-directed teams that analyze and improve their jobs. The result has been improved product quality, the curtailing of unnecessary paperwork, and the reduction of factory rework rate to record lows. Having joined Grumman as a flight test analyst in 1954, O'Brien is facing some of the most challenging years in the history of the business.

GEORGE L. PLA
Cordoba Corporation
Los Angeles, California

Pla founded the business in 1982. He now leads a fast-growing company that specializes in providing consulting services throughout California in real estate development, urban transportation, and computer information systems. A former economic advisor to Gov. Jerry Brown, Pla is a leading member of the Hispanic business community.

JACK D. REHM
Meredith Corporation
Des Moines, Iowa

CEO since 1989. Faced with rising printing, paper, postage, and television programming costs as well as increased advertising competition, Rehm is directing a growth-oriented strategy. He's adding new magazines to the fold (anchored by "Ladies' Home Journal" and "Better Homes & Gardens"), launching children's projects books and a new book club, expanding real estate activities in Canada, and pooling magazine, book, custom publishing, commercial printing operations, and broadcasting resources to generate new business.

JOSEPH A. RICE
Irving Bank Corporation
New York

Rice served as CEO from 1984 to 1988. Confronted with a hostile takeover attempt by Bank of New York while he was leading Irving Bank to record levels of growth, Rice directed a tough, complex defense, including a shareholder rights plan, reorganization, a white knight, and proxy battles. The 14-month struggle was a bitter one. In the end, Irving Bank was taken over. But Rice says, "While we eventually lost, we never wavered from our resolve and the basis for it."

CHARLES E. RICE
Barnett Banks
Jacksonville, Florida

CEO since 1979, Rice says, "Barnett is at a crossroads entering the 1990s. I see the new decade as an era of possiblities for the company in which we will focus on quality over size, excellence over growth alone. To put it simply, we want to be the best, not necessarily the biggest."

THURMAN J. RODGERS
Cypress Semiconductor Corporation
San Jose, California

Rodgers founded the business in 1983. "We're American—an advantage, not an excuse," says Rodgers who has guided the company to record sales and earnings in each year the company has been in business. He's accomplished this by providing high-quality, highly sophisticated products for niche markets of the semiconductor industry. Rodgers is attempting to keep the entrepreneurial spirit alive and well at Cypress by developing "remote design centers" and "independent start-up subsidiaries," semi-autonomous operations within the corporation.

JOHN W. ROWE
New England Electric System
Westborough, Massachusetts

CEO since 1989, Rowe came to New England Electric after a five-year tenure as CEO of Central Maine Power Company. During that time, he restored Central Maine's balance sheet and redirected its energy sources toward conservation and cogeneration. Two major challenges this former railroad lawyer will be concentrating on in the 1990s are increasing the utility's return on equity and expanding the load growth.

GERARD R. ROCHE
Heidrick and Struggles
New York City

CEO since 1978, Roche leads an international firm specializing in executive recruiting. During the past two decades, he has placed some 200 top executives, more than a quarter of them presidents and chief executive officers.

JOHN J. SCHIFF
Cincinnati Financial Corporation
Cincinnati, Ohio

CEO since 1987. This insurance business experienced the largest single catastrophe loss in its history from the damage caused by Hurricane Hugo. Schiff is helping position Cincinnati Financial for growth in the 1990s by expanding the agency force and the number of field representatives.

LAWRENCE J. SCHOENBERG
AGS Computers
Mountainside, New Jersey

He co-founded AGS Computers in 1967. AGS provides automated solutions, particularly in software, to a variety of markets including government, telecommunications, computer, and finance. Now that he has acquiesced to a friendly takeover by NYNEX, the software segment of AGS has become a separately operated subsidiary of the telecommunications company while AGS's microcomputer segment has become an independent public company. Schoenberg and his management team have stayed on to lead AGS toward further growth in the 1990s.

JOHN A. SCHUCHART
MDU Resources Group
Bismarck, North Dakota

CEO since 1980, Schuchart has helped transform MDU Resources from a regional, public utility to a network of energy-oriented companies, including coal mining, oil and gas exploration and production, pipe line operations, and utility operations.

BENJAMIN J. SOTTILE
Gibson Greetings
Cincinnati, Ohio

CEO since 1989, Sottile has been bucking strong tides in a highly competitive, increasingly cost-conscious market. But he has always accepted tough challenges. Brooklyn-born and raised, Sottile enlisted in the Navy right out of high school. He persisted in getting an appointment to the Naval Academy, spent 10 years as a Naval officer, then left the Navy to take on a number of jobs in civilian life—from plastic bathroom accessories salesman to senior vice president at Warner Communications—before becoming CEO. He says that a key reason for his success is his willingness to take on responsibility. "I operate on the 'green light principle'," he says. "I declare, 'This is what I'm going to do until you stop me.' "

VINCENT SOTTOSANTI
Aniforms
New York City

CEO since 1989, Sottosanti leads both Aniforms and its parent company Comart-KLP: Aniforms, a corporate communications company, and Comart-KLP, a marketing promotions agency. Sottosanti was a captain in the United States Air Force in Japan and has done community work for the Boy Scouts of America and the New York Chapter of the Association for the Help of Retarded Children.

JERRE L. STEAD
Square D Company
Palatine, Illinois

CEO since 1989. Reorganizing, cutting costs, expanding worldwide organizations, improving product quality, and speeding products to the marketplace are a few of the advances Stead is directing to enable this electrical products manufacturer to become more competitive. He asserts that the key advantage of his business is its focus. "None of our large worldwide competitors are as focused as we are. They're all much more diversified. They're tough, and I like competing against them, but if we can't beat them then shame on us, because for us, our business is the only game in town."

C. Jim Stewart II
Stewart & Stevenson Services
Houston, Texas

Grandson of a blacksmith who cofounded the business, C. Jim Stewart II turned the company around in the 1980s by redirecting its stategy from supplying offshore drillers with diesel and gas turbine power systems to supplying such systems for cogeneration power plants. An alliance with a Dutch manufacturer will help the company market its gas turbine generators in Europe. With the U.S. and the rest of the world squeezed between the pincers of power shortages and the need to protect the environment, Stewart's commitment to clean-burning, high-efficiency gas turbine power plants should provide solid growth for the business.

David S. Tappan, Jr.
Fluor Corporation
Irvine, California

CEO since 1984. After restructuring and reducing the size of this international engineering and construction company, he has positioned it for growth during the 1990s. Today, his company designs, constructs, and maintains buildings and equipment in more than 30 industries. Fluor's strong global infrastructure provides rich opportunities for the business to reassert itself around the world. Son of educational missionaries, he was born and raised in China, attended Swarthmore College, served in the Navy during World War II, and went to work for Fluor in 1952 as a marketing executive.

JAMES G. TREYBIG
Tandem Computers
Cupertino, California

Founded the company in 1974. Treybig is enhancing Tandem's growth by broadening niche strategies that have made this supplier of online computer systems and enterprise networks a billion dollar company 13 years after it was founded. He says: "Growth has always been a part of our culture. We proved to our employees that high growth is necessary by sharing an understanding of growth .... If you are a $2 billion company . . . you can still grow at 50 percent a year."

BARBARA WALDEN
Barbara Walden Cosmetics
Toluca Lake, California

Founded the company in 1968 when she and an advertising executive pooled a $750 investment and she began selling cosmetics door-to-door in the Watts section of East Los Angeles right after the riots. Today her line of cosmetics is sold in leading department stores and beauty clinics in the U.S. and other countries.

INDEX

ABOUT THE AUTHOR

B RENT FILSON first learned about leadership and communication as a Marine Corps infantry officer. Since then he has published 14 books on a variety of subjects, from physics to phobias, and more than a hundred magazine articles. He is president of Brent Filson Communications and lives in Massachusetts with his wife and children.